Half Sound,
Half Philosophy

Half Sound, Half Philosophy

Aesthetics, Politics, and History of China's Sound Art

Jing Wang
王婧

BLOOMSBURY ACADEMIC
NEW YORK • LONDON • OXFORD • NEW DELHI • SYDNEY

BLOOMSBURY ACADEMIC
Bloomsbury Publishing Inc
1385 Broadway, New York, NY 10018, USA
50 Bedford Square, London, WC1B 3DP, UK
29 Earlsfort Terrace, Dublin 2, Ireland

First published in the United States of America 2021
This paperback edition published in 2022

Cover design: Louise Dugdale
Cover image © Lu Lei, *The Square (2005/2015)*, *Pretending Egomania* (2015), *The Night*
(2015), solo exhibition *Echo*, Shanghart Gallery, Shanghai, 2015. Courtesy of the artist and
Shanghart Gallery.

Library of Congress Cataloging-in-Publication Data

Names: Wang, Jing, 1982 November 25- author.
Title: Half sound, half philosophy: aesthetics, politics, and history of
China's sound art / Jing Wang.
Description: New York City: Bloomsbury Academic, 2021. | Includes bibliographical
references and index. | Summary: "Maps the aesthetic, cultural,
and socio-economical networks of a variety of sound practices
and discourses in contemporary China"– Provided by publisher.
Identifiers: LCCN 2020036734 (print) | LCCN 2020036735 (ebook) | ISBN 9781501333484
(hardback) | ISBN 9781501333491 (epub) | ISBN 9781501333507 (epub)
Subjects: LCSH: Music–China–21st century–History and criticism. | Music–China–20th
century–History and criticism. | Music–China–Philosophy and aesthetics. | Sound art–
China–History and criticism. | Qi (Chinese philosophy) | Sound (Philosophy)
Classification: LCC ML336.9 .W36 2021 (print) | LCC ML336.9 (ebook) | DDC 780.951–dc23
LC record available at https://lccn.loc.gov/2020036734
LC ebook record available at https://lccn.loc.gov/2020036735

ISBN: HB: 978-1-5013-3348-4
PB: 978-1-5013-7477-7
ePDF: 978-1-5013-3350-7
eBook: 978-1-5013-3349-1

Typeset by Deanta Global Publishing Services, Chennai, India

To find out more about our authors and books visit www.bloomsbury.com and
sign up for our newsletters.

To my grandma (1935.5–2020.7)

CONTENTS

FIGURES

ACKNOWLEDGMENTS

This book took three years to write but the research began about ten years ago. The last year of writing is the most intense and dramatic when I spend one year at MIT anthropology as a visiting scholar. It all began with peacefully reading and writing in a few regular corners of libraries of MIT and Harvard. Walking along the Charles River to and from the library became the most relaxing and creative time everyday. With the eruption of coronavirus, the window-sized Charles River and the cloud far above the apartment studio became my everyday writing view. An increasing self-doubt and the feeling of powerlessness as a scholar accompanied the completion of the book. As I am writing this acknowledgment, I am ten days into my fourteen days' quarantine at a hotel in Shanghai with barely any internet connection, four more days to finally travel back home in Hangzhou.

What can a scholar of (post)humanities do in this global crisis of coronavirus? Probably nothing directly and immediately. This pandemic should have been faced with globally joint effort among countries, but the situation now exactly reveals the stubborn and selfish mode of thinking and operation all based on separations. The global pandemic is worsened by our own crisis, that of racial, national, economic, religious, ecological. Therefore, to change modes of perception and thinking is the responsibility of a scholar of (post)humanities. It takes time to make correlation and mutual care the fundamental base of living, sensing, and thinking. It is nonetheless worth working for.

I am eternally grateful to professor Marina Peterson at the University of Texas at Austin for inspiring me to a scholarship in anthropology, sound, and art while I was still a graduate student. From Marina, I learnt the value of critically testing intellectual rigor with and against anthropological materials. Without Marina's introduction of my work to the editor at Bloomsbury in the first place, this book would not have been possible.

I give my heartfelt thanks to professor Stefan Helmreich at MIT for his kindness, wisdom and deep intellect. Stefan not only granted me the opportunity of visiting MIT but always generously shared inspiring sources, provided immediate feedbacks to my writing, connected me to the brilliant intellectual community of anthropology and sound in Cambridge, and made it possible for me to present my work in progress at the intellectual forum of MIT anthropology. I would like to thank everyone at the forum who read a part of the manuscript and make suggestions: Hector Beltran, Michael M.J. Fischer, Christine Walley, Graham M. Jones, Beth Michelle Semel; Heather Ann Paxson, M. Amah Edoh, Paul Roquet, and Caroline A. Jones. All the comments made it a much stronger book than it otherwise would have been. I thank both Stefan and Graham for family dinners and generative conversations.

And a special thanks to professor Jing Wang of Chinese language and culture at MIT for suggesting me to rethink the name of the book, while the old one is too obtuse and hard to remember. I am also grateful to staff at Dewey library for introducing me to the library's powerful database and to the useful citation tool Zotero. Thank Seth Riskin, the manager of MIT Museum Studio, for introducing me to the studio's community and for all the provocative conversations over art, light, and perception at Wednesday's open studio nights.

Also great appreciation to artists and musicians who have created sound works that inspire me: Deng Yuejun, Feng Cheng, Feng Hao, Fujui Wang, Geng Jianyi, He Chi, Jiang Zhuyun, Li Jianhong, Li Zenghui, Lin Chi-Wei, Lin Tianmiao, Liu Chuang, Lu Lei, Maimai, Mei Zhiyong, Meng Qi, Shao Yi, Shi Qing, Sheng Jie, Shen Piji, Wang Changcun, Wang Chung-Kun, Wang Fan, Wang Tian, Wang Ziheng, Wei Wei, Xu Cheng, Xu Zhe, Yan Jun, Yi Xin Tong, Yin Yi, Jun-Y Chao, Zhang Ding, Zhang Peili, Zheng Bo, Zhu Wenbo. I am grateful to galleries that gave me permission for using images of artworks: SPURS gallery, M+, Hunsand Space, Imagokinetics.

Thank Margaret Romoser for being a dear and caring friend over fourteen years and for making me and Yue feel like a part of the Romoser family. Also, great appreciation to my colleagues at Zhejiang University for cultivating a community of teaching, researching, debating, and mutual caring. I'd especially like to thank my colleague Fan Yun for recommending books of Chinese intellectual history, aesthetics, and ethics. Also thank my friend, professor of philosophy Jiang Yuhui at East China Normal University for making French philosophy accessible.

The project is indebted to the funding of Chinese Scholar Council that sponsored my visit at MIT and to the support of the Fundamental Research Funds for the Central Universities.

Most part of Chapter 4 of the book has been drawn from "Shanshui-thought in Experimental Music Practices: China and beyond" published in *Organized Sound* 2020, 25(3). I am grateful to Cambridge University Press for their permission.

I would also like to thank the editor Leah Babb-Rosenfeld, editorial assistant Rachel Moore from Bloomsbury and the anonymous book reviewer for supporting this book.

Finally, I offer my special thanks to my parents for unconditional love, to my husband Yue for coming all the way from Hangzhou to Cambridge to be with me for Christmas and Chinese Spring Festivals, for taking care of me during the coronavirus lockdown, and for providing inexhaustible support and love every step of the way.

Introduction

The British biochemist, embryologist, and sinologist Joseph Needham in *Science and Civilisation in China, Vol. 4: Physics and Physical Technology* (1965), collaborating with Kenneth Robinson, makes a significant yet brief claim about Chinese notions of sound (acoustics), offering that Chinese acoustics is an acoustics of *qi*. This brief claim has been forgotten in histories of modern acoustic technology. Listening back to ancient Greek philosophy, one finds some concepts similar to *qi*—particularly around the notion of the *pneumatic* (air, breath of life, spirit)—which informed medicine in the first century AD. As the historian of medicine Shigehisa Kuriyama discusses, the notion of *pneuma* takes central position in the Hippocratic treatise, including *On Breaths*, *On the Sacred Disease*, *Air, Water, Places* suggesting that *pneuma* flows both outside of the body and inside through the mouth, nose, brains, veins, limbs, and nerves (1999). A fascination with "the pneumatic character of life" is also prevalent in Greek tragedy (Kuriyama, 240). Needham, in fact, applies the figure of the pneumatic in his discussion of *qi* and of ancient Chinese acoustics. In the Western tradition, air eventually becomes an object of scientific study—as in aerobiology, aerodynamics, aeronautics, aerostatics. As modern China developed its science and technology, however, the notion of *qi* continued to be kept apart from acoustics, and was treated instead as a more general philosophy of life in cultural, medicine, ritual, health, and art practices.

My first fieldwork encounter with sound art in China happened in Beijing a few weeks before the Beijing 2008 Olympic Games. Experimental musicians were hosting concerts at home or in semi-private studios, while clubs and venues were ordered to stay closed. I was fascinated with how grassroots practices of experimental music, noise, improvisation music, and sound art had given rise to a subculture working toward communal and alternative ways of living in post-Mao China, forming a contrast with the dominant form of life shaped by accelerated commercialization, commodification, and individualization. With training in anthropological methods and with a simultaneous interest and participation in Chinese art and music, I became aware of an urgent and anxiety-ridden need among artists to figure out their relation to "sound art"—to identify with or disidentify with this form of aesthetic practice. With them, I wanted, using Chinese materials, to expand the notion of *sound* itself.

These two concerns—retrieving an understanding of ancient Chinese acoustics as the acoustics of *qi* and asking how sound as a creative medium registers in China's contemporary art and music practices—motivated me to conceive this book project.

Dajuin Yao, curator, artist and professor of sound art at China Academy of Art, argues that one of the most distinctive characteristics of sound art practice in China is its engagement with Chinese social media platforms, formats that have subtly taught the society how to listen (2019, 651–2). Without negating the category of "sound art," Yao nonetheless downplays it, and suggests that we hear China's contemporary sound art as part of "Chinese auditory culture" and as "an extension of one of the oldest and most important heritages in world auditory culture" (2019, 652). Yan Jun, the poet, musician, and independent curator of experimental music, expresses a more casual but radical attitude, calling China's experimental music "loser-music" (Yan 2017). In recent two experimental music and sound art compilations Yan Jun curated—*There Is No Music From China* (2017) (cocurated with the musician and event organizer Zhu Wenbo) and *Music Will Ruin Everything* (2020)—a humorous negation of categorical identities of the national and the musical can be clearly felt from both their titles and from the strange, bold, and hard-to-categorize music tracks.

I have found both Yao and Yan's insights and attitudes about the value and development of China's sound art and experimental music inspiring. However, in this book project, I want to listen beyond such existing evaluations and beyond already-charted territories. In what follows, I return to contemporary Chinese visual art from the 1980s (Chapter 2), to electronic music, which was introduced as a target of critique in the 1950s, to electronic instrument building fever in the late 1970s and early 1980s, and to the origins of both academic and nonacademic electronic and experimental music activities (Chapter 3). This expansive tracing of sound in the arts meets with another goal of this book, to understand sound and its artistic practice through notions of resonance (Chapter 1), *shanshui* (mountains-waters) (Chapter 4), *huanghu* (elusiveness and evasiveness) (Chapter 5), and diffusive politics and immanent control (Chapter 6), all of which I take to be informed by a classical philosophy of *qi* (Chapter 1). I turn back to deep history to learn about the meaning and function of sound and listening in ancient China, particularly to understand how a scholar such as Needham would arrive at the statement that "Chinese acoustics is acoustics of *qi*." Curiously, *qi*-philosophy, while underlying current sound practices in China, may be heard as in dialogue with contemporary cybernetic theory, providing insights into today's life world that is increasingly shaped by ambient technology, ambient marketing, and ambient governance, in which sound proves to be a long-used tool of manipulation and control.

The title of this book, *Half Sound, Half Philosophy*, came to me when I was trying to find a way to synthesize the two seemingly incompatible goals of the book: taking account of the recent history of sound practiced in the arts in China, and understanding sound practices through the philosophy and cosmology of *qi*. The book might easily have opened up into two book projects. But to let either one stand on its own seemed incomplete to me. Without a database of *practices* (sound art), it would be empty to talk about *concepts* (*qi*). Without identifying hidden philosophical lineages, practices by Chinese artists would have to be filtered through theoretical frameworks derived more from sociocultural-intellectual milieus of the global North. I have no intention of denying any theoretical frameworks, but I feel the need to give voice to a philosophy and cosmology that has too often remained unheard in the analysis of sound art in China.

So, as I wrote this book, I thought: why not let the two coexist? The idea was to let each exist in the other even as they operate as two independent polarities, as in *qi*-philosophy. The relation between practice and thinking should be the relation of what the Chinese painter Shi Tao (1642–1707) calls *huwei tuotai*, that is, mutual birth, mutual resourcing, or *coenfantement*.

The split suggested by my title also hopes to capture the nature of sound art and experimental music practices at large. Sound art and experimental music practices as known today originate from expanding the conceptualization of music and visual art. The English terms "sound art" and "experimental music" are not simply names for art practices; they carry baggages of philosophy, history, ethics, and politics, and names of notable artists. These baggages would not easily contextualize practices in non-English speaking cultures. The development of acoustic technology, I urge, is often tightly related to its cultural cosmology, epistemology, ontology, and ethics.

Qi-Philosophy

Is there philosophy in China? The Chinese philosopher Mou Zongsan (1909–1995) opens his book *Characteristics of Chinese Philosophy* (牟宗三 2007) with this question. The book is comprised of a collection of twelve lectures Mou gave at Hong Kong University with a focus on Confucianism. From the beginning, Mou makes it clear that there is no philosophy in China that answers to the precise definition developed out of ancient Greek sources, but that it would be ignorant and narrow-minded to therefore say that there is no philosophy in China. For Mou, philosophy is an intellectual and conceptual reflection on activities related to human nature. Every cultural system has its own philosophy, without which a culture will not take form. For Mou, Western philosophy can be seen as knowledge-centered and as a game of rationality. Chinese philosophy or Eastern philosophy at large is life-centered. Despite varied versions of academic accounts of the history of Chinese philosophy, this observation is shared.

Works by contemporary Chinese scholars including Mou Zongsan, Feng Youlan (1895–1990), Zhang Dainian (1909–2004), Li Zehou (1930–), Ying-shih Yu (1930–), and most recently the young philosopher of technology Yuk Hui, as well as sinologists Francios Jullien (1951–) and Benjamin I. Schwartz (1916–1999), have been my major guides in beginning to understand the rich and complex history of Chinese philosophical thinking. Yuk Hui's most recent project in developing a Chinese "cosmotechnics" that develops from both Western and Eastern thinkers is inspiring. Drawing from Heidegger, Simondon, and Steigeler's works, Hui points out that current technological convergence and synchronization has resulted in a homogeneity in technology. Only through what he calls cosmotechnical thinking—unifying the cosmic order and moral order through technical activities—can anthropocentrism be overcome and can we save ourselves from the risk that modernization has delivered to the world (Hui 2016). Although my project is far from a purely philosophical one, I share a similar concern and aspiration with Hui by turning back to ancient Chinese acoustic thinking to find solutions—and new questions—for the status quo of the contemporary.

Qi plays a pivotal role in the classical holistic and organic Chinese worldview (Ames and Hall 2001; Cheng 1987; Kim 2015). As Joseph Needham points out, just as form and matter dominated European thought from the age of Aristotle onwards, the notion of *qi* has molded Chinese thinking from the earliest times (Needham 1965, 133). In ancient China, *qi* was considered both the vital source breath for life and the driving force in the cosmic world. *Qi* was used to describe the human body as used in *qi*-blood, explaining how the human is a part of the resonant cosmic cycle, forming into a union with the heaven and earth. The notion of *qi* refers to the ceaseless fluctuation, interpenetration, and transformation of *yin-qi* and *yang-qi*. Through different historical periods, *qi*, from a vague idea, was developed into a cosmological, aesthetic, social, medical, moral concept, and eventually a philosophical system, reaching its maturity in the Song Dynasty.

It is very easy to think of *qi* materialistically today. The visuals of steam, gas, or fog easily reduce *qi* to simply a material force, blocking the possibility of thinking of it as a movement, a process, or an experience. However, as heavily influenced by *Yijing* (*The Book of Change,* allegedly created by Fu Xi, a legendary hero in Chinese mythology), the Song Dynasty scholar Zhang Zai (1020–1077), known as the philosopher of *qi*, defines *qi* as change, mutation, propensity, and transformation. As Zhang Zai writes, *gui-shen* (literally translated as ghosts-spirits, also means movements of contraction and expansion) is the intuitive and intrinsic nature of *qi* (鬼神,二气之良能). The contraction of *qi* is *yin* and hence *gui* (return); the expansion of *qi* is *yang* and hence *shen* (outstretch). For ancient Chinese from Han Dynasty, as Ying-shih Yu explains (1987), the soul consists of two kinds, the *hun*-soul

(魂) and the *po*-soul (魄). *Hun* is seen as the arising *qi*, light and ethereal; *po* is the descending *qi*, connected to the flesh and heavy. Life is not being but condensation of *qi*. Death is not nonbeing but dispersion of *qi*. When one dies, the *hun-qi* ascends quickly and hence there were ancient rituals of *hun*-soul summoning in which the summoner calls aloud, "O! Thou so-and-so, come back!" (Yu 1987, 365).

As one of the essential concepts in Zhang Zai's *qi*-philosophy, *gui-shen* not only suggests the ceaselessly mutating and transformative nature of *qi* but also emphasizes the virtue and the sensation of reverence in *qi*-philosophy. That is, one should always have reverence for transformation, mutation, and resonance of nature and the myriad things (including humans). Following Zhang Zai's *qi*-philosophy, the neo-Confucian scholar Tang Junyi (or Tang Chün-I) (1909–1978) argues that *qi* is not a matter or spirit, but is rather a becoming. "An existential process, within which there is the mutation of forms, or as an existence within which there is the process of the mutation of forms" (121). Zhang Zai uses the perspective of *qi* to interpret the cosmos and human experience. Instead of using words like being and nonbeing, existence or nonexistence, Zhang Zai's *qi*-philosophy favors another set of vocabularies, condensation and dissolution, coming to be and passing away, moving and resting, contraction and expansion, ascending and descending.

Mostly uniquely, *qi*-philosophy, as well as *qi*-cosmology, highlights a sixth sense—resonance (感)—beyond but also underlying the five senses of sight, smell, hearing, taste, and touch, a notion essential to *Yijing* (*The Book of Change*). Yuk Hui calls resonance a "moral sentiment" and "a moral obligation" that "emerges from the resonance between the Heaven and the human" (27). Based on the Confucian scholar Jung-Yeup Kim's interpretation of Zhang Zai, it is one primary goal of Zhang Zai to realize in the cosmos and the myriad things the capacity for resonance, which is often veiled or hidden. This capacity for resonance is creativity. As Zhang Zai writes, that which interpenetrates through resonance (感) is creativity (诚) (感而通诚也). Resonance as a transformative interaction among polarities of *qi* leads to the great harmony, which further produces and sustains life vitality.

Qi-philosophy suggests an organic, holistic, and enchanted worldview that the cosmos and the myriad things (including humans) are a correlated organism that are constantly resonating, condensing, disintegrating, and forming unity with one another. It is an enchanted worldview that holds a reverence for transformations, mutations, and resonance.

Sound as *Qi*

Zhang Zai (1020–1077) describes sound as a result of *qi* riding each other. Song Yingxing (1587–1666), a Chinese scientist and encyclopedist during the late Ming Dynasty, extends Zhang Zai's statement and adds that sound is *qi* disturbed in a certain way. Song stresses that to make sounds, *qi* has to possess *shi* (the advantage of position of force). Considering Zhang Zai and Song Yingxing's interpretations of sound through *qi*, together with Needham's discussion of ancient Chinese acoustic technology, the relation between sound and *qi* in ancient China can be summarized as: (1) sound is produced by qi; (2) sound is a manifestation of qi; and (3) acoustic technology is a facilitator of qi.

To understand sound through *qi*-philosophy is hence to take the organic and holistic worldview of *qi*. *Qi*-thinking shares similarities with contemporary cybernetics. Norbert Wiener in his book *Cybernetics* in 1948 originally coined the word "cybernetics" drawing from the ancient Greek work *kubernete*, meaning governor and steersman. Both suggest a holistic method, and both can be seen as an art of control. Cybernetic theory inspired the French economist and scholar Jacques Attali to conceive his model of socioeconomic change through a history of noise by placing music/ noise relation within the frame of information/energy, suggesting that noise as unformed energy gives rise to new forms of social organization (Attali 1985). Cybernetics also inspired the British musician and artist Brian Eno to invent the genre of ambient music, a music system that generates atmospheric music loops to create a sense of place. *Qi*-philosophy, essentially a life philosophy, intuitively informs Chinese sound art creativities. Experimental music that operates through principles of tacit resonance and strives for the aesthetics of *dan* (quiet and bland) and *you* (inward expandedness) can be understood through *shanshui*-thought, which is informed by *qi*-philosophy and *qi*-cosmology. Praise for strange sounds and shamanism in experimental music and sound art resonates with the mythical dimension of *qi*-philosophy, a mystified spiritual state known as *huanghu* in Daoism, advocating a dissolution of divisions among senses, a withdrawing to the background, into the realm of non-distinction, seeking life forces in the dark and dim, the impure and afterlife.

Qi-philosophy circumvents the divide of nature-culture, a division around which Christoph Cox develops a philosophy of sound art that defines sound as an immemorial flux (2018). Drawing from Schopenhauer, Nietzsche, and Deleuze's conception of "flux" and extending Manuel Delanda's realist ontology, Cox suggests that sonic flux, as matter-energy-information, always has a resistance to human interpretation that the natural history of sonic flux precedes its cultural history. Through sonic ontology, Cox suggests that we see the sound artist as someone "who samples from the sonic flux" (an expression Cox borrows from Deleuze) (30).

Cox's philosophy of sonic art is insightful. However, the idea of the temporal precedence of nature over culture, as well as the very image of artists sampling from the flux of becoming remains dissatisfying. The artist and scholar of sound and listening Salomé Voegelin expresses her discomfort in the suggested distance between matter and human in Cox's sonic materialism, which is informed by new materialism and speculative realism. Voegelin rethinks sonic materialism, through Karen Barad, Rosi Braidotti, and Luce Irigaray, as a "sonic-feminine new materialism" that "reads objectivity not as a distance but as responsibility, and develops an embodied materiality that performs an 'agential realism' of the world through the 'diffraction' and 'intra-activities' of listening as a creative engagement in the between-of-things" (Voegelin 2019, 152–76).

The nature/culture divide and the temporal precedence is a highly Western way of thinking. Acknowledging the theoretical rigor of Cox's sonic materialism, Voegelin's moral stance informed by sonic feminist materialism, I propose Chinese *qi*-thinking as another way to understand sound and sound art practices. Through *qi*-thinking, myriad things (including humans) are constantly changing and resonating to known and unknown forces. It does not therefore make sense to ask "what it is." Rather, what is important to ask is "what is its propensity?" or, in other words, to ask "what and how it is going to become." Different from phenomenological "intertwining" that runs through Voegelin's philosophy of sound art, *qi*-thinking places things in relation to each other through resonance, an innate capacity of the cosmos and of myriad things, the secret of creativity.

I am not proposing *qi*-philosophy as an alternative theory, because the very term *theory* must be questioned. Theories encapsulate, abstract, and generalize phenomena, while *qi*-thinking suggests, hints, and insinuates. Theories are related to truth, while *qi*-thinking is eventually about living a life.

This book consists of six chapters. The first chapter is a preliminary attempt to investigate sound through the philosophy of *qi*. It can be read first or the last. The second and third chapters are historical accounts of the use of sound in contemporary Chinese art practices and in electronic, experimental music. The remaining chapters, four, five and six, can be read as thematic analysis of China's contemporary sound art practices. In these three chapters, I reinterpret various sound practices through notions informed by *qi*-philosophy, under three themes, *shangshui*, *huanghu*, and immanent control.

Chapter 1, "Sound, Resonance, and the Philosophy of *Qi*," recontextualizes sound studies in a different worldview, that of *qi*, which emphasizes correlationality, resonance, process, and transformation. As difficult as it is to grasp the complex and diverse definitions of *qi*, I begin with a close reading of Joseph Needham's discussion in ancient Chinese acoustics, focusing particularly on sound and *qi*. I then trace translations of the term *qi* in different languages and follow its development from a vague idea in prehistoric China to a cosmological, aesthetic, social, medical, and moral concept in ancient and imperial China and to a philosophical system in Song Dynasty. According to Zhang Zai's philosophy of *qi*, sound is a result of and a manifestation of resonating *qi*. It is one of the primary goals of *qi*-philosophy to unveil the capacity of resonance among things to enhance creativity and at the same time to restore reverence for transformation, mutation, and resonance.

Chapter 2, "A Brief History of Sound in China's Contemporary Art," goes back to the initial stage of the development of China's contemporary art in mid-1980s and discusses how sound already by then played a role in art making. Inspired by Bill Viola's observation that like sound, video evolves out of the electromagnetic and hence video art bears a closer relation to audio art than to film and photography, I reexamine earlier video art for its acoustic mechanism and make evident the essential role sound has played in earlier video artworks. The year 2000 marked the origin of recognizing sound as a unique art medium in mainland China through two consecutive exhibitions *Sound* (2000) and *Sound 2* (2001). Through an analysis of sound art works by categories—sound installations, sound in performance-oriented conceptual art, sound objects/machines, public sound art, and sound and net art—developed after 2000, this chapter unveils the rich creative field of China's sound art practices.

Chapter 3, "A Brief History of Electronic and Experimental Music in China," traces developments of electronic instrument building, academic electronic music, and grassroots experimental music practices. Each of the three has its own distinct resources, agendas, leading figures, and ethical-aesthetic preferences. Instead of seeking a unification, I endorse keeping "a sonorous archipelago" to borrow Francois J. Bonnet's expression, to allow highly creative and original collectives (both unprofessional and professional) to have a chance to develop following their own desires and standards in music making.

Chapter 4, "Shanshui-thought in Experimental Music Practices," discusses how experimental music of Chinese musicians including Yan Jun, Li Jianhong, Jun-Y Chao, Shen Piji, and the tea Rockers Quintet, embodies a particular mode of thinking rooted in *qi*-philosophy known as *shanshui*-thought, which conceives nature and the environment as secret and nurturing. *Shanshui*-thought cultivates an existential gesture of following rather than obeying or conquering; it requires tacit resonance rather than objective knowing. *Shanshui*-thought enables us to recognize the cosmic, aesthetic, and moral values of music qualities of *dan* (淡)(quiet and bland) and *you* (幽)(inward expandedness), once described as "poverty" and "darkness" by the composer Christian Wolff of what he calls ascetic minimalism.

Chapter 5, "*In Praise of Strange Sounds of the Shamanistic*," is inspired by the increasingly shamanistic reference and mysticism in contemporary new music practice, sound art, and experimental music. Drawing from China's own shamanic cultural past, I identify two tendencies in mystical sound artists and musicians, taking works by Tan Dun, Xu Cheng, Wang Fan, Lin Chi-Wei, and Sheng Jie as examples. One treats the shamanistic as a cultural gene and plays the role of cultural inheritor; the other continues a particular aesthetic sensibility shared with the shamanistic known as *huanghu* in ancient Daoism and presents a particular resonance with the old, deserted, and noisy.

The last chapter, "Ubiquitous Control: From Cosmic Bell, Loudspeakers to Immanent Humming," attends to diffusive forms of control that are prevalent in today's political, economic, and technological regimes. How do we negotiate with what has already been shaping, changing, and synchronizing us, like the data cloud and our humming acoustic infrastructure? Sound works by Zhang Peili, Zhang Ding, and Liu Chuang seek to detect, repurpose, exaggerate, and speculate on the increasingly cloud-like, atmospheric, and ubiquitous form of power and violence in everyday life. As "weapons of the weak" to borrow James C. Scott's expression, these artworks embody a holistic worldview of *qi* or a cybernetic brain, suggesting artistic ways of exercising the power of anti-control and of acquiring the quality of anti-monumentality.

*   *   *

Breathing is the simplest manifestation of the fact that we are composed of *qi*, the original creative potency accessible to myriad things in forms of resonance. *Qi*-thinking is in a way prevalent in other cultures, in science, arts, philosophies, and even politics. However, identifying *qi* as a global component in all thinking and cultural practices is different from claiming its global universality.

I am pushing for a reinterpretation of sound and listening through a philosophy of *qi* and at the same time confirming that no philosophical system is universally applicable, including *qi*-philosophy. Any philosophical system needs to work with a set of concepts and within particular historical and cultural contexts. It is to follow the anthropologist Stefan Helmreich's insight in his study of sound, life, and water, remembering that we should not fall into the trap as if we are offering "the final, most meaningful account of the biological world" or "the final answer to what sound and life really are" (2015, xix).

I like how François Jullien describes a scholar's work as a gardener taking care of her own garden, checking how a plant of concept grows, fixing it now and then and observing what kind of function it serves or stops to serve. It is with this kind of caution, care, and responsibility that I begin with *Half Sound, Half Philosophy*.

1

Sound, Resonance, the Philosophy of *Qi*

Sound has been interpreted as numbers (Pythagoras), vibration (Galileo), objects (Pierre Schaeffer), sonic flux (Cox 2018), waves (Helmreich 2015), and events (O'Callaghan 2007). These different (sometimes overlapping) ways of understanding sound suggest different lineages of theories, methodologies, and even worldviews. To an already rich collection of theoretical discussions of sound, I am going to propose another one, informed by Chinese *qi*-philosophy unfortunately undervalued in modern and contemporary times.

To think of sound through the philosophy of *qi* is to recontextualize sound studies in a worldview that emphasizes correlationality, resonance, process, and transformation. In this chapter, I trace back to ancient and premodern China to learn how sound is perceived, conceived, and practiced through *qi*-philosophy and *qi*-cosmology. Joseph Needham has done substantial research and discussion on the history of Chinese acoustics. His observation that Chinese accoustics is the acoustics of *qi* has been an inspiration for this project. While finding Needham's discussion on Chinese acoustics original and substantial, I find it unsatisfying for a lack of thorough discussion of essential acoustic notions, which I believe are long-lasting and still influential in today's sound practices. This is not to blame Needham since it has never been a project for him to pursue from the very beginning.

To begin, it is necessary to point out two commonly made mistakes in discussing *qi*. Almost unavoidably, in contemporary time, the notion of *qi* has been framed within a discourse of materialism or been reduced into the formula of matter-energy. As the American sinologist Benjamin Schwartz reminds, the notion of *qi* "embraces properties of psychic, emotional, spiritual, numinous, and even 'mystical'" and hence neither Western definitions of "matter" and the physical which systematically exclude these properties from their definition nor the word "energy" used in the West to describe a force that relates to physical mass corresponds to *qi* (1985, 181). Another mistake is related to a critique in Chinese thinking in general in the confusion of subject and predicate in classical Chinese philosophical writing. That is, Chinese thinking never consolidates on the notion of a subject and does not distinguish the thing and its medium or the thing and its action. As the art historian John Hay points out, Chinese conceptual language is more precise in identifying functions rather than things (John Hay, 1985). For example, in the sentence by Song Dynasty scholar Zhang Zai we will be discussing later "*gui-shen* is the intuitive and intrinsic nature of qi," *gui-shen* can be understood both as subject (ghosts-spirits) and actions (contraction and expansion). For some, this may be a defect in Chinese thinking, but it can also be a valuable resource to circumvent issues in another thinking system. As François Jullien has convincingly argued that there is no ontology in Chinese thinking in the sense that Chinese thinking does not concern much with questions of being but more with the ungraspable, the evasive, and allusive (Jullien 2018b).

In this chapter, instead of rehearsing Needham's discussion on acoustics, I only focus on sections where he discusses sound and *qi*. I will begin with ancient Chinese acoustics based on Needham's discovery and proceed with discussing how sound is understood through the philosophy of *qi*, particularly emphasizing the notion of resonance. The ancient Chinese distinguished *sheng* (sound)(声) from *yin* (notes)(音) and from *yue* (music) (乐). My focus is on *sheng* (sound) and its experience, but as Needham also noted, it is sometimes difficult to separate in classical texts the primarily acoustic works from those primarily musical (127).

Ancient Chinese Acoustics

In the opening of the discussion of Chinese acoustics in *Science and Civilisation in China, Vol. 4: Physics and Physical Technology* (1965), Joseph Needham, together with Kenneth Robinson, uses a story of resonance to demonstrate the general difference between the Chinese and European approaches. It was a story narrated in *Chunqiu Fanlu* (春秋繁露, *The Luxuriant Dew of the Spring and Autumn Annals*) by the Western Han Dynasty (202 BC–9 BC) thinker Dong Zhushu (179 BC–104 BC), who Needham speaks highly of as "among the most scientific and philosophical minds of his age" (130).

> Try tuning musical instruments such as the *chhin* [*qin*] or the *se*. The *kung* [gong] note or the *shang* note struck upon one lute will be answered by the *kung* or the *shang* notes from other stringed instruments. They sound by themselves. This is nothing miraculous, but the Five Notes being in relation: they are what they are according to the Numbers (whereby the world is constructed). (130)

For Needham, the story is exemplary in showing ancient Chinese thinking as correlative and the ancient Greek as analytic (128). It surprises Needham that Dong Zhongshu did not find the phenomenon of resonance bemused; "This is nothing miraculous." It means for Needham that the seemingly mysterious phenomenon of resonance fits well into ancient Chinese organic worldview.

With this difference (correlative versus analytic) identified, Needham proceeds to propose his observation that Chinese acoustics is the acoustics of *qi*. It is worth confirming that Needham not only attends to classical writings by scholars but also stresses the value of the oral tradition of craftsmen (130). According to Needham, the earliest hint of sound being produced through *qi* appeared in *Yue Ji* (乐记, *Record of Music*, second and first centuries BC). He quotes:

The *chhi* [*qi*] of the earth ascends above; the *chhi* [*qi*]of Heaven descends from the height. The Yang and Yin come into contact; Heaven and Earth shake together. Their drumming is in the shock and rumble of thunder; their excited beating of wings is in wind and rain; their shifting round is in the four seasons; their warming is in the sun and moon. Thus the hundred species procreate and flourish. Thus it is that music is a bringing together of Heaven and Earth."[1] (205)

Written in Western Han Dynasty, *Yue Ji* is still one of the most important texts of Chinese aesthetics. The above passage from *Yue Ji* establishes a direct relation between the heaven-earth and sound-music. In *Yue Ji*, music plays an essential role in regulating and maintaining social, political, and moral hierarchy for the ruling class. For example, sound, notes, and music are classified through hearing, "Music is connected to human relations and morality. Hence, beasts only know sound and do not know notes. The common people know the notes, but they do not know music. Only the noble man knows music."[2] The cosmic relation between music and the heaven-earth precisely legitimizes music's social, political, and moral functions.

Yue Ji is a chapter collected in one of the Confucian classics *Li Ji* (礼记, *Book of Rites*, 202 BC–9). *Li* (rites, ritual) (礼) is one of the most important concepts for Confucius. The Chinese philosopher Li Zehou identifies three characteristics of *Li* (2015/2018). First, *li* needs to be carried out in practice, specifically referring to "the behavior and

---

[1]地气上齐，天气下降，阴阳相摩，天地相荡，鼓之以雷霆，奋之以风雨，动之以四时，暖之以日月，而百化兴焉。如此则乐者天地之和也。《乐记》
[2]凡音者,生于人心者也。乐者,通伦理者也。是故知声而不知音者,禽兽是也;知音而不Z知乐者,众庶是也。唯君子为能知乐。《乐记》

etiquette of the individual in actual life," including "actions, bearing, speech, and even appearance . . . to be carried in proper and regulated sequence" (108). Secondly, *li* requires normalization of all aspects of social life through rituals, including the way to treat guests or getting married. Even greeting, eating, walking, and leaving home has ritual regulations. The third and most important characteristic is *li*'s sanctity. Li Zehou explains,

> Ritual comes from shamanism, and shamanism involves the divine. Because of this, *the norms of "ritual regulations" are not simply laws among humans*. The *Zuozhuan* connects the "ritual" enacted by humans with the principles and rightness of heaven and earth. They are given by heaven and earth to regulate human life. Thus violating ritual regulations is not merely transgressing customs, regulations, or laws of the human realm, but more severely offends the deities. That, of course, results in various calamities and punishments. . . . Thus, people's "actions" (behavior, activities, demeanor, speech, appearance, and so forth) must accord with the norms of "ritual regulations" in order to be in harmony, accordance, and connection with the natural cosmos and the divine . . . *the divine lies within this world, including within the "ritual regulations" of the human realm. Human ritual ceremony is the prescript of the divine. Humans and deities occupy a single world, and therefore "ritual edification" became China's "religious teachings."* (112)

Music originates before *li*, but is later incorporated into *li* in the school of Confucianism. Music serves the same function as artificial objects known as *li qi* (礼器) which is to "nurture moral sensibility" and "to stabilise and restore the moral cosmology through ritual" (Yuk Hui, 109–10). Moreover, *Yue Ji* suggests that ritual is for the earth and music is for the heaven. "The sages make music in response to heaven, and frame rituals in response to earth. In the wisdom of completeness of their rituals and music, we see the directing power of heaven and earth."[3] In general, *Yue Ji*'s discussion of music fits into what the contemporary Chinese Confucian thinker Du Weiming calls anthropocosmic worldview of Confucianism, a vision that addresses the interplay between heaven's creativity as expressed in the cosmological process and human's creativity as embodied in heaven's life-generating transformation (Tu 2010).

Since *Yue Ji* mainly discusses music in relation to ritual rather than technology, Needham spend relatively less time on it. Although he admits that the neo-Confucian scholar Zhang Zai from Song Dynasty discusses exactly

---

[3]故圣人作乐以应天，制礼以配地。礼乐明备，天地官矣。《乐记》

how sound is produced by *qi*, Needham does not speak highly of Zhang's contribution. According to Zhang Zai, to use Needham's translation,

> The formation of sound is due to the friction (lit. mutual grinding) between (two) material things, or (two) chhi [*qi*] (or between material things and chhi [*qi*]). The grinding between two chhi [*qi*] gives rise to noises such as echoes in a valley or the sounds of thunder. The grinding of a material thing on chhi [*qi*] gives sounds such as the swishing of feathered fans or flying arrows. The grinding of chhi [*qi*] on a material thing gives sounds such as the blowing of the reeds of a mouth-organ. These are the inherent capacities in things for response. People are so used to these phenomena that they never investigate them."[4] (206)

For Needham, this discussion of formation of sound is far from satisfying. It even reflects weakness in traditional Chinese thought: "To say that the formation of sound is due to friction is obviously as much a defect of language as of thought." He continues seeking explanations behind this "defect" and writes reflectively, "perhaps it would not be too sweeping a generalization to say that medieval science was as much handicapped by the failure of the Chinese language to make transitive and intransitive verb functions always explicit, as it was by the inability of some European languages to resolve verbs into specific physical operation" (206). The verb Needham refers to is *xiang zha* (mutual grinding). The word *zha* describes the action of grinding or pressing against each other.

Zhang Zai's brief explanation of sound as produced by *qi* is unclear for Needham. Instead, Needham believes that Tan Qiao, a Daoist in Tang Dynasty before Zhang Zai, provides a clearer understanding of *qi* in *Hua Shu* (化书, *The Book of Transformation*, 907–76), a book about internal alchemy and spiritual transformation. The preference for a Daoist over a Confucianist is not surprising considering Needham's overall conviction of Daoism's importance in Chinese science and technology (Cullen 1990; Sivin 1978). For Needham, "Tan Qiao anticipated Zhang Zai's theory of grinding of *chhi* [*qi*] and material things, but by-passed the problem of how sound is formed by the use of a linguistic side-step, in this case 'riding' instead of 'grinding' or 'friction'" (207). Tian Qiao writes, as quoted by Needham (207–8),

> The void (*hsü*) is transformed into (magical) power (*shen*). (Magical) power is transformed into *chhi* [*qi*]. Chhi [*qi*] is transformed into material things (*hsing*). Material things and *chhi* [qi] ride on one another (*hsing*

---

[4] 声者，形气相轧而成。两气者，谷响雷声之类；两形者，桴鼓叩击之类；形轧气，羽扇敲矢之类；气轧形人声笙簧之类。是皆物感之良能。人皆习之而不察者尔。《正蒙动物篇第五》

chhi hsiang chheng), and thus sound is formed. It is not the ear which listens to sound but sound which of itself makes its way into the ear. It is not the valley which of itself gives out echoing sound, but sound of itself fills up the entire valley.[5]

Also,

An ear is a small hollow (*chhiao*) and a valley is a large hollow. Mountains and marshes are a 'small valley' and Heaven and Earth are a 'large valley.' (Theoretically speaking, then) if one hollow gives out sound ten thousand hollows will all give out sound; if sound can be heard in one valley it should be heard in all the ten thousand valleys[6].

Tan Qiao's notion of sound is conceived in *yin-yang* thinking, which is made most clear in his following statement.

Sound leads (back again) to *chhi* [*qi*]; *chhi* [*qi*] leads (back again) to (magical) power; (magical) power leads (back again) to the void. (But)the void has in it (the potential for) power. The power has in it (the potential for) *chhi* [*qi*]. *Chhi* [*qi*] has in it (the potential for) sound. One leads (back again) to the other, which has (a potential for) the former within itself. (If this reversion and production were to be prolonged) even the tiny noise of mosquitoes and flies would be able to reach everywhere.[7] (Needham, 208)

Yin-qi and *yang-qi* correlate with each other; one transforms into another without losing the potential of what it transforms from. For Needham, these paragraphs explain the mechanism of thunder and lightning and Tan even anticipates modern physics, "Than [Tan] would have little difficulty in understanding the way in which today the tiny sound of mosquito or a fly may be 'led back again' into electric power 'having in it the potentiality for' amplification of sound by means of 'agitation of the chhi'[qi] through a loudspeaker" (208).

Compared to Zhang Zai, Tan Qiao indeed offers more comments on sound by explaining how sound is produced, how sound is independent of hearing, as well as the phenomenon of amplification. But it is hardly convincing how the verb *cheng* (ride) is better or clearer than *zha* "friction." In fact, in my opinion, what is more important in Zhang Zai's discussion

---

[5]虚化神，神化气，气化形，行气相乘而成声。耳非听声也，而声自投之。谷非应响也，而响自满之。《化书》。
[6]耳小窍也，谷大窍也。山泽小谷也，天地大谷也。一窍鸣，万窍皆鸣。一谷闻，万谷皆闻。
[7]声导气，气导神，神导虚，虚含神，神含气，气含声。相导相含。虽秋蚊之翻翻，苍蝇之营营，无所不至也。

of sound is not the verb *zha* but the verb *gan* (resonance) as appeared in the second to last sentence: "These are the inherent capacities in things for response."[8] That is, sound is a result of the resonating interaction among things. Needham translates *gan* as response, as well as resonance. The verb *zha* is used in the beginning of the sentence to specify the more abstract verb *gan*.

It is Needham's criticism of Zhang Zai's use of the verb *zha* and his negligence of Zhang's use of the verb *gan* that give me the first hint that Needham might have missed an important notion in understanding *qi* and sound. Later in the discussion, Needham's comments on a text from *Guan Yinzi* (关尹子), arguably written by a Daoist named Tian Tongxiu in Tang dynasty, further confirms my speculation.

Tian writes, "It is like striking a drum with a drumstick. The shape of the drum is possessed in my person (in the form of the ear)[9]. The Sound of a drum is a matter of my responding [resonance] to it[10]." For Needham, this proves the medieval Chinese' recognition of the psychology of hearing, "it is the response [resonance] (*gan*) of a sentient being which enables one to describe this process as sound" (209). Here, Needham reduces the notion of resonance to simply a psychological aspect of hearing. However, *gan* (resonance) in ancient Chinese thinking goes far beyond the psychological; it is one of the most essential concepts in Chinese correlational cosmology of *qi*. In order to first complete tracing how Needham arrives at his another important claim that premodern Chinese acoustic technology is a facilitator of *qi*, I leave a further discussion of resonance for later.

Needham first noticed in classics of *Zhuangzi* and *Zuozhuan* (左传, *The Commentary of Zuo*, ca. fourth century BC) the interchangeable use of the term "channel" and "*qi*." The term "six channels" is sometimes used as a synonym for the "six *qi*." This suggests for Needham a connection important for early Chinese acoustic theories. "If *qi* is something which can be canalised or piped off, the obvious instrument for the purpose would be a bamboo tube, such as is used in China for irrigation" (Needham, 134).

Humming Tubes

Humming tubes is called *lv guan* (律管). *Guan* (管) means pipe. The word *lv* (律) is more complicated. *Lv* is the name of humming pipes used by shamans. *Lv* also means regulating dance steps or setting the pitch for other instruments. In *Yue Ji*, as Needham quotes, "Eight winds follow the *lv* and

---

[8]是皆物感之良能。
[9]鼓之形者我之有也。
[10]鼓之声者我之感也。

will be without any turbulence."[11] This expression again reveals the ancient Chinese belief in sound's function of regulating the cosmic order. Wind was an important form of *qi*. In pre-*qin* period (2100–221 BC), wind and *qi* was often used interchangeably. The sound of winds/*qi* coming from different directions were named differently in musical terms. According to Eastern Han (25–220) scholar Zheng Zhong as quoted by Needham, the northern wind is *jia zhong* (夹钟) and *wu yi* (无射), while the southern wind is *gu xi* (姑洗) and *nan lv* (南吕). *Jia zhong, wu yi, gu xi,* and *nan lv* are four major notes of Chinese twelve-pitch scale, known as *shi er lv* (十二律). In ancient China, pipes were made of animal bones[12]. The bone flute was in the beginning not played to entertain or perform, but to predict the secret of the heaven and earth. Needham gives examples of the application of humming tubes in military divination, agriculture, and astronomy.

From the Daoist classic *Lie Zi* (列子, ca. fifth century BC), Needham quotes a story of the great naturalist Zou Yen using humming tubes to control the weather. "In the North, there was a valley of good earth but so cold always that the five grains would not grow there. Zou Yen blew on his pipe however and (permanently) warmed its climate, so that grain and miliet could be raised abundantly" (29).

Shaman-diviners use humming tubes in the battle field to predict conditions of the enemy, their morale, and the outcome of the battle. Needham quotes from Tang Dynasty scholar Sima Zhen (司马贞, 679–732) in explaining how military divination works, "Above every enemy in battle array there exists a vapour-color (*chhi-se*) [*qi se*][气色]. If the *chhi* [*qi*] is strong, the sound (note) is strong. If the note is strong, his host is unyielding. The pitch-pipe (or humming-tube) is (the instrument) by which one canalises (or communicates with) *chhi* [*qi*], and thus may foreknow good or evil fortune" (Needham, 138). Humming tube also follow the *yin-yang* principle. "In the *Chou Li* it is said: 'the grand instructor (Ta Shih) takes the Yin-tubes and the Yang-tubes, listens to the army's note, and predicts good fortune or bad'" (Needham,136).

Needham cites another example of using four humming tubes in divination from *Zuo Zhuan*. The officials of the state of Qin asked the music-master Kuang to predict if the troops of the Southern State of Chu besieging Zheng should march north. Kuang replies: "there is no harm. I repeatedly hummed the northern 'wind'; I also hummed the southern wind. The southern wind was not vigorous. The sound signified great slaughter. (The state of) Chu will inevitably fail to gain a victory" (Needham, 136).

While providing an impressively rich collection of examples of humming tubes being used in divination, Needham mixes his explanation of the

---

[11] 八风从律而不奸。《乐记》
[12] The bone flutes excavated in 1986 from an early Neolithic tomb in Wuyan county of Henan province proves to be the oldest known instrument from China, about 6000 BC.

working mechanism with his judgment of how divination is pseudoscience. Here, I will try to offer my interpretation.

Through the principle of resonance, it is easier and clearer to understand how the humming tube's sound blown by the musician-shaman Kuang manifests the *qi* of the enemy. When Kuang blows the pipe and the sound is weak, it means the *qi* of the enemy which Kuang's *qi* resonates to is weak. Hence it is of crucial importance in the first step of divination that the shaman-musician reaches and keeps the state of nothingness or void to enlarge one's capacity to resonate. To recall Tan Qiao's writing, "sound leads (back again) to *chhi* [qi]; *chhi* [qi] leads (back again) to (magical) power; (magical) power leads (back again) to the void. (But)the void has in it (the potential for) power. The power has in it (the potential for) *chhi* [qi]. *Chhi* [qi] has in it (the potential for) sound." Zhang Zai also stresses the importance of the void, as interpreted by the Chinese philosopher Tang Junyi (1909–1978), "from the fact that one thing can prehend another we can see that the thing must have the void within itself in order to be able to absorb the other. And this void must be within the thing or within the ether [*qi*] out of which the thing is generated, but never outside" (Tang, 124). This is also what Zhuang Zi means by "empty the heart-mind to wait for qi" in demanding "don't listen with your ears, listen with your mind. No, don't listen with your mind, but listen with your spirit. Listening stops with the ears, the mind stops with recognition, but spirit is empty and waits for all things. The Way gathers in emptiness alone. Emptiness is the fasting of the mind."[13]

Shaman-musicians are not only the operator of the humming tube; they are part of the humming tube in the sense that they are the conduit of *qi* as well. This is what Needham neglected.

Humming tubes are also used in astronomy. Needham mentions a unique technique used in ancient Chinese astronomy called *lv guan chui hui* (律管吹灰). According to *Qian Han Shu* (前汉书, the *Book of Pre-Han*, ca.82), wind is produced by the combination of the *qi* from the heaven and the *qi* from the earth; if the *qi* of the winds from the heaven and earth are correct, the twelve-tone pitches are rectified. Therefore, the twelve-pitch scale is set when the *yin* and *yang* of the month reaches its harmony, which is reflected from the *qi* of wind. The twelve-pitch scale corresponds to twelve months. *Lv guan chui hui*, also known as *hou qi* (waiting for the *qi*) is a method used to test the arrival of the proper *qi* of a month[14]. According to the Chinese archaeologist Feng Shi (1958–), Sima Biao's description of the method in *Xu Han Shu · Lv Li*

---

[13]"无听之以耳而听之以心，无听之以心而听之以气。听止于耳，心止于符。气也者，虚而待物者也。唯道集虚，虚者，心斋也"。《庄子·人间世》 Burton Watson's translation in *The Complete Works of Zhuangzi*, Columbia University Press, 2013.

[14]The method of *lvguan chuihui* was recorded in Bei Shi · Xin Du Fang Zhuang (北史·信都芳传), Lv Li Zhi Shang (律历志上), Xu Han Shu · Lv Li Zhi Shang (续汉书·律历志上), Jin Shu · Lv Li Zhi Shang (晋书·律历志上), and Lv Lv Xin Shu (律吕新书).

Zhi Shang (续汉书 • 律历志上, 445) was too advanced to be practiced, while the astronomer in Sui and Tang Dynasty Li Chunfeng (602–670) records a method of *hou chi* (*waiting for the qi*) in *Jin Shu · Lv Li Zhi Shang* (晋书 • 律 历志上, 648), which is easier to be practiced (Feng, 262).

> Place twelve pitch pipes inside of a room according to the position of twelve earthly branches, *zi, chou, yin, mao, chen, si, wu, wei, shen, you, xu, hai*. The top of each pipe is placed at the ground level. Fill each pipe with ashes of reeds, the top of each pipe is covered with silk. When the ch'i [*qi*] for a given month comes, the ashes from its corresponding pipe will fly out.

Lv guan chui hui is used to learn about changes of months and is also applied in measuring if the pipe is made in the right length. Unfortunately, this technique has never been popular, partly due to its complicated operation and strict requirement of tools in ancient times. The technique is also believed to be a trick played to please the emperor. But the significance of this method in revealing the ecological and astronomical function of acoustic instruments makes it nonetheless worthy of our attention.

Needham's research into the history of Chinese acoustics is of great value to enrich our knowledge of sound technology in Chinese history. However, it is also important to notice his reduction of the notion of resonance and his materialistic understanding of *qi*. Needham reminds the reader, "Chinese acoustics . . . was from the first, if not analytical, highly pneumatic." and "We must not forget that they thought of chhi [*qi*] as something between what we should call matter in rarefied gaseous state on the one hand, and radiant energy on the other" (135). Pneumatic is a Greek word for breath, spirit, or soul, often used in a religious context. Defining Chinese acoustic as pneumatic steers Needham away from understanding some of the early examples of acoustic practice; it also explains Needham's proposition that Chinese's acoustics originates from Babylon. Chen Cheng-Yih, a professor of physics, while confirming the significance of Needham's work, challenges Needham's proposition. In his book titled *Early Chinese Work in Natural Science: A Re-examination of the Physics of Motion, Acoustics, Astronomy, and Scientific Thoughts*, Chen demonstrates that China has its own acoustic thoughts and that similar concepts may have paralleled and disbursed independent development (Chen 1996/2007). To further engage with Chinese acoustics through the perspective of *qi*, it is necessary to turn to the notion of *qi*.

The Philosophy of *Qi*

What is *qi*? In contemporary time, for the Chinese philosopher Li Zehou, *qi* is the rationalization of the mysterious and at the same time realistic life force felt and mastered in shamanistic practices (2015, 37). For the Japanese architect Masayuki Kurokawa, *qi* is that which resides inside of humans, objects, and cosmos; it supports life force and enables a sense of union among human, thing, and the cosmos (Kurokawa 2006/2014). Musicians like to use *qi chang* to describe the kind of atmosphere or force field of a performance space, which one can only feel in certain state of mind/body. In Chinese medicine, *qi* is used to describe the human body in terms of *qi*-blood, to connect the human to nature and to the movement of heaven-earth. As the American sinologist Nathan Sivin writes, "the physical vitality of the newborn child is drawn before birth from the ch'i [*qi*] that fills the cosmos" (1987, 48).

Although today *qi* is no longer a focus of contemporary philosophy, it continues as a common-sense concept and expression in uncountable ways. Most importantly, *qi* still functions as a way of thinking that underlies creative and practical works in the arts, architecture, gardening, and everyday life situations. The prevalent care for the invisible among artists and musicians who work with sound also hint at the pertinent of *qi*-thinking. It is after all impossible to understand "*qi*" in one grasp. Its meaning varies in different contexts for different people.

Translations of the Chinese Character *Qi*

Translations of the word "*qi*" in different languages give us a general idea of how *qi* is understood in different cultures. In French, citing from the *Dictionary of Chinese Classical Language* (*Dictionnaire Classique de la Langue Chinoise*) edited by F. S. Couvreur S. J., *qi* is explained as *air atmospherique, suffle du vent, vapeur, emanation, gaz, fluide, esprits vitaux, vigueur, energie, disposition ou sentiment de l'ame, maniere d'etre, intelligence*, and so on. The sinologist Marcel Granet translates *qi* into *le souffle*, which becomes a common usage among French scholars. In German, the sinologist Otto Franke translates *qi* as *wirkungskraft* (effective force, influence). W. Grube and W. Eichhorn instead propose *odem* (breath, respiration) as the most appropriate translation that would work in most occasions.

In English, *qi*, sometimes written as *ch'i*, is usually translated into vital energy, air, or ether. Wing-Tsit Chan, a scholar of Chinese philosophy, lists three major ways of defining *qi*: (1) *qi* is a "subtle, incipient, activating force," an "inward spring of movement," and "incipient movement not yet visible outside"; (2) *qi* is a "concrete thing" to be understood philosophically as opposed to the concept of Dao which has no physical form; and (3) *qi* is "material force" as opposed to *li* (pattern, principle, form) (1973, 784). It is also interesting to notice that Joseph Needham uses "subtle spirit" to refer to *qi*.

Some of these translations suggest a materialist tendency, which is susceptibly a result of visuocentrism (the visuals of steam, gas, or fog). This materialist point of view not only is prevalent when *qi* is translated into other languages but also was dominant in modern China after the May Fourth movement in 1919, also known as the new culture movement to replace traditional Confucianism and Daoism, calling for "Mr. Science" and "Mr. Democracy."

The philosopher François Jullien warns that translating *qi* as energy reduces it to an ancient Greek thought (Jullien 2015). Jullien however, does not expand on this particular comment. A possible explanation could be found in an earlier writing by Nathan Sivin. Sivin observes that premodern Chinese thought lack separate concepts to distinguish energies from their carriers. Sivin instead proposes that, as quoted by Christopher Cullen, "we might define [*qi*] . . . as simultaneously 'what makes things happen in stuff' and (depending on context) 'stuff that makes things happen' or 'stuff in which things happen'" (Sivin 1987, 47; Cullen 1990).

In general, it will be helpful to think of *qi* as a big verb, a proposition, and a small noun. Now let us turn to the cultural, historical, and intellectual contexts in which the idea of *qi* develops into a philosophical system.

Qi, the Word and the Idea

According to *Shuowen Jiezi* (说文解字, 100–21) by the Han Dynasty scholar Xu Shen (58–48), the oracle character *qi* originally meant the *qi* of the cloud or the *qi* of the earth. The primordial worship of cloud and wind in pre-*qin* era (2100–221 BC) marked the early stage of the development of the idea of *qi*. Specifically, in Shang dynasty, cloud, wind and earth were believed closely related to agriculture as well as to the stability of the society and everyday life. People worshipped the cloud and wind and relied on shamans to command winds, which was believed to bring clouds and rain. It was believed that winds coming from different directions affect life in different ways. Wind was considered a prototype of *qi*. This explains why in early manuscripts including *Zhuangzi* (庄子), *Chuci* (楚辞), *Shanhaijing* (山海经), *Huainanzi* (淮南子), characters of wind and *qi* are used interchangeably. Wind coming from different directions in different seasons produce different type of sounds. Hence there developed a practice known as *ting feng* or *xing feng* (listening to winds or examining winds). *Xing feng* later was developed to *houqi*, meaning waiting for and inspecting *qi*.

Qi was also written as 氣, with 米 *mi* (rice) underneath, indicating the connection of *qi* to food. Food is considered the major provider of *qi* for the body; different kinds of food connect the four seasons and different types of earth to different states of human bodies. *Qi* is considered both the vital source of life and the driving force in the cosmic world.

Since Zhou dynasty (1046–256 BC), the idea of *qi* was already omnipresent in Chinese thinking. The character *qi* appears in both Daoist and Confucian texts. In the Daoist classics *Zhuangzi*, it reads, "when *qi* is condensed, there is life, when *qi* is dispersed, there is death . . . . Hence it is said, all under the sky there is *qi*"[15]. Different foods provide different kinds of *qi*, light or heavy. Daoism believes that grains bring heavy *qi* that prevents one from becoming saints or *xian* (仙, immortals or sages), hence the tradition in Taoist practices known as *bigu* (辟谷, grain avoidance)—not eating five grains, only air and water. For example, in *Zhuangzi A Happy Excursion*, we see a paragraph reads like this,

> there is a Holy Man living on faraway Gushe Mountain, with skin like ice or snow and gentle and shy like a young girl. He doesn't eat the five grains but sucks the wind, drinks the dew, climbs up on the clouds and mist, rides a flying dragon, and wanders beyond the four seas. By concentrating his spirit, he can protect creatures from sickness and plague and make the harvest plentiful.[16]

Zhuangzi contributed to later philosophical development of *qi* by explaining the life and death of the myriad things through the condensation and dispensation of *qi*. *Yijing* and *Yizhuan* (a book that annotate *Yijing*) establishes *yin-yang* thinking, connecting human life to the *yin-qi* and *yang-qi* of the cosmos. For Daoism, human beings are only one element in the vast universe, sharing with other myriad things the same origin and affected by the same *qi* of *yin-yang*.

Huainanzi, a complied text mainly used for the ruler in Western Han Dynasty (202–9BC) with Taoist thinking as its basis, extends the idea of *qi* to cultural geography, arguing that the *qi* of the earth has a close impact on human characters, intelligence, body states, and so on. *Huainanzi* also incorporate medicine book like *Huangdi Neijing Suwen,* bringing Daoist thinking into everyday life practice.

Daoism tends to thinks of *qi* through cosmological questions (how the cosmos and the myriad things came to be and how to cultivate oneself to be immortal), while Confucianism concerns more with cultural and political problems. In the Waring States Period (475–221 BC), blood-*qi* as a kind of *qi* in humans was considered more closely related to the human body than with the human spirit. Confucianism believed that only through cultivating the blood-*qi* can one acquire virtues, and consequently a strong state can be guaranteed. In *Sunzi Bingfa* (*the Art of War*) (fifth century BC), *qi* was often

---

[15] 人之生，气之聚也，聚则为生，散则为死。若死生为徒，吾又何患！故万物一也，是其所美者为神奇，其所恶者为臭腐；臭腐复化为神奇，神奇复化为臭腐。故曰：'通天下一气耳。'圣人故贵一。《庄子知北游》

[16] "藐姑射之山，有神人居焉。肌肤若冰雪，绰约若处子，不食五谷，吸风饮露。乘云气，御飞龙，而游乎四海之外；其神凝，使物不疵疠而年谷熟"。Burton Watson's translation in *The Complete Works of Zhuangzi*, Columbia University Press, 2013.

considered as the collective psychology of the entire army. The technique of *wang qi* (inspecting *qi*) was popular during war times to learn about the enemy and to predict results of battles. Liu Bang, the founder and first emperor of the Han Dynasty, was known for his extraordinary ability of *wang qi*.

When Buddhism was introduced to the late Han Dynasty, the idea of *qi* as informed by both Daoism and Confucianism was incorporated into Buddhism through translation and eventually giving form to *Chan* Buddhism, unique to Chinese culture. Through different historical periods, *qi*, from a vague idea was developed into a cosmological, aesthetic, social, medical, moral concept, and eventually a philosophy, reaching its maturity in Song Dynasty.

Zhang Zai and the Philosophy of *Qi*

Zhang Zai (1020–1077) is known as the philosopher of *qi*. Although Zhang's contemporaries Zhu Xi, Cheng Hao, and Cheng Yi (known as Cheng-Zhu school) were more recognized than Zhang Zai in neo-Confucianism, Zhang Zai's significance however is rediscovered by contemporary scholars, including Tang Junyi (1909–1978), Zhang Dainian, Feng Youlan, and later Jung-Yeup Kim and Ira E. Kasoff.

Zhang Zai studied Buddhism and Daoism before he abandoned both and turned to books on medicine and astronomy. His most important writing *Zheng Meng* (正蒙, *Rectifying the Ignorant*) is set to achieve two goals, to critique Buddhism as misleading and to speculate on the myriad things. For Zhang Zai, Buddhism's nihilist perspective that considers the world we live in as illusion is misleading. According to Siu-Chi Huang, Zhang Zai replaces terms frequently used by Buddhists like "existence and non-existence, production and annihilation" with his favorite terms like "appearance and disappearance, coming to be and passing away, moving and resting, contraction and expansion, ascending and descending" (1968). Zhang Zai's terms, as Huang explains, "connote the idea that in spite of the constant change of the myriad things in the universe, nothing will be lost or completely destroyed quantitatively" (1968, 250).

Zhang Zai's work is challenging to interpret and has thus produced different interpretations. Modern Chinese philosopher Zhang Dainian recognized Zhang Zai as a *qi* monist materialist, confirming his philosophy of *qi* as an original contribution to Chinese thinking. Another Chinese philosopher, neo-Confucianist Tang Junyi, however, speaks against the materialist perspective of Zhang Dainian, convincingly arguing that *qi* is not a matter or spirit, it is a becoming. Tang pointed out that *qi* is a conception prior to form and matter, as understood in Western philosophy or science before modern physical quantum theory and relativity theory (Tang, 120).

In Chinese thought ether [*qi*] is invariably active, or, in other words, there may be said to be force within it. It is not an absolute formlessness or a sub-formal matter or potentiality, but a real existence that is capable of motion or quietude, and of assuming a definite form while also capable of transcending one form to assume another form. (121)

What is essential to Zhang Zai's notion of *qi* is its movement, transformation, and mutation. For Zhang Zai, there is never existence or nonexistence, but only condensation and disintegration, hidden (*you*) or manifested (*ming*). Tang suggests that *qi*, particularly informed through Zhang Zai's philosophy, should be defined as "an existential process, within which there is the mutation of forms, or as an existence within which there is the process of the mutation of forms" (121).

Along with existing critiques of materialistic readings of Zhang Zai's philosophy of *qi*, Jung-Yeup Kim makes it clear that the prevalent assumption "that *qi* is a singular substance and that the myriad things and dimensions of this world are merely different manifestations of it" never exists in Zhang Zai's position. Instead, building on Tang Junyi's interpretation of Zhang Zai's *qi*-philosophy, Kim suggests that Zhang Zai develops the concept of *qi* through the notion of polarity, correlativity, and organic unity. Hence, it is more accurate to call Zhang Zai an organic pluralism (x). According to Kim, to say that "x" is *qi* and "y" is *qi* is to say that "x" and "y" are correlative polarities mutually resonating, interpenetrating, and forming an organic unity with one another (34).

Both Tang and Kim's interpretations of *qi* help us to better understand one of Zhang Zai's known statement about the nature of *qi*, "*gui-shen*, the intuitive and intrinsic nature of *qi*."[17] *Gui-shen* (鬼神), literally translated as ghosts-spirits, also means movements of contraction and expansion. The contraction of *qi* is *yin* and hence *gui*; the expansion of *qi* is *yang* and hence *shen*. Death is not nonbeing but dispersion of *qi*. Life is not being but condensation of *qi*. "Mutation of forms" in Tang's words or "mutual resonance" in Kim's description, both describe a *qi*-philosophy that emphasizes ceaseless movements and correlativity.

As one of the essential concepts in Zhang Zai's *qi*-philosophy, *gui-shen* not only suggests the transformative nature of *qi*, but also emphasizes the virtue and the sensation of reverence in *qi*-philosophy. That is, for Zhang Zai, one should have a reverence for transformation, mutation, and resonance of nature and the myriad things. As the Chinese scholar Zhou Yun explains, while opposing the superstitions of personification of ghost and spirits in folk cultures, Zhang Zai strongly advocates restoring shamanic rituals through which one can truly resonate to *gui-shen*, the great movement of the cosmic *qi* (2014).

---

[17] 鬼神，二气之良能。

This statement also reflects the deep influence of the ancient cosmic resonance theory on *qi*-philosophy. Kim insightfully points out that echoing the neo-Confucian philosopher Zhu Xi's (1130–1200) observation, Zhang Zai inherits more from *Yijing* than other Confucian texts. *Yijing* is the first classics that brought up the notion of *gan* (resonance) and *gan* is the guiding motif for Zhang Zai's philosophy of *qi*. It has to be stressed that it is the notion of resonance that makes Zhang Zai's philosophy of *qi* pertinent to an understanding of Chinese acoustics.

Sound Explained through *Qi*-Philosophy

Based on previous discussions of the history of Chinese acoustics and the philosophy of *qi*, it can be generalized that the relation between sound and *qi* comprises three dimensions: (1) sound is produced by *qi*; (2) sound is a manifestation of *qi*; and (3) acoustic technology is a facilitator of *qi*. *Qi*-philosophy suggests an enchanted worldview that the cosmos and the myriad things (including humans) are a correlated organism that are constantly resonating, condensing, disintegrating, and forming unity with one another. It is an enchanted worldview that humans keep reverence for transformations, mutations, and resonance.

Sound *Qi*, Song Yingxing

As stated before, Zhang Zai's writing on sound is rather limited to one paragraph, but his philosophy of *qi* and his understanding of sound has deeply influenced Song Yingxing (1587–1666), a Chinese scientist and encyclopedist in late Ming Dynasty. Needham somehow leaves Song Yingxing out of his discussion on Chinese acoustics, while mentioning him in sections on mechanical engineering and nautics. Song wrote an important essay on sound and *qi*, which can be seen as a further demonstration of the ancient proposition—sound is produced by *qi*—found in *Yue Ji*, *Hua Shu*, *Zeng Meng*, and *Guan Yinzi*.

In his book *Lun Qi (论气, On Qi)*, Song offers a rather interesting discussion of sound through the philosophy of *qi* in the section titled *Qi Sheng* (气声, *Qi* Sound). Song's basic idea on sound seems to be inherited from Zhang Zai, because there are a few places where Song directly copies Zhang. For example, in *Qi Sheng* 2, Song writes, "*Qi* fills the heaven and earth. When two *qi* rubs each other arises sound. It is wind." However, Song provides more detailed and well-argued discussions on sound as produced by *qi*.

Song suggests that *qi* itself doesn't make a sound. Sound is not simply the vibration of *qi*. To make sound, *qi* needs to be disturbed in a certain way.

That is, *qi* has to possess *shi* (势, the advantage of position or force), which is an important and unique concept in Chinese thought as François Jullien later identifies (Jullien 1999). Song asked why a high waterfall produces a loud sound whereas the fall of water from a pot hardly make any sound although the water and the process is the same. He explains it is because they have different *shi*. The *qi* of the waterfall possesses *shi* by reason of height and speed.

Song also gives a few examples to prove that *qi* is what produces sound. He asks, "When one strikes a bell or a drum, is the sound produced by the bell or the drum, or is it produced by *qi*?" To prove that it is *qi* that produces sound, Song argues, "Let's suppose that sound is not produced by *qi*. Try stretching a drum skin on the ground, and fill up the bell with earth. What sound is there?" Song then gives a counter example:

Someone might ask "if you hang up a sounding-stone and strike it, it emits penetrating note despite the fact that it has no hollow inside it. What do you make of that? I reply that what is going on is that the suspended stone forms a barrier between the continuous *qi* on either side of it. If you strike it from one side the *qi* on the other side responds. It is the same principle as the bell and drum. Supposing that the sound was produced by the stone rather than by the *qi*, what kind of sound is produced when the stone is placed flat up against a wall and struck?" (Cullen, 308–9)

Song provides an essential addition to our understanding of *qi* and human sound. He writes:

Human beings live because they have received [an endowment of] *qi*. When there is *qi* there can be sound, and sound returns to *qi*. Now when solid body (*xing*) transforms to *qi* it returns to it very slowly, while when sound returns to *qi* it does so in an instant. The sound produced by human beings come forth from the viscera [where the body's *qi* is stored], are modulated by the lips and tongue, and then have to make contact and harmonise with the *qi* in empty space [outside the body]. [To see that this is necessary] if the mouth and nose are blocked what is outside cannot enter and harmonise [with what is within] and what is within can only rise up to the roof of the mouth and make an obscure grunting noise. In the human body the father's seminal essence and the mother's blood are conserved in the "reservoir of qi" and in the "gate of life." Whether an individual's "sound *qi*" is large or small, short or prolonged, depends on the embryonic endowment and not on the strength of effort made. (Cullen 1990, 307)

In this paragraph, Song only states that *qi* resides in the body. Later, he specifies that the vital *qi* resides in the gallbladder of the body and communicates with the exterior through the ear. The *qi* that resides in the gallbladder possesses *liang zhi* (良知, intuitive knowledge), which enables innate moral judgment of the human being. Interestingly, Song believes that one's sound *qi* is innate; like gene, it "depends on the embryonic endowment." However, not so much different from his predecessor Zhang Zai, Song Yingxing's perspective on the function of sound and music is also a moral one, that is, to cultivate *liang zhi*. "*Liang zhi* can tell if the sound is good or evil, thus the saint makes music to cultivate it."

It is important to notice Christopher Cullen's reminder that it is rather tempting to read modern physics back into Song's writing. If we do so, "much of the real character of Song's thought will be obliterated in the process" (Cullen, 306). This warning is also helpful to keep in mind while working through Chinese *qi*-philosophy.

Resonance

Essential to both ideas of sound and *qi* is the notion of *gan* (感 resonance), which was recorded as first appeared in *Yijing (Book of Changes)* in Zhou dynasty, later developed in encyclopedic classics *lvshi chunqiu* (吕氏春秋), a collection of different schools of thoughts by the end of Waring States Period (481–403 BC). Roger T. Ames and David I. Hall observe that "the vocabulary of *qi* and *yin-yang* emphasizes acoustic resonance and response" (Hall & Ames 260). From *Yijing*, we learn that to know the nature of a thing, for example, the earth, one needs to recognize the resonant nature of the earth, that is, what the earth is resonating to and what it is in relation to. The valley resonates to sounds and gives echo in response; Laozi calls it *gu shen* (谷神, the creative indeterminacy of the valley). Resonance also applies to humans. *Jing qi* (精气), the most refined form of *qi* is what makes one thing resonate with one another. Parents and their children, despite different bodies share the same *qi*. Therefore, they resonate with each other even if they are at different locations. The notion of resonance reached its highest popularity in Han Dynasty. In *Huainanzi* (125 BC), it reads, "the mutual resonance between various things is deeply mysterious and profound. It cannot be evaluated through knowing, nor understood through explanation . . . this is perhaps the emotional resonance between things . . . this is perhaps the dynamic movement among things"[18]. Dong Zhongshu (179–104BC) further consolidated the notion of resonance in his theory of *tianren ganying* (天人感应 resonance between the heaven and the human). Resonance theory implies, as Yuk Hui summaries, "A homogeneity

---

[18]淮南子: "夫物类之相应，玄妙深微，知不能论，辩不能解…或感或动"

in all beings" and "an organicity of the relation between part and part, and between part and whole" (27).

Resonance is also the major principle through which music is understood in *Yue Ji* (The Record of Music). Music notes correlate to seasons, compass points, raw materials, body organs, and social matters. For example, the five basic notes *gong* (宫), *shang* (商), *jiao*(角), *zhi* (徵), and *yu* (羽) were originally decided and arranged correlatively through the principle of resonance between material of instruments, seasons, and directions. According to Dong Zhongshu, the sound of each notes corresponds to particular natural phenomenon: *gong*—the thunder sound in the fall; *shang*—the fierce lightening sound in the fall; *jiao*—the wild wind in the summer; *zhi*—the lightening in the fall; and *yu*—the wind in the spring and summer. Each note symbolizes different people or things: *gong*—the emperor; *shang*—the minister; *jiao*—the people; *zhi*—events; *yu*—living and nonliving beings. *Gong, shang, jiao, zhi,* and *yu* correspond to five notes—do, re, mi, so, and la. However, the order of the five notes often appear as *shang, jiao, gong, zhi,* and *yu* (re, mi, do, so, and la). This is because, as Needham argues, "this tradition of the notes being ranged not by pitch but by some sort of ceremonial array," that is, "the *gong* position for the house-fame, which was lord; the *shang* position for the *xiang* drum (相鼓) regulating the proceedings like a just minister; the *jiao* position for a stand dressed with horns, the *zhi* or summoning position, possibly associated with the *ying* bell (应钟) or *ying* drum (应鼓); and the *yu* (羽) position where the post or stand was adorned with feathers" (159). These correlations are more clearly listed in Table 1.1.

Zhang Zai's contribution in developing the notion of resonance lies in working resonance into a philosophy of *qi*. Most significantly, Zhang Zai defines creativity through resonance. It is necessary to clarify that creativity corresponds to the Chinese word *cheng* (诚), which in contemporary Chinese language often means sincerity or integrity. However, in classical Confucian texts including Zhang Zai's, *cheng* is believed to be better understood as creativity. Roger T. Ames and David I. Hall suggest, "The dynamic of becoming whole, construed aesthetically, is precisely what is meant by a creative process. It is thus that *cheng* is to be understood as *creativity*" (2001, 32). Following Ames and Hall, Kim translates *cheng* in Zhang Zai's text as creativity. For Zhang Zai, quoting Kim's translation, "that which interpenetrates through resonance (*gan*) is creativity" (感而 通诚也)。

According to Zhang Zai, what we call *xing* (性, nature, instinct), is that which is not able to not resonate (不能无感者谓性). A double negative is used to confirm the ingrained nature of resonance in nature and myriad things. In his earlier work *Yishuo,* Zhang Zai discuses different causes for resonance: similarities, differences, attractions, fear, and correspondence (Xin, 130). As Kim summarizes, Zhang Zai's understanding of creativity

TABLE 1.1 *Correlations among Five Chinese Notes, Sense Organs, Five Elements, Directions, Western Notes, and Natural Phenomenon*

Five notes	Five body organs	Five sense organs	Five elements	Five Directions	Western notes	Myriad things	Natural phenomenon
Gong	Spleen	Nose	Earth	Middle	do	Lord	Thunder sounds in the fall
Shang	Lung	Eye	Gold	West	re	Minister	Fierce lightening sound in the fall
Jiao	Liver	Ear	Wood	East	mi	People	Wild wind in the summer
Zhi	Heart	Tongue	Fire	South	so	Events	Lightening in the fall
Yu	Kidney	Mouth	Water	North	la	Things	Wind in the spring and summer

consists three dimensions: creativity as resonance (gan, 感), creativity as the capacity to resonate (性), and creativity as emptiness (xu, 虚). *Xu* (emptiness) is interpreted as the capacity to resonate with the multiplicity of things.

Through this relation of resonance and creativity, we can say that resonance functions as a particular sensibility, the sixth sense so to speak. The ability to resonate is innate to myriad things but often remains hidden or blocked. If we follow Zhang Zai's teaching, it is crucial to recognize that as part of the myriad things, we the humans are constantly resonating/ affecting and resonated/affected by one another and by the cosmos. Creativity is not only necessary but fundamental in unveiling and increasing our capacity of resonance and ultimately forming an organic unity with the cosmos (天人合一*tianren heyi*). To recall what Zhang Zai says about sound, "sound is a result of and manifests the inherent capacity of resonance among things. People are only so used to resonance that they never notice them" (声者…是皆物感之良能。人皆习之而不察者尔). Zhang Zai's philosophy of *qi* articulates how the myriad entities of this world are simultaneously differentiated yet interrelated organically, and his goal is to maximize the vitality of human experience through creativity (the capacity to resonate with one another).

Resonance in Modern Times

In the 1950s, through mathematical means, physicist Winfried Otto Schumann calculated that the earth has an atmospheric frequency at 7.85 hz. This frequency happens to be similar to the frequency of the neural oscillation of the human brain known as the alpha wave when one closes eyes and stays in a relaxed state. The resemblance is curiously intriguing. It makes one wonder if humans are, indeed as the ancient Chinese believe in, intrinsically intertwined with myriad things to form and sustain an organic unity with the cosmos.

Classical Western physics discovered that anything with certain degree of elasticity and a shape has a natural frequency. Resonance occurs when a periodicity force matches the natural frequency of the thing. Later a discovery of the mechanism of resonance in quantum mechanics by Werner Heisenberg inspired the chemist Linus Pauling to apply the word "resonance" in his valence bond theory in 1930s to describe certain chemical species consisting of more than one Lewis structure. That is, the electron can jump from one nucleus to the other, forming a more stable bond in the molecule. The notion was later challenged for its misleading meanings derived from physics and was suggested to be replaced by "dislocalization" (Kerber 2006). It is beyond my capacity to go in depth to chemistry and quantum mechanics. What is interesting to me is the conceptual similarity between Pauling's and Zhang Zai's theories, the idea that a molecule contains an unstable structure with two shifting/interchanging Lewis structure to be stable recalls Zhang Zai's notion that it is through the resonating nature of the myriad things that the great harmony is achieved.

Other than its discovery and application in science, resonance is argued to be the key to the definition of reason and the key vehicle of modern self-fashioning (Erlmann 2010). After meticulously reworking with Descartes's philosophy and the development of acoustic physiology, Veit Erlmann shows that the notion of man has shifted from this self-reflexive and self-resonant ego of romanticism and idealism to the echoless ego in the twentieth century sketched out by Heidegger, Günther Anders, and Peter Sloterdijk. Artworks in the twentieth century, by the composer Arnold Schoenberg, the poet Rainer Maria Rilke, as Erlmann cited, present the hopeless situation of man (as in Rilke's essay) and an utterly inhuman and self-contained system (as in Schoenberg's composition) to mirror the social system the artists find themselves in.

According to Erlmann, philosophers including Heidegger, Sloterdijk, and Anders have left us an echoless, panicked, and autovibrating Dasein, no matter how much they value the existential value of music or the acoustic. "Where we are when we listen to music"—Peter Sloterdijk poses this existential question, which also inspired Erlmann to draw comparison between Heidegger and Anders. For Heidegger and later Sloterdijk, music is the "acoustic uterus" where the primal sympathetic resonance is regained (337). Hence Heidegger's answer to the question "where we are when we listen," as Erlmann postulates, is that we are in resonance (338). For Anders, as Erlmann quotes, "the situation of being in music is an extraterritorial," similar to situations of sleep, shock, play or dreams. In music, "one fall out of the world" (325–6). Like being shocked, or in sleep, one falls out of the historical self, the sense that one is continuous with the I of the previous day. Music plays the role of midwifery who cuts the umbilical cord connecting the Dasein to the world.

Heidegger and Anders have subtracted the listening man from its resonant and reflexive and hence reasoning self. They sent their listening subjects to exile in a nonresonant and solitary process of returning (to either an acoustic uterus or an extraterritorial situation). The difference between the two remains in that for Anders, as Erlmann interpreted, "the resolution of our longing for timelessness, according to Anders, is not a question of ontology or of Heidegger's pseudohistorical phantasm, but of a well-lived life, of the successful handling of time in the satisfaction of our vital needs" (339).

Curiously, Günther Ander's thinking as interpreted by Erlmann has a closer resemblance to Chinese qi-thinking that works with vocabularies such as condensation-disintegration and hidden-manifestation. Ander claims that music is transformative in the sense that one engages in a double/paradoxical movement of Mitvollzug (co-performance) and Umstimmung (returning). Returning contains three types: dissolution, detachment, and released. In the ever-changing movement of the myriad thing, dissolution, detachment, and release is always essential for resonance and for reconnecting. This movement of co-performance and returning, interpreted both conceptually and phenomenologically, would be readily embraced by readers of Lao Zi, Zhuang Zi, and Zhang Zai.

How would Chinese philosophers like Zhang Zai approach the question of where we are when we listen?

In *Yijing,* a book that deeply inspires Zhang Zai, we read that everything is in a constant movement. Things do not take up a space-time, but can only be described by their temporary location and orders. As scholar Fong Sai Ho (n.d.) elaborates while analyzing Zhang Zai's texts, in Chinese thinking, the order and position of things are constantly changing. When a thing's position and order changes, its form changes too. Thus, the form, position, and nature of a thing are never independent. For Zhang Zai, a thing's position and order is decided by the process of its responsive relation with others. A thing does not take a position alone. Things are always related to their past and future, therefore it is incorrect to say that a thing takes up a space-time. With the example of grass, Fong (n.d.) explains that grass is what grows in the entire living system. Thus, a seed and the earth in which it is planted have a resonant relation. The seed feels the difference of the earth from itself and discovers that it can grow in it. Jullien uses the concept of propension to describe this unique feature in Chinese thinking, that is, things never are, but lean toward (Jullien 2015, 14). Behind the concept of propension is the philosophy of *qi*. Through *qi*-philosophy, to know means not only to know the current state of things but also more importantly to discern stages of networks of things, that is, not only to grasp the shape of things but also the *xiang* (象, the intensity and propensity of the shapeless), the diffusive and immersive.

Therefore, Zhang Zai's *qi*-thinking challenges the existential question of where we are when we listen. Instead of focusing on destinations, *qi*-thinking attends to tendencies, correlations, and processes. Instead of focusing on the subject that listens, *qi*-thinking returns us to the background, the network, or the system through which a resonating event arises and in which listeners are also creators.

Conclusion

Through sound—a result and manifestation of resonating *qi*—we perceive the world as in ceaseless transformation and mutation. Zhang Zai's *qi*-philosophy suggests that it is in the nature of the cosmos and the myriad things not able to not resonate. Barry Allen emphatically writes, "Taking resonance seriously implies a connection of things that is not exhausted by logic and experience, or even by logic and causation. Things are connected through their becoming, the mere fact that they come to be. From this becoming they receive a duration, a temporality, and cannot fail to resonate with, ultimately, everything" (2015). Like it or not, we are always parts of more than one circuit of mutation and transformation. Through *qi*-philosophy, questions of fixation like "who we are" or "what a thing is" give way to questions of propensity and tendency. The latter questions are also asked by what is now called system-thinking or cybernetics. Both *qi*-philosophy and system-thinking or cybernetics attend to processes and transformations. The difference may be that *qi*-philosophy is still endowed with reverence and embodies an enchanted worldview.

The philosophy of *qi* does not work as a higher mode of thinking that explains sound art and music. It suggests a moral, intellectual, and somatic sensibility, with which we listen, feel, think, create, care, and live. It is a resource of living a creative life. To repeat myself, breathing is the simplest fact that we are composed of *qi*. Breathing is resonating.

2

A Brief History of Sound in China's Contemporary Art

The initial stage of China's contemporary art was filled with noise, from the avant-garde art group The Stars staging Star Art Exhibition without official permission along the street outside of the China Art Gallery in 1979,[1] to members of Xiamen Dada[2] burning their own artworks in front of the Cultural Palace of Xiamen in 1986, to the preplanned gun shot fired by the Chinese artist Xiao Lu that gave a thriving contemporary Chinese art scene a temporary pause in 1989. Other than being a background noise, sound has been a part of the creative practices of contemporary Chinese artists since the 1980s. Unfortunately, sound, as an artistic medium, somehow has slipped away from art historians' account. The goal of this chapter is, therefore, to examine sound in the history of China's contemporary art, both before and after the application of Chinese translation of the English term "sound art."

---

[1]The Stars (1979–1983) was founded by Huang Rui and Ma Desheng. Its members include Wang Keping, Qu Leilei, A Cheng, Ai Weiwei, and Li Shuang. The Star Art Exhibition attracted crowds upon its opening and was forced to close by the police for public safety reasons. Artists put up a protest asking for the freedom of art. For more on the Stars art group see Wu Hung's *Contemporary Chinese Art: A History, 1970s-2000s*. Thames & Hudson, 2014.
[2]Xiamen Dada (1983–1989) was founded by Huang Yongping as a radical art group emerged during the '85 New Wave movement. Its major members include Lin Jiahua, Jiao Yaoming, Yu Xiaogang, Xu Chengdou, Cai Lixiong, Lin Chun, Chen Chengzong, Li Shixiong, Zeng Yinhong, Wu Yimng.

Conditions and Precursors

Before 2000

During the 1980s, the beginning of China's economic reform, Chinese artists found themselves gaining increasing access to new media technologies, tools, as well as imported art and culture products. Mixed with a pent-up desire for knowledge and creativity, artists in the 1980s were bold and adventurous, experimenting with all possible ways of art making. Sorting through artworks created during and after the '85 New Wave movement (a series of art groups and provocative art exhibitions created between 1985 and 1989 as a reaction to the dominant socialist realism in art academies), I come to realize that sound has already been part of new art mediums used by artists, although the awareness of sound as a unique and independent art material came much later in the year 2000 in mainland China. During the mid and late 1980s, conceptual and experimental art often appeared in the format of mixed media, engaging with the material and notion of sound for its performative, emotive, and conceptual forces.

Geng Jianyi (1962–2017), one of the leading artists in the '85 New Wave movement, worked with oil painting, photography, video, installation, and performance. Sound has never been a pronounced focus in Geng's work. However, curiously in 1989, Geng made an installation titled *Tremble with Fear* using sets of clock hearts, which strikes me as probably the earliest exhibited contemporary art work in mainland China that affected audience through its sounding (Figure 2.1). This work was re-exhibited in his solo exhibition titled *Wuzhi, 1985–2008 Geng Jianyi's Work* in 2012 at MinSheng Art Museum. It was a remade piece because the original one was affected by rust. Unfortunately, there was barely any video or audio documentation of this work. From a review article written by a sinologist and researcher Jeanne Boden, we get a glimpse of this work. Boden writes, "More surprises come from the noise being used in this installation. Audience will hear an unsettling background noise when they are looking at the artworks. Once one comes closer to the installation, minor interruption becomes strong opposition" (Boden 2015).

Zhang Peili (1957–), another leading artist in the '85 New Wave movement, a good friend of Geng Jianyi, is most recognized for his pioneer video art works in China. Zhang and Geng were former schoolmates in Zhejiang Academy of Fine Art (renamed China Academy of Art in 1993) in Hangzhou. They later worked together to cofound the New Media Art department at China Academy of Art. Qiu Zhijie (1969–), graduated from China Academy of Art in 1992, once commented that the whole aura of China Academy of Art was bold and cool in the 1980s. Students dared to reject many things and they dared to belittle techniques of oil painting that were popular in art academies and in the art world at the time.

FIGURE 2.1 *Geng Jianyi*, Tremble with Fear, *2012, restored 1989. Electrical machine, steel plate, and copper, dimensions variable. M+, Hong Kong. [2012.1644]. © M+, Hong Kong.*

In 1991, Zhang made a video titled *Water: Standard Version from the Cihai Dictionary*, in which standard broadcasting voice was heard out of its usual context of national news report. The work's statement reads,

> Xing Zhibin, the female television announcer who once represented the image of the official state media in China, reads aloud from the standard *Cihai* dictionary the terms beginning with the character *shui*, or water, with impeccably standard speed and diction. The video itself is shot according to the standard style of television news in China with the production facilities of the Beijing Media Center, making this an exercise in absurdity and suggesting something of the actual content or rigor of typical news broadcasts. (Gladston et al. 2012, 114)

The standard broadcasting voice of Xing Zhibin constitutes a collective memory of ordinary Chinese individuals, especially those born before the early 1980s who would watch CCTV news every day seven o'clock in the evening. The voice is also held as the standard of spoken Mandarin, perpetuated in schools and universities where local dialects were discouraged all over the country (see Chapter 6 for more analysis of this work).

In 1996, Qiu Zhijie and Wu Meichun, both alumni of China Academy of Art and residing in Beijing by then, curated a video art exhibition in Hangzhou titled *Phenomena and Image Video Art*. This exhibition was seen as the first of its kind in mainland China.

Most artworks in this exhibition used sound as a complimentary medium to the visuals. This made Geng Jianyi's video installation *A Complete World* stand out as a unique piece, wittily playing with the relation between the audio and the video. Four television screens were placed at each of the four walls of a room. On the screens were video documentation of different parts of the room. A fly appeared still in one of the videos. When it flew away (not seen on screens), one heard a buzzing sound. When it appeared on one of the screens resting, the buzzing sound stopped. The buzzing sound became a medium through which the physical space and its representation on the screen connected. The artist seems to suggest that only when paired with an audio perception, the visual world can be complete.

Although sound has always been a part of video art works, video art is largely categorized as visual art and evaluated primarily according to visual criteria. However, speaking from its working mechanism, the artist Bill Viola insightfully remarks, "The video image is a standing wave pattern of electrical energy, a vibrating system composed of specific frequencies as one would expect to find in any resonating object" (2013, 43–4). And hence, Viola argues that video has a closer relation to sound than video's normally assumed association to film and photography.

> Video has evolved out of sound (the electromagnetic) and its close association with cinema is misleading is since film and its grandparent, the photographic process, are members of a completely different branch of the genealogical tree (the mechanical/chemical). The video camera, as an electronic transducer of physical energy into electrical impulses, bears a closer original relation to the microphone than to the film camera. (43–4)

Video has also been used in documenting performance art in the 1990s. In his video art *Shouting* (喊) (1998), the artist Xu Zhen (1977–) placed a camera at the back of moving crowds in different busy public spaces of Shanghai, including subway station, train station, and commercial shopping centers. The camera documented people in the forward-moving crowd turning back, shocked by a sudden eruption of a shout. The shouts of the artist and his friends generated the most spontaneous human reaction, to respond. The artist deftly interrupted and took control of the flow of the crowd through a simple shout, circumventing meanings. A series of interesting relations were evoked through this piece, call and being called upon, control and being controlled. The art critic and curator Tian Feiyu even went as far as to relate the work to the Chinese revolutionary writer Lu Xun's essay

Scream (呐喊). *Shouting* was later shown at the fifty-first Venice Biennial—The China Pavilion, curated by the known Chinese contemporary artist Cai Guoqiang. Xu Zhen studied art in Shanghai Gongyi Meiyuan (Shanghai Art and Design Academy). After graduation in 1996, he went to Beijing for a year and a half, earning his living by selling *dakou* CDs[3]. It was a time (1996–1998) when the rock music scene was rampantly growing in Beijing, but there was hardly a contemporary art scene by the time. In 1998, Xu Zhen returned to Shanghai to begin his art career.

Always a radical and provocative artist by nature, Xu Zhen often employs performance that involves sound and music as his artistic outlet. Video is mainly used as a means of documentation in these cases. In the three-channel video installation *Road Show* (2002), Xu Zhen dressed up as a hip hop performer on tour. In the performance piece *Baba Mama (Daddy and Mommy)* (2003), Xu Zhen asked two performers to wear the costume of wild men wandering around at the exhibition opening of *Second-Hand Reality Contemporary Art Exhibition* at Today Art Museum in Beijing. Once the performers encountered an audience face to face, they immediately kneeled and shouted "daddy" if the audience was a male and "mommy" if female. In a similar spirit, Xu Zhen's performance piece *We Are Coming* (2003) performed by two young individuals wearing police caps installed with a police alarm launched a sonic attack at an exhibition opening in Hangzhou.

On November 6, 2000, the third Shanghai Biennale took place at Shanghai Art Museum. For the first time, the Shanghai Biennale decided to include a series of unofficial art activities organized at local commercial galleries. The known Chinese art historian Wu Hung considered this year of Shanghai Biennale "a milestone in the history of contemporary Chinese art" (2014). Wu explains, "It formally announced the official acceptance of international style exhibitions of contemporary art and opened the doors of a major government museum to experimental artists" (2014, 352). These artists include Ai Weiwei, Xu Zhen, Yang Fudong, and Yang Zhenzhong.

Other than Shanghai and Hangzhou, Beijing is another major city where there began to emerge a new media art scene from late 1990s. Feng Mengbo (1966–), an accomplished new media artist, is not only a pioneer in computer art in mainland China but also a fervent collector of analog and digital sound devices. Feng bought his first Macintosh (Macintosh LC II) in late 1993, two years after he graduated from the Central Academy of

---

[3]Dakou, or saw-gash, describes the small punch hole cut into the excess CDs by Western record companies prior to shipping them to China as trash, presumably unsellable. Dakou CDs soon found a market in China, despite their ragged packaging and missing tracks of music. They became the main source of Western music for Chinese youths, satisfying a growing desire for new and different types of music before internet and personal computers became available in mainland China after 2000.

Art in Beijing with the money he earned through painting. He bought his first synthesizer Korg M1 on the second day after he bought the Macintosh. With these new tools, Feng created a series of computer-based artworks, including the interactive CD-ROM installation *My Private album* (1996), recognized as the first computer-based artwork in China. *My Private Album* narrates the family history of Feng through old family photos, images of household objects of different generations, hand-drawn sketches of family members, LP records, private tape recordings of the elder's storytelling, and video recordings. To break the linear narrative line, Feng thematized the family history into four categories titled "Grandparents," "Parents," "Xiaozheng and Me," and "Hong Xiaobing's Cinema" and let the audience choose which one to open. Each category unfolds with an animation of operating a device that marked the era: the LP player with "Grandparents," camera with "Parents," television with "Xiaozheng and Me," and cinema with "Hong Xiaobing's Cinema." Transitions in sound and music vividly convey particular social spirits in different eras, from *shidai qu* (时代曲, a unique music genre that combines Chinese folk music with American Jazz originated in Shanghai in the 1920s), to *yangbanxi* (样板戏, "model opera" during the Cultural Revolution), from LPs to tapes, to CDs, to loudspeakers hung in public spaces during the Cultural Revolution period, and from individual star singers to unanimous collective singing.

In1999, contemporary artist Lin Tianmiao (1961–) created a mixed-media installation *High!!!* (嗨!!!) (Figure 2.2) using video projection, sound, and cotton threads. In the work, a video of Lin Tianmiao's portrait shot from the shoulders up was projected onto a white canvas. It was a moving image played in loop, showing Lin Tianmiao changing from a contemporary female outlook to androgynous images of a naked and bald person. The back of the projection screen was connected to more than ten thousand single strands of white cotton threads with the other side connected from a wall. Behind the wall were speakers and amplifiers playing high and low frequencies, causing thousands of suspended threads to vibrate. The art work's note reads, "This movement is never fixed image; transformation is the only constant state; and that the connection between ideas and events remains as fragile as the threads themselves." The vibration of the cotton threads not only made the fragility tactile but also added both acoustic and spatial dimensions to the constant transformation often too subtle to detect.

In the same year of 1999, Lin Tianmiao together with her husband, contemporary artist Wang Gongxin (1960–), returned to Beijing after living in New York for eight years and founded the art space *Cang Ku* (藏酷) in Beijing. *Cang Ku* (1999–2003) quickly became a popular place among artists to host the coolest art shows, art and culture forums, screenings of independent and art films in Beijing, including a few of Qiu Zhijie's "Post-sense Sensibility" exhibitions, which prove to be essential to the origin of China's sound art.

FIGURE 2.2 *Lin Tianmiao,* High!!! *1999/2018. Installation view Rockbund Art Museum, Shanghai, 2018. Photo by Author.*

Post-Sense Sensibility Movement and the Origin of Sound Art

Sensing an increasingly conceptual trend in China's contemporary art world in the late 1990s, the artists Qiu Zhijie and Wu Meichun initiated the "post-sense sensibility" movement to rival against conceptual art. There are two driving factors paving the way for the formation of the Post-sense Sensibility group (active between 1999 and 2003). One is the controversial exhibition of YBA (Young British Artists) *Sensation.* The other is the artist Qiu Zhijie's interests in philosophy and another member of post-sense sensibility group, Shi Qing's interest in theater.

Sensation: Young British Artists from the Saatchi Collection (opened in September 18, 1997, in London) showcased the collection of contemporary art works owned by Charles Saatchi. It later toured in New York and Berlin. The exhibition included works by Young British Artists including Marcus Harvey, Damien Hirst, Chris Ofili, and Yinka Shonibare. Due to several controversial artworks, including Damian Hirst's life-size shark suspended in a tank of formaldehyde, Marcus Harvey's image of the child killer Myra Hindley, Chris Ofili's painting the Holy Virgin Mary, and Jake and Dinos Chapman's installation of child mannequins with noses replaced by penises and mouths in the form of an anus, *Sensation* provoked criticism and protests in London and later in New York. Qiu Zhijie revealed that it is this controversial exhibition *Sensation* that inspired post-sense sensibility group in his interview with new media art curator Li Zhenghua.[4]

Qiu Zhijie graduated from Zhejiang Academy of Art in 1992. He moved to Beijing in 1994 to study philosophy, particularly to understand the philosophy of Ludwig Wittgenstein through the renowned Chinese philosopher Chen Jiaying, whose translation of Heidegger's *Beijing and Time* was highly popular among Chinese readers in the 1980s. While still studying at China Academy of Art, Qiu Zhijie, Gao Shiming, Jiang Zhi, Gao Shiqiang, Lu Lei, and Liu Yi formed a private study group and spoke against academic authorities who at that time held firm that a good conceptual art should clearly and precisely deliver a concept through artistic language. The group held an opposite position, insisting that art was not to deliver any messages. Instead, artwork should create a sense or an effect that would make one cry, angry, or calm. In 1994, Qiu Zhijie published several articles on *Jiangsu Huakan* (江苏画刊, Jiangsu Pictorial), an influential art magazine that supported new art forms in the 1980s, arguing for the importance of maintaining a sense of presence, liveness, and embodiment in the process of art making.

Post-sense Sensibility group consisted artists including Qiu Zhijie, Shi Qing, Wu Ershan, Wang Wei, Liu Wei, Zhang Hui, and Gao Shiming. The term "post-sense" made its debut with the exhibition titled *Post-sense—Distorted Body and Delusion*, held on January 8, 1999, in the underground compartments (eighteen altogether) of a residential building named *Shaoyaoju* (芍药居) in Beijing. It presented works by Qin Ga, Wang Wei, Feng Qianyu, Sun Yuan, Peng Yu, Jiang Zhi, Chen Wenbo, Zhu Yu, Yang Fudong, Qiu Zhijie, and Wu Ershan. Despite being a one-day show, the exhibition caused a scene in China's contemporary art world, inviting as much criticism as praise. Two of the most notorious pieces in the history of Chinese contemporary art came from this exhibition—Zhu Ming's installation *Miniature Theology* with an arm cut from a dead body hanging on the ceiling holding a rope that covered the entire floor of the room and Sun Yuan's *Honey* with a frozen dead fetus placed on a gigantic ice bed.

With the spirit of challenging conceptual art, Post-sense Sensibility group put emphasis on the body, liveness, and immersive experience that is nonreplicable and nonrepeatable. Sound was seen as a fit medium in creating a field with affective propensity that could directly impact audience emotionally and somatically.

---

[4]http://www.bjartlab.com/read.php?17

—Sound (2000)

Two group exhibitions titled *Sound* (2000) and *Sound 2* (2001) were part of the Post-Sense Sensibility exhibition series. *Sound* (2000) was organized by Li Zhenghua when he was working as the art director of *Cang Ku*, organizing music concerts and art activities. In 1999, Li Zhenghua was selected to attend an art training program at ICA in London. He took the chance to see contemporary arts in and near London. During his stay in London, ICA organized a contemporary art exhibition titled *Beijing in London*, showing works by artists including Qiu Zhijie, Shi Qing, Wang Gongxin, and Zhang Hui. Li Zhenhua worked as an assistant to organize the exhibition and he met Wang Gongxin and Qiu Zhijie there. When Li returned to Beijing by the end of 1999, Wang Gongxin invited him to be the art director of *Cang Ku* space.

On December 9 and 10, 2000, Li curated the exhibition *Sound* at Beijing Contemporary Art Museum on Longfusi street, inviting "Post-sense Sensibility" artists Wang Wei (1972–), Zhang Hui (1967–), and Shi Qing (1969–). As a self-financed exhibition, *Sound* was later identified as the first sound art exhibition in mainland China. Using sound as the main creative focus was clearly expressed as the curatorial intention. It was a time when neither Western theories of sound nor institutional models of sound art as an independent genre were available to mainland art world. The three artists had to rely on their own interpretations of sound in combination with their own experience with art making. The absence of Western sound art category makes artworks in this exhibition even more interesting.

Shi Qing's multimedia work *Oral Period* was based on his childhood memory of kindergarten when the kindergarten teacher (called *a yi* or auntie) was constantly watching or inspecting restless young kids during night times (see Figure 2.3). The artist statement for the work reads:

Imagination and delusion accompanied my childhood in kindergarten. Before I sleep at night, the child minder's ghost would come out of her white uniform and fly into our bedroom. Where does the ghost hide? I guess she must stayed on the baby-bike, I can't say why. She will come out while we sleep and collect our souls like gathering toys in the day time, she puts our souls in little bottles and covers them, puts them in the wardrobe, and now we won't be able to play at night. She will use a torch to check if anyone's soul has already been collected. When torch light passes over my face, I quickly shut my mouth and tightly close my eyes.

Oral Period staged such a situation in which the audience reexperience what kindergarten kids' feel like under the watch of the auntie. Sound in this work is used as a sign of threat (the whistling sound blown by the auntie) and fear (increasing heartbeat sound). The work consisted of a projector

FIGURE 2.3 *Shi Qing,* Oral Period, *2000, Beijing. Photo Courtesy of the artist.*

showing a video of the artist himself riding a child bike fully naked in a dark room, a bike installation next to a wooden baby bunk bed video installation (showing a baby doll on the upper level and a video on the lower level), a baby bed video installation, a chair video installation, and a sculpture with a baby bust on top of a hollow wooden cylinder. When a visitor came closer to the twin bed, people shown in the video would close their eyes with a flashlight flashing on their faces. At the same time, one heard the sound of an increasing heartbeat. When the visitor left the area, people in the video opened their eyes. On the chair video installation, the screen showed an auntie whistling and sucking a baby nipple interchangeably. When the whistle was blown, the artist riding the bike stopped and turned around. *Oral Period* was a complicated interactive system rather rare at the time. According to Shi Qing, the work was made to create an immersive ambience to suite the overall theme of Post-sense Sensibility exhibition series. The artist used sound as one of the central mediums to build a theatrical and immersive experience. Li Zhenhua describes the work as a time machine to take audience back to the artist's childhood time.

Wang Wei's video installation *75 kg and 3.2 Cubic Meters,* the loudest one among the three, explored reactions and conflicts between human body and space. An enclosed steel case measuring 3.2 cubic meters was installed in the exhibition space with its floor fully graveled and with strips of pork skin scattered around. Two or three holes were carved out on the cube through which one can get a glimpse of a video installed inside, documenting the naked artist Wang Wei trying to break away from the same steel case cube by jumping and bumping against the steel wall. The clashing noise from the video, together with noises generated by audience walking around while avoiding strips of pork skins on the floor created an intense sense of anxiety and annoyance. More than just being a spectator of an artist trapped inside struggling to break out, the audience was involved in the work as an immediate part of the sound sources.

In his early art works, Wang Wei consistently attempted to generate a sense of discomfort by creating a situation in which the audience has no choice but to confront the artwork. *1/30th of a Second Under Water* was an even earlier work by Wang Wei that used sound. This work was exhibited in the first Post-sense Sensibility exhibition titled *Post-sense—Distorted Body and Delusion* in 1999. Installed at the only entrance to the exhibition space, the work consisted a series of luminous light boxes with images of a man trapped underwater facing upward. In a documentary of the exhibition *Sound*, Wang Wei commented, "For me, sound has a memory. When we are in an empty swimming pool, we hear a strange sound when sinking down under the water. It gives a feeling of fear. I want my audience to walk with this kind of feeling through my work." In both artworks, *1/30th of a Second Under Water* and *75 kg and 3.2 Cubic Meters*, Wang Wei used the affective power of sound to generate a certain sensation among viewers. However, the acoustic dimension of Wang Wei's artworks were left out in several records of Chinese contemporary art history. For example, in writing about this particular work, Wu Hung described the visual of this photo installation but neglected the sound (2014). In the publication that accompanies the first comprehensive exhibition of China's contemporary art in the UK titled *The Real Thing: Contemporary Art from China* (Groom, Smith and Xu 2007), Wang Wei's earlier works that involved sound stay completely muted (2007, 123–5).

Different from Shi Qing and Wang Wei's interactive and immersive installations, Zhang Hui's *Sound Lost* explored the intricate relation between spaces where art works were produced and exhibited, using sound as the means of this exploration. The work consisted two parts, a performance in streets of Beijing before the exhibition and a multimedia installation inside of the exhibition space. For the performance part, Zhang Hui went out to sites including shopping centers, streets, and subways, asking random people for directions. Dialogues together with environment sounds were recorded by an anonymous sound engineer.

Hello, how do I get to *Kuanjie?*
Go ahead, pass the Big Buddha Temple and there it is.

The recordings were then mixed and reproduced in the studio, with spatial references in the dialogues replaced by artificial sound without meaning.

Hello, how do I get to (artificial sound without meaning).
Go ahead, pass the (artificial sound without meaning) and there it is.

Zhang Hui also boiled 1000 sound recording cassettes in colored water. The sound of boiling is combined with previously post-produced sound of the dialogues. Each of these boiled cassettes were sealed in plastic bags. Zhang Hui then went to a shopping district and asked for permission from vendors to hang one of the cassette bags among other commodities on their vender booths. He explained to the vendors how it was part of an artwork and how the cassette was becoming useless but at the same time regained its new function.

The second part of *Sound Lost* was a multimedia installation. Zhang Hui divided the exhibition space into half black box and half walking tunnel. Inside of the black box was a video-audio installation with a front shot of the artist's eyes closed and mouth murmuring. The video looped the artist's face fading into the background of a blank screen, with the soundtrack playing a post-produced sound (the artist asking for directions on the streets mixed with water boiling noise). In the walking tunnel was a pile of fur and boiled cassettes, creating a mood that is both quiet and cold. Through this work, Zhang Hui tried to understand the usefulness and uselessness of an object (in this case the cassette tape) as a result of spatial divisions and transference (between exhibition space and performance space, exhibition space and vendor booths on streets, studio and exhibition space).

These three artworks in *Sound* (2000) focus on creating a scene to involve audience through video, audio, installation, and performance. Sound added a temporal duration and psychoacoustical dimension to both the artworks and experiences of the works. One had to go through the length of the work to complete looking at it and hence it was in a way resonating with Post-sense Sensibility's emphasis on experience, rather than concepts.

Sound 2 (2001)

In 2001, Li Zhenhua left *Cang Ku* to found his own space *Mustard Seed Garden Art Center* in the outskirt of Beijing, where he organized exhibitions once a week. At *Mustard Seed Garden Art Center*, He cocurated with Qiu Zhijie the second exhibition on sound titled *Sound 2* (July 14–21). In this exhibition, Qiu Zhijie curated the sound installation section, while Li Zhenhua curated live music performances by Feng Jiangzhou and the music duo FM3. The installation section presented works by Li Yong, Li Pinghu, Li Chuan, Wang Wei, Shi Qing, Wu Ershan, Liu Wei, Zhang Hui, Ma Jie, Qiu Zhijie, Song Dong, Wang Peng, and He Yingyi (Rania Ho).

In *Sound 2*, Wang Wei's installation *Close Contact* continued his experiment with breaking personal comfort zones by creating a spatial situation. The artist installed a narrow glass labyrinth at the entrance of the exhibition space. Its size only allows one person to squeeze through at one time. On the top of the labyrinth installed speakers that played a sound recording of one's naked back being stroked and rubbed during massage in a Chinese bathhouse. An image of a naked man was projected onto the glass as well. Compared to the image, the sound more easily evoked an intimate and un-dodgeable tactile feeling making the audience uncomfortable upon entering a public space.

Both Feng Jiangzhou and FM3 are among the first generation of musicians practicing electronic and experimental music in mainland China. Feng graduated from the art education major at China Academy of Art but he has earlier found his interest in music. After graduation, in 1992 he went to Beijing and in 1993 with his classmates Song Yonghong, Wang Jingsong, and Yan Lei from China Academy of Art he formed the punk band *The Fly* (1993–1998) which soon became one of the most radical avant-garde bands in Beijing's underground rock music scene. In 1997, the band released their first album *The Fly >1* in Taiwan. The album was listed in the annual Top Ten records by a Hong Kong journal *Music Colony* in 1998. *The Fly* disbanded after the second release of the band's CD in 1998. Feng Jiangzhou moved on to focus on electronic music and later multimedia theater. In 2001, the music duo FM3 (1999–) had just began developing their meditative and ambient electronic music, experimenting with fusing Chinese classical instruments with electronic music devices (see more discussion of FM3 in Chapter 3).

In the same year of 2001 in January, before *Sound 2*, Qiu Zhijie's solo exhibition *The Sound of Sound* took place in the gallery *Gen* in Koshigaya, Japan. All three exhibited works, *Ya Zhong (Dumb Bell)*, *Nian Dao (Murmur)*, and *Jiugong Lvlv*, intentionally avoided emitting audible sound in the external space, except for the friction sound of devices in operation. Qiu Zhijie even added a muffling treatment to the floor. *Dumb Bell* was a spinning paper lantern, motor-driven, with its interior made of double-layered thin film and with Chinese onomatopoeia characters printed on the outside. *Murmur* was a bicycle installation with its tire treads designed in Chinese characters. In the third work *Jiugong Lvlv*, the artist carved names of the twelve pitches in classical Chinese music on the soles of Japanese clog shoes. Audience were asked to wear the clogs to leave their foot prints on the *jiugongge* (nine palace chart)-printed floor. These works generated an acoustic imagination for the viewers through silent reading of changing Chinese characters, from the spinning lantern, prints left by the bicycle tires, and foot prints left in *jiugongge* on the floor. The exhibition however required one to know the Chinese language and even to know classical Chinese music notation to fully engage in the art works. Qiu Zhijie later reflected, "I don't know if the interest is sound or Chinese characters." Without using any audio devices or intentional sounding, the exhibition's silence formed an interesting contrast with *Sound 2* filled with visual and audio noises.

The Sound of Sound stands out uniquely from existing sound art works in China for its play with silent reading and acoustic imaginations. Thinking is, after all, sonorous.

During the Post-sense Sensibility movement, the use of sound in artworks was largely inspired by an emphasis on "live art." Artists spontaneously turned to sound as an expressive medium to deliver affective memories and as a material to create and control the propensity of the "energy field" of artworks. Artists who participated in *Sound* (2000) and *Sound 2* (2001) continue with their art making, without an intentional emphasis on sound in particular. Shi Qing later founded the nonprofit platform *Jilie Kongjian* (Intensive Space) in Shanghai, which specialized in socially engaged art. Shi Qing himself continues making multimedia works focusing on geopolitical politics and everyday life politics. Wang Wei's artistic attention has shifted from performance to site-specific art and space art. Together with Rania Ho and the curator Pauline Yao, Wang Wei ran an alternative art space *Jian Chang* (Arrow Factory) (2008–2019) in Beijing, supporting non-commercially oriented experimental art creativities.

On November 5, 2016, at Beijing Minsheng Art Museum, Qiu Zhijie, together with Guo Xiaoyan, curated *Post-sense Sensibility: Trepidation and Will* to exhibit works by twenty-one artists who were once involved with Post-sense Sensibility exhibitions and nine young artists. As Qiu remarks, "Post-sense Sensibility is the never-completed mirror image, a never-ending puberty that lasts the entire life."

Sounding Beijing (2003), the Sound Festival

One of the unique features that makes sound art distinct from traditional art genres is the diversity of its exhibiting platforms. Sound art can happen in gallery spaces just as video installations, sculptures, and even paintings, but it can also take place in music festivals, concerts, and radio broadcasts.

From the year 1999 to 2003, the art space of *Cang Ku* played an important role in fostering a vibrant art and cultural scene in Beijing. Without much similar spaces like it during that time in Beijing, almost everyone involved in the arts, including film directors, writers, scholars, artists, and musicians all came to events at *Cang Ku*. *Cang Ku* ended its art and music activities by the end of 2003 when more art spaces and galleries became available in places like 798 Art District.

Before its closing, *Cang Ku* hosted *Sounding Beijing* during November 1 and 4 in 2003, curated by Dajuin Yao, who was by then known to new music fans in mainland China mainly through his online radio program *Foretaste Radio Program* (2000–2002). Yao produced the radio program while he studied art history at UC Berkeley in the United States. Through *Sounding Beijing*, Yao introduced to the mainland audience the curatorial idea of formatting experimental music and sound art as festivals. *Sounding Beijing* invited French sound artist Laetitia Sonami, Austrian composer Helmut Schafer, American noise musician Randy Yau, noise musician Zbigniew Karkowski from Poland, and Atsuko Nojiri from Japan. From mainland China, Yao invited the multimedia duo 8gg, field recordist/musician Zhong Minjie, noise musician Zhou Pei (Ronez), experimental musician Wang Fan, digital hardcore musician Sulumin, electronic musician Lou Nanli (B6), and Ding Dawen (cy). *Sounding Beijing* also invited musicians from the music conservatory, including the American composer Kenneth Field, professor of electronic and computer music in the Center for Electroacoustic Music of China at Central Conservatory of Music, together with China's leading erhu (a two-stringed bowed traditional Chinese musical instrument) performer Yu Hongmei, who was also a professor at Central Conservatory of Music (CCoM). The curatorial format resembled the Sónar Festival in Barcelona, combining electronic music, computer music, noise, audiovisual performance, and sound art performance. It was the first time when Chinese music fans saw sound performances through gestural controller by Laetitia Sonami's *Lady's Glove* and experienced the high intensity live sound/noise performance by Zbigniew Karkowski. Yao also performed during this self-financed festival. Yan Jun helped checking tickets on the door.

In May 2004, at the first Dashanzi International Art Festival (DIAF), Yan Jun collaborated with the artist and curator Huang Riu and organized sound and music events involving twenty or so art spaces. In October 2004, the international art curator Hou Hanru invited Chinese musicians to perform at *Nuit Blanche à Paris*, including Dajuin Yao, Li Jianhong, Zhong Minjie, Wang Changcun, FM3, Wu Quan, and Yan Jun. This was the first time when Chinese experimental musicians performed outside of mainland China. After Paris, Dajuin Yao, Wang Changcun, FM3, Wu Quan, and Yan Jun toured in Belgium, Holland, and Germany.

Sounding Beijing (2003) established contact points between music and art, nonacademic musicians and academic artists; it inspired series of curatorial projects and salon events. It at the same time opened another stream of development that seems to go on a separate (occasionally intertwined) path from that of contemporary art world. The festival format however, further suspends sound art over existing categories of contemporary art and music. Sometimes, sound art fit into both, sometimes neither seem appropriate.

New Media Art after 2000

In southern China, with Shanghai being the leading city for the development of China's contemporary art, a new media art scene was taking its form with resources from commercial galleries and independent art spaces, exhibitions, and academic institutions. By the end of 1998, one of the earliest nonprofit art spaces, BizArt Art Center, was cofounded in Shanghai by Davide Quadrio and Huang Yuanqing. The artist Xu Zhen was invited to become its first art director. In 2004, BizArt Art Center moved from a factory building in Huaihai Xilu #610 to the contemporary art district M50 converted from a textile factory complex. In 2010, BizArt Art center changed its name to Meiding art space.

The first academic new media art center was founded in China Academy of Art in 2001 in Hangzhou, with Zhang Peili acting as the dean, who was by then working at Hangzhou Normal University. Tired of traditional art education methods used in training students under a dominant ideology and under the teacher's way of art making, Zhang had the ambition to revolutionize the art education format and to enrich students' perception of different art mediums. New media artist Shen Ligong and artist Geng Jianyi were involved in designing a curriculum for the undergraduate program to establish the Department of New Media Art. In order to come up with a proper curriculum, Zhang Peili set up new media art seminars (workshops) as a pilot course, recruiting students from all over China. In the pilot course, Zhang Peili taught video art while Geng Jianyi taught photography. Artists including Zhang Ding and Shao Yi attended the seminar. During this period of time, Zhang Ding and Shao Yi created their first sound art pieces. In 2003, the Department of New Media Art was officially founded at China Academy of Art, indicating the acceptance of new forms of contemporary art pedagogy into the national art education system.

During those pilot seminars, besides teaching, Geng Jianyi and Zhang Peili organized art events intensively. There was no professional contemporary art space in Hangzhou by that time. They had to be creative in finding exhibition sites, which included the coffee shop "Coffee Box," *ling yinlu* #31 bar, anonymous basements and deserted buildings. In 2003, a few artists and designers rented factory buildings as personal studios in LOFT 49, which was an art district remodeled from desolate warehouses and factory buildings of a printing and dyeing factory called *Jinlun Branch of Hangzhou Blue Peacock Chemical Fiber Co., Ltd*. In 2004, more artists opened their studios in LOFT 49. They invited Geng Jianyi to organize an exhibition there. The name of "Lost ING, no Lost" came up during a meeting among Geng Jianyi, Shao Yi, and Shen Ligong. In this exhibition, Shao Yi's sound performance work *Shi Sheng (Lost Voice)* had gained much attention and praise (Figure 2.4).

In *Shi Sheng (Lost Voice)*, Shao Yi invited *Yue* opera (a Chinese opera genre, also known as *shaoxing* opera) singers to stage a normal opera performance only with their voices suppressed. The actors and actresses were asked to make vocal gestures with their mouths without making any sound. The dialogues were instead displayed on both sides of the stage. Without hearing any vocal sounds, audience members had to focus more on body gestures, facial expressions, interactions, and all kinds of details that

FIGURE 2.4 *Shao Yi*, Lost Voice, Performance, 2003. *Courtesy of the artist.*

are normally neglected due to the dominance of oral narratives. *Shi Sheng* was later selected to attend the group exhibition *The Elegance of Silence: Contemporary Art from East Asia* at Mori Art Museum in Japan, March 29–June 19, 2005. According to the museum catalogue, *The Elegance of Silence* "examines the relationship between contemporary art and the East Asian artistic traditions that increasingly have become 'silent' in contemporary culture." *Lost Voice* was no doubt a perfect match for the curatorial team and was exhibited as a three-screened video installation instead of live performances.

To enrich the breadth and depth of students' knowledge of new media art and to cultivate students' creativity, Zhang designed a course titled "free creation," inviting notable practicing artists, including Xu Zhen, Yang Zhenzhong, Chen Shaoxiong, Wu Wenguang, Shi Hui, Fei Pingguo, Zhou Xiaohu, Tang Maohong, Jing Feng, and Cao Kai, to the department as visiting professors to guide students' art works. Students were divided into groups led by individual artists. Over the process of the course, students had a chance to decide a direction, to search for materials and eventually actualize an art work. Students' artworks, if selected, would attend an exhibition organized by the department by the end of the course. Other than choosing an art medium, students were encouraged to select a "non-artistic" technique going beyond new media tools, which may include carpentry, *tai chi*, knitting, gardening, wine mixology, or bricklaying. Jiang Zhuyun created his installation *Scale of Sound* (2006) (Figure 2.5)

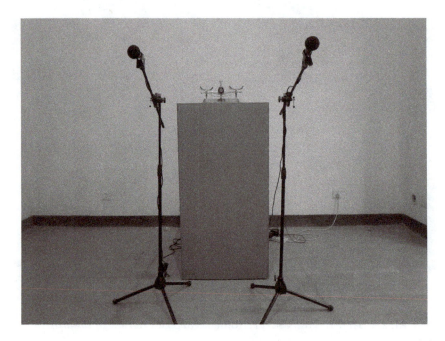

FIGURE 2.5 *Jiang Zhuyun,* Figure of Sound, *Installation, 2006. Courtesy of the artist.*

at Zhang Peili's mechanical installation course. Intrigued by a popular game in Chinese variety shows in which the audience took the challenge of screaming and the voice that reached the highest decibel won, Jiang decided to change the judging criteria to measuring the weight of sound. Through movements of the scale's two ends, one seemed to be able to tell the weight of sounds generated by audience through two microphones. *Scale of Sound* intentionally fakes visualization of sound and provokes the audience to ponder: does sound really carry mass?

Through Jiang Zhuyun's introduction, Zhang Peili invited Dajuin Yao to give a guest lecture in New Media Art department on sound art. By the end of his course, Yao organized a group exhibition titled *Sound Imagination: A Sound Installation Exhibition* (December 9–16, 2005), featuring more than twenty sound art works by students from the New Media Art Department. In this exhibition, Jiang Zhuyun did his acclaimed sound performance *Sound of Temperature* (2005) (Figure 2.6). Despite being a southern city, the winter of Hangzhou can be freezing and most public buildings including schools are not well equipped with heating systems. Jiang sat half naked indoors on a winter night, with his hands holding contact microphones, one against his heart and another his cheek. As the temperature dropped, his body began to quiver. The artist reflects, "It was a state of total relax during

FIGURE 2.6 *Jiang Zhuyun,* Sound of Temperature, *Live Performance, 2005. Courtesy of the artist.*

the process, coldness has become something like electricity that makes my teeth quiver, my body falls into irregular trembling, until it becomes a kind of pattern, I'm just following."[5] Sound of the quivering was picked up by contact microphones, processed through a computer software and converted back to audible sound, involving everyone present with the artist into an organic system of quivering.

By the end of 2006, Geng Jianyi and a few artists learnt that a deserted factory building of *Huqing Yutang* Chinese Traditional Medicine Museum was about to be dismantled. For the artists, it was a perfect place to host exhibitions. Geng made contacts, looked for commercial supports and asked artists to submit art proposals. With the support of the Department of New Media Art and BizArt Art Center, the exhibition *It's All Right, Contemporary Art Exhibition* opened during December 16–20, 2006. The exhibition presented up to thirty-seven artists' works, ranging from already established artists like Zhang Peili and Geng Jianyi themselves, emerging young artists Xu Zhen, Fei Pingguo, Yang Zhenzhong, as well as thirteen undergraduate students and five graduate students' works.

Zhang Ding's first sound installation *To the West N Kilometers* (Figure 2.7) was created for this exhibition. It was a ball-shaped structure covered with

---

[5]https:www.jiangzhuyun.net/works/st.html

FIGURE 2.7 *Zhang Ding, N Kilometers towards the West, 2006, Sound Installation.*
Courtesy of Astrup Fearnley Museum.

wool blanket, with the diameter of 165 cm. Sixteen high-pitched speakers
were directly welded to the ball. Bass and medium speakers were connected
to CD players, amplifiers, and frequency divider circuits. The CD players
play sixteen field recordings recorded by the artist in difference places,
including a restaurant, a public square, streets, riverside, and an old mosque
in Linxia Hui Autonomous Prefecture located in southwestern central
Gansu province. Linxia is a multiethnic city with 50 percent Hui Muslims,
3 percent minorities of Dongxiang, Sala, Bonan, and Tibetan, and is hence
known as the little Mecca of China.[6]

In 2008, Geng Jianyi was invited to take the position of the chief director
of the opening performance titled *Streaming Objects* of the 2008 Shanghai
eArts Festival. Dajuin Yao curated the music performance section. Sulumi,
Laetitia Sonami, Wang Changcun, and 8gg, who had performed in *Sounding
Beijing* (2003), were invited back to stage. Electronic media artist Frank
Bretschneider from Germany, Japanese artists Ryoichi Kurokawa and
Masayuki Akamatsu were also invited to the performance section. It was
the first outdoor live media art show in mainland China. In the following
years, Yao continued curating live sound art/music festivals and exhibitions,

---

[6]In the research project led by Rachel Harris from University of London titled "Sounding Islam
in China: A multi-sited ethnographic study," one can find a more substantial discussion on the
soundscape of the city of Linxia. http://www.soundislamchina.org/?page_id=1282

including *Sounding Hangzhou: Live Media Art* in 2011, *Revolution Per Minute: Sound Art China* in New York, Shanghai, and Hong Kong in 2013, and *Schizophonia: Sonic Alienation* in Sheng Zhen in 2015.

In the same year of 2008, Zhang Peili's solo exhibition took place at OCAT Shenzhen. This exhibition only presented one artwork, an event-scene installation titled *Mute*. Zhang Peili recreated a sewing workshop of a clothes factory in the exhibition space, measuring 300–400 square meters. The setup of the factory gave an impression that the factory was suddenly stopped for some unknown reason in the middle of production. A projected video (12'59") appears to be a documentation of the production scene of a real sewing workshop. A video wall consisting of 40 screens (10 horizontal, 4 vertical) showed on each screen the surveillance video of individual sewing worker. Background noise of a sewing factory in production was played interchangeably with silence. As the curator Huang Zhuan commented, the absence of sound of the work had apparently been the logical starting point for the artist to express doubts about the rationality of social event scenes reported in the news. Zhang Peili commented on this work, "is it completely mute, or momentarily mute? Is it appropriate to add to the work the background sound of the process of clothing manufacturing? The momentary mute suggests that background sound can be added and it can be intermittent." Fitting to the artist's long-time concern with power structures, the work is to make the audience realize the control over reported reality by mainstream news media, revealing the constructed nature of news production (see more discussions of Zhang Peili's work in Chapter 6).

Sound Art after 2000

The year 2000 marked the origin of publicly recognizing sound as a unique art medium in mainland China through two consecutive exhibitions *Sound* (2000) and *Sound 2* (2001). The year 2000 was also the year that marked "a new beginning" of China's contemporary art with the launch of the third Shanghai Biennale (Wu 2014); it was also the year after which internet became an accessible tool for communication and information in mainland China (Groom, Smith, and Xu 2007), the year when 798 Art District rented out its factory space to artists as studios, expecting a quick growth of art communities in following years. It can be said that, in 2000, Sound made its entry to China's contemporary art world through Post-sense Sensibility movement and the new media art development led by China Academic of Art.

For the convenience of discussion, I divide sound art practices into following categories: sound installations, sound in performance-oriented conceptual art, sound machines/object installations, public sound art, and sound and net art. These categories are not exhaustive. Also, artworks discussed in one category may easily fit into other categories.

Sound Installation: Collective Memories and Public Loudspeakers

Sound installation art is a term notably used by American artist Max Neuhaus to distinguish his sound works from music. For Neuhaus, sound in installation art is placed in space while in music sound is placed in time. Comparing to sculptures, installation art indicates a different ideology and aesthetics; it is often site-specific, theatrical, immersive, and experiential (Bishop 2012). Installation art usually cannot be installed anywhere, it has its fit space. The Chinese-French artist Chen Zhen (1955–2000) preferred the term "site-specific installation" to describe installation art. According to Chen, "Site-specific installation is the kind that is designed for a particular space. It is *feng shui*. *Feng shui* is the system of knowledge in selecting the best natural and cultural time and space when Chinese build houses, tombs or even a city. The alignment of the window and the door, placement of furniture, and their inter-relations in space is all considered by *feng shui*."[7] Before installing an artwork, the first step for Chen Zhen was always to analyze all kinds of elements of the exhibition space, including its physical aspects, visual and spatial awareness, and historical background.

Sound installation art in its Western context originated from several influences, including artists like Marcel Duchamp, John Cage, Joseph Beuys, and Allan Kaprow, as well as art genres like readymade, Happenings and Fluxus, social sculptures, conceptual art, and site-specific art. Sound installation art became a more stable art genre in the context of the avant-garde and experimental art movement in the West in the 1970s and 1980s.

For Chinese artists born in the 1950s and 1960s, political propaganda music, political speech and news reports played through public loudspeakers or home radios constitute a unique collective cultural memory. Loudspeakers, which almost disappeared in the public space in urban cities in the new millennium, are given a new life in sound installation works, including Zhang Peili's *Collision of Harmonies* (2014), *A Standard, Uplifting, and Distinctive Circle Along with its Sound System* (2015), and *Sound Installation with Transistor Radio And Trumpet Speaker* (2019), Shao Yi's installation *Broadcast* (2008), Lu Lei's solo exhibition *Echo* (2015), as well as Chen Zhen's *Resonance* (1994). A fuller discussion of Zhang Peili's sound works will be found in the last chapter. Here I will discuss works by Chen Zhen, Lu Lei, and Shao Yi.

Chen Zhen was born in Shanghai to a family of doctors. He studied art at Shanghai Fine-Arts and Craft School in 1973 and specialized in stage design in Shanghai Drama Institute in 1978. After graduations, he shortly taught

---

[7]http://www.artlinkart.com/cn/article/overview/081izBm/about_by2/Y/9cchwAl

in both schools before moving to Paris in 1986. He stayed in Paris ever since. His family's background in medicine, his own health condition, and his cross-cultural experience were consistent themes in his artworks. Sound, both as a medium of collective memory in his earlier works and later as an indispensable therapeutic element, was used throughout his installation artworks.

Chen Zhen's memory of growing up in communist China was vividly acoustic, with the sound of political propaganda speech and people reciting the Little Red Book (*Quotations from Chairman Mao Zedong*). In the installation *Resonance* (Kröller-Müller Museum, 1994), Chen Zhen used a gigantic bell, loudspeakers, and burned chairs to symbolize power and everyday living conditions under dictatorship. The bell symbolizes power of the state during ancient times, when the bell was used for regulating time of the public. Loudspeakers, instead, symbolize power of the Party in modern China. More interestingly, Chen Zhen did not install sound in this work. He preferred silence. "She is totally silent, like the people who live under dictatorship. Silence is the cruelest aspect of the violence of power." However, as Chen Zhen revealed, when the work was finally installed in the museum's park, he decided to add a sound track of recorded natural sound to resonate with sounds of the site.

Daily Incantations (1996) was an installation that used the structure of Chinese chime bell (*bianzhong* 编钟) with bells replaced by 101 wooden bucket toilets (*matong* 马桶). Speakers were installed in these buckets, playing sounds of political speeches one would easily hear during the cultural revolutionary time, mixed with recordings of everyday sounds of Shanghai women cleaning bucket toilets. At the center of the bracket that hang those bucket toilets, was a ball made of metal wire and electrical cord containing electronic equipment including used television sets, radios, and speakers. The work embodied dialectical relations between the sublime and profanity, high taste and low taste, political propaganda and everyday life, and the ancient and the modern. Additionally, the structure of ancient Chinese chime bell and used old objects bring a mysterious atmosphere to the work.

In 1999, Chen Zhen began a lifelong project: "I want to be a doctor." Since then, using sound objects and sound systems as a therapeutic method that purifies the body and the spirit has become persistent in Chen's art works, including *Bathroom* (2000), *Bibliotheque Musical* (2000), *Cocon du Vide* (2000), *Six Roots-Souffrance* (2000), *Danser la Musique* (2000–2009). In 1998, Chen began using drum skin, recycled wooden chairs and beds in installations *Un-Interrupted Voice* (1998), *Jue Chang-Fifty Strokes to Each* (1998) and in the installation-based performance project *Jue Chang-Dancing Body, Drumming Mind* (1999). Professional musicians and dancers, as well as audience members, were invited to strike the drum skin surface to acquire a therapeutic experience through drumming.

The Hangzhou-based artist Shao Yi's installation *Broadcast* (2008), without using the object of loudspeaker, is also related to the collective memory of a similar historical period of the 1960s and 1970s. During the Cultural Revolution period, broadcast radio was a primary device used in a household as a way to receive radio broadcasting programs. People living in the rural areas used self-made radios and often individualized the device by adding pictures or images to it. Shao put audio clips of field recordings of private conversations and conference speeches inside sixty recycled radios collected from villagers in Zhejiang province. *Broadcast* delivers a message from the artist, a comment on the particular historical era when the private and personal can no longer be distinguished from the political.

Loudspeaker has been a special medium for the younger artist Lu Lei (1972–). While the other artists grasp the realistic and symbolic power of memory-ridden public loudspeakers, Lu Lei hinges upon the super-realistic and even the metaphysical dimension of the acoustic experience of the era of the 1970s and 1980s. Lu Lei's solo exhibition *Echo* (2015) (Figure 2.8), with three independent artworks, *The Square* (2005/2015), *Pretending Egomania* (2015), and *The Night* (2015), creates a public space with an industrial ambience yet inhabited by nonhuman species, emitting an eerie yet strangely tranquil vibe. In *The Square* (2005/2015), 100 galvanized oil barrels installed with high-frequency loudspeakers constitute a speaker-wall with a flagpole, a gray silk banner, and a concave mirror in front, generating

FIGURE 2.8 *Lu Lei,* The Square (2005/2015), Pretending Egomania *(2015),* The Night *(2015), solo exhibition* Echo, *Shanghart Gallery, Shanghai, 2015. Courtesy of the artist and Shanghart Gallery.*

an intense industrial and military ambience. The visual forms a curious relation with pigeon sounds played through the speakers controlled by a reel-to-reel tape recorder placed on top of the oil barrels. Opposite *The Square*, are *Pretending Egomania* and *The Night*, strange animals with the body of dog, bear, mouse, donkey, and pig, but with faces shaped in horn loudspeakers. Inside of each horn is a light bulb signaling morse codes that says no memory, no smell, no conscious, no sights, no words. Twenty-one bats hung on two coat racks in the shape of king-chess and the queen-chess, adding an even more mysterious and nocturnal atmosphere to the entire field. These horn-faced bats are ready to fly, signaling the fall of the night, leaving the audience immersed in the sculpted acoustic memory of both the collective and the individual. Lu seems to indicate that echo is a sound that never disappears once issued; echo is a memory that navigates one through the darkness.

Sound in Performance-Oriented Conceptual Art

Conceptual art prioritizes idea or concept more than the actual art object through the process of art making. Its precursors can be traced back to Marcel Duchamp's readymade and minimalism art that reduces emotions to its minimum through mathematical or industrial operations. Conceptual art is subversive in the sense that it often disregards the quality of art in terms of good or bad as a way to challenge the art market and art institutions (Harrison 2003). Language is an important medium for conceptual art. In 1961, the American theorist and composer Henry Flynt proposes the term concept art in his essay "Concept Art" (1961).

> "Concept art" is first of all an art of which the material is "concepts," as the material of for ex. music is sound. Since "concepts" are closely bound up with language, concept art is a kind of art of which the material is language. That is, unlike for ex. a work of music, in which the music proper (as opposed to notation, analysis, a.s.f.) is just sound, concept art proper will involve language.

A similar idea is shared by the British art group Art & Language which derives its name from the journal *Art-Language* (1969–1985), advocating for text-based theoretical art works. The group Art & Language describes conceptual art as "modernism's nervous breakdown" and "the homeless art of the culturally displaced" (Corris 2004, 1). Sol Lewitt's list of definition/manifesto "Sentences on Conceptual Art" (1967) has further expanded the definition of conceptual art and largely popularized Anglo-American conceptual art in the late 1960s and 1970s. Artists identified as conceptual artists are associated with a wide span of art genres, including Sol Lewitt from minimalism, John Cage from music composition, Richard Long from Land art, Joseph Beuys and Vito Acconci from performance art, and artists involved with Fluxus and Happenings.

Besides using languages, conceptual artists also use nonlinguistic medium to create art, such as body and sound. If text-based conceptual art suggests rational thinking, performance-based or sound-based conceptual art advocate more for embodied mode of knowing. Performance-oriented conceptual art can be self-contained, focusing on self-enlightenment and self-cultivation. It can also go beyond the existential to address social and political concerns. Philosophy, literature, and social science play a significant role in making, experiencing, and understanding conceptual art.

In China, from the '85 New Wave movement, according to Wu Hung, conceptual art was seen practiced by art groups including Xiamen Dada, the Pond Society, The New Measurement Group, Big Tail Element, and by individual artists such as Geng Jianyi, Zhang Peili, Gu Dexin, Wang Jianwei, and Huang Yongping (Wu 2014). Chinese artists of contemporary art draw inspirations from Western art practices, philosophy, and literature, but they also draw (perhaps more) from Eastern philosophical thoughts of Buddhism and Taoism. For example, Geng Jianyi's art is often subtle, witty, and profound, inviting audience to enter an uncertain and almost meditative state, known as *guan xiang* (contemplation) in Buddhist practice, to eventually achieve enlightenment. His use of the audio and the visual in *Complete World* (1996) pushes the audience to rethink the question of what is a complete world through setting up a perceptual game of the actual space and its representation. In his installation *Hole* (1999), a loud noise of crashing a wall was first heard, followed by a sudden beam of light shooting in through a hole cracked open on the wall. Although the sound seemed to be an assisting element for the final arrival of light, the artist still well captured and manipulated the perceptual and intellectual charm of both mediums.

Yan Jun (1973–), who more prefers to be identified as a musician than a sound artist, has created a range of performance-oriented conceptual art over the years. After experimenting with feedback noise on his DIY no-input synthesizer set, he added a performative aspect to his work by engaging the movement of his body, sometimes as simple as breathing, sometimes dancing, and even sleeping. His works are performed in a variety of venues, including music clubs, galleries, and art spaces, and also in individual audience's living room.

Time Sections (2018) (see Figures 2.9.1–2.9.5) is a unique piece by Yan Jun, a solo project lasting four hours in the art space known as The Bunker in Beijing (more discussion on The Bunker can be found in Chapter 6). The work consists of five performances occurring at the same time in five separate rooms, including an installation of a plastic bag spinning above an

FIGURE 2.9.1 *Yan Jun,* Time Sections, *2018. Room 1 Performer Wei Guo, The Bunker, Beijing. Courtesy of the artist.*

FIGURE 2.9.2 *Yan Jun,* Time Sections, *2018. Room 2 Performer Ake 5. The Bunker, Beijing. Courtesy of the artist.*

FIGURE 2.9.3 *Yan Jun,* Time Sections, *2018. Room 3 Performer Anzi. The Bunker, Beijing. Courtesy of the artist.*

FIGURE 2.9.4 *Yan Jun,* Time Sections, *2018. Room 4 Performer Li Yingwu, photography, The Bunker, Beijing. Courtesy of the artist.*

FIGURE 2.9.5 *Yan Jun,* Time Sections, *2018. Room 5 Performers Huang Hao (left), Li Weisi (right). The Bunker, Beijing. Courtesy of the artist.*

air purifier, a photographer taking photos now and then, a seated performer shaking legs, random water dropping, and a continuous about-to-play-but-not-yet-playing performance. Although *Time Sections* is packaged as an art exhibition, Yan Jun suggests that the work still be considered music, not performance art or theater. It is music, because for Yan Jun music is not only about sound. On the exhibition booklet he writes, "music is the presence of the performers, the participation of audience, as well as the air, background noise, and the smell of the entire environment." In the same booklet, commenting on the concept of time in relation to this work, Yan Jun writes,

> "Time" is not a word. Isn't it often said that time is an illusion? We could only experience this concept in illusion; let the body become the maternal body for concept. Body is always the original interface for language. We have to return where language was born. This is reality. The pressure from the society and the confusion caused by sexual desires and my wallet command me to go inside of those spaces and try to stay a bit longer. I have to believe what I want to hear, every sentence, are there, including those I do not want to hear. People should believe in logic and instinct, right? Then doesn't it make the two things the same thing?

Yan Jun's desire to go beyond or before language is similar to existentialists' critique of the limit of language and Yan suggests that body-based experience be given the most important value. Using the body to probe open the definition of music and to push audience to rethink music in relation to time makes this work both experiential and conceptual. *Time sections* reminds us of Happenings developed by Allan Kaprow by combing sculptures, performance, objects to blur boundaries between art and life and to give significance to non-significant mundane events. Similar to Happenings' conceptual art practices in the 1970s, Yan Jun's art work in general resists the notion of professionalism in music and art making. Instead, he often creates situations when skills are the least necessary element.

Philosophically minded, performance-oriented conceptual artists usually treat art not as an end in itself but as a way to understand the world or a way to live in the world. Beijing-based artist He Chi's (1978–) work *Sound Segregation* (2018) (see Figures 2.10.1–2.10.2) is existentially mundane, poetic, and yet thought-provoking. Different from Geng Jianyi's witty manipulation of acoustic and visual experiences to provoke a certain degree of enlightenment, different from the avant-gardist playfulness in Yan Jun's *Time Sections*, He Chi's *Sound Segregation* is down to earth,

FIGURE 2.10.1 *He Chi,* Sound Segregation, *Installation view, Hunsand Space, Beijing, 2018. Courtesy of Hunsand Space.*

FIGURE 2.10.2 *He Chi,* Sound Segregation, *Installation view, surveillance video screenshot, Hunsand Space, Beijing, 2018. Courtesy of Hunsand Space.*

kitsch, and somewhat romantic. Over 2017, He Chi sang one and another popular song through *chang ba*, a cellular karaoke application highly popular among users particularly from lower-tier cities. Without deploying any visible pain actions as often seen in performance art, *Sound Segregation* is touching for its simplicity and sincerity. He Chi's voice, with a heavy Tong Wei accent (a town in Gansu province), was far from professionally trained singing voice. He tried hard to sing to the original soundtrack, attempting to match emotions suggested by those popular songs. Singing alone can be a romantic gesture but singing alone through a cellphone app in one's room somehow gives this romantic gesture an absurd realistic twist.

Sound Segregation can be better understood when placed back to the repertoire of He Chi's artworks. In *I am Quite Thoughtful* (2011), he picked up leaves fallen off from a tree and glued them back on. In August 2014, He Chi's father passed away. He went back to his hometown, a village county in Tong Wei to take care of his father's funeral. He decided to live there for a period of time just like his father, to live a meaningless life. He asked his mother to document him with a video camera and later simply put these document videos together in time sequence without any post-editing and titled it *So Forget* (2014). In *Next Door* (2016), he stayed in the art space (less than 10 square meters) of Arrow Factory for the whole spring. He painted the inside of the space in green color everyday accordingly as the old elm tree behind the art space grows greener. The art space stayed empty and clean over the span of the artist's residency, only that it became greener with the elm tree. The seemingly simple artistic actions in He Chi's works is always profoundly evocative. The exhibition of *Sound Segregation* extended

He Chi's usual artistic style—simple, clean, and powerful. The exhibition statement reads:

> The everyday life of the individual has broken away from the oppression and kidnap of meaning—perhaps it is due to this that the texture of life, its warmth and coldness, as well as its numbness and pains can transmit artlessly and vividly when one listens to He Chi's singing alone, as if it were a part of one's own secret and private life. . . . If the life during the creating of "Sound Segregation" is denial or self-segregation, "Sound Segregation" as an artwork is communication, exchange, embrace, care, and recognition between specific individuals.

The exhibition space was intentionally kept empty, with only two speakers fixed on the wooden beam of the room. Only one audience was let in at one time. On the wall was printed a line that read, "There is a sound segregating me from us." Segregation, a classical Chinese aesthetic concept in poetry and painting, has been a persistent concept for He Chi. In this work, singing foregrounded a separation between the singing self and the listener. At the same time, listening creates an "us." Through listening, sound that segregates connects.

Sound Machine/Object Installations

With sound installation art, while the generations of the 1950s, 1960s, and 1970s seem to be more concerned with the cultural-political acoustic milieu or collective and individual acoustic memories of certain period in modern China, the younger generation is found more perceptual and object-oriented, with attention to topics of the public, gender, system, human, and nonhuman relations.

New York-based Chinese artist Yi Xin Tong's work *Cello* (2011) (Figure 2.11) consists a silent video of a female cellist playing cello shot from the back against an almost all-white background. A cello bridge of an enlarged size was placed on a stool at the eye level, facing the video. The artist writes,

> The shape of the isolated bridge is easily associative of a masculine body, which has a rather opposite aesthetic in comparison with a cello, whose shape is on the contrary reminiscent of the female torso. Both sexes are incarnated and having parallel existence in a single piece of instrument.

Cello (2011) seems to be a distant comment on the surrealist Man Ray's photography *Ingre's Violin* (1924), in which May Ray transformed a female body into a musical instrument by painting a cello sound-holes on her

FIGURE 2.11 *Yi Xin Tong*, Cello, *installation, 2011. Courtesy of the artist.*

naked back. While objectification of the female body was a popular trend among surrealist artists, through *Cello* Tong brings up the fact that the real sector that makes the cello sound is a male body-shaped object. By taking away its sound, the work shifts one's habitual mode of perceiving a classical instrument from its sounding to its visual, further complicating the gender stereotype imposed to the instrument.

Similarly being a silence piece, Jiang Zhuyun's installation *A Disappearing Answer* (2017) (see Fig. 2.12) shares the neutral and simplistic aesthetics of minimal installation art. An orange-colored black box sat at the bottom of a large square-shaped water container, almost filled up with water. Black box was a misnomer for Flight Data Recorder (FDR), used in an aircraft to record the last thirty minutes of things happened during the flight. FDR is usually painted in bright color (i.e. orange) to make it easier to be found. The FDR also contains an underwater acoustic beacon usually triggered by water immersion. The beacon emits an ultrasonic 10ms pulse at 37.5 kHZ once per second for over thirty days in order to be located. *A Disappearing Answer* is in response to the missing flight MH370. The artist writes, "The mysterious disappearance of the flight MH370 in 2014 left me a great impression. With rapid technology development in this age of information, the sudden disappearance of a Boeing airplane seems especially unbelievable. The following failure of a multinational search and the spreading rumors reflected the particular tension of this digital age, until the public attention shifted to another major event." The large water tank, and the comparatively

FIGURE 2.12 *Jiang Zhuyun,* A Disappearing Answer. *Installation view Hunsand Space, Beijing, 2017. Courtesy of the artist.*

tiny industrial-looking metal flight recorder generates a complex sense of solemness, helplessness, and suspense. "A black box, preserving two hours of cockpit voice recording and twenty-five hours of flying data, implies an underlying answer, a truth waiting to be found," the artist writes.

Jiang Zhuyun's another inaudible sound installation *Current Monologue* (2017) (Figure 2.13) is a tape recorder with a tape that is set to loop ad infinitum. The recorder records sound which will be erased in the next loop and hence sabotages the most celebrated function of audio tape recorder—to capture the acoustic ephemeral and stores it as an acoustic object. Back to 1971, a similar work was conceived by the New York-based conceptual artist Christine Kozlov, titled *Information: No Theory.* The artist set the tape to record any sounds in exhibition room for two minutes. Through looping, the old recording was replaced by the old one. In both works, the information recorded on the tape cannot be heard and hence one's knowledge of the recorded acoustic information can only be derived from probability.

More young artists tend to make sound machine installations that either play prerecorded sound or make sounds. Taiwanese artist Wang Chung-Kun (b.1982) and Hangzhou-based artist Deng Yuejun (b.1986) both work with kinetic sculptures. Wang Chung-Kun began with an interest to bestow the warmth of life to machines through sound by making his very first kinetic

FIGURE 2.13 *Jiang Zhuyun,* Current Monologue, *Installation, 2017. Courtesy of the artist.*

sculpture *wood-fish* (2005). After *wood-fish,* inspired by vintage portable sound devices and box-type instruments, Wang Chung-Kun began to develop his *Sound.of.Suitcase* series (2011–) to build sound making kinetic systems inside of custom-made wood boxes. *Noise Box* (2014) (see Figure 2.14) in the series hacks the working mechanism of Thomas Edison's phonogram by replacing the wax cylinder with gears of different numbers of teeth. In *3 Little Wood-fish* (see Figure 2.15), three window-doors were carved on a wooden suitcase, through which wood-fish pops out and performs at half beat or whole beat in a random manner. With *Sound.of.Suitcase series,* the artist intends art works to be carried along just like carrying a suitcase to travel to any place of the world. The whole system operates automatically,

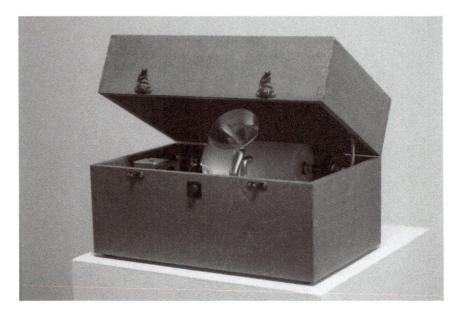

FIGURE 2.14 *Wang Chung-Kun,* Noise Box, *Installation 2014, 35.5 × 23 × 24 cm,* Sound.of.Suitcase *series. Courtesy of the artist.*

FIGURE 2.15 *Wang Chung-Kun,* 3 Little Wood-fish, *Installation 2014, 26 L × 26 W × 44 H cm,* Sound.of.Suitcase *series. Courtesy of the artist.*

announcing the death of the author/musician. Wang Chung-Kun calls them "over-complex musical instrument."

Different from Wang Chung-Kun's consistency in working with sound kinetic sculptures, the new media artist, graduate of the New Media Art department at China Academy of Art, Deng Yuejun's kinetic installations are not limited to sound making, but focus more on blurring differences between organic and nonorganic things. Sound is one of the mediums to suggest such indistinction. In his sound installation O (2016) (Figure 2.16), he samples 100 individuals pronouncing the vowel O at one breath and puts the recordings into 100 custom-made chips. The chips are then installed in round-shaped granite tops that stand on four short legs; Deng calls them photovoltaic insects. Flocks of these photovoltaic "insects" make O sounds when they get light. The loudness, duration, and intensity of O is completely orchestrated by a system of light and shadow. By making the sound of O (the chemical element that symbolizes oxygen or the sound of om, the sound that is believed to contain cosmic energy in Buddhism), the 100 mechanical parts form a sentient mini-universe, in constant resonance with passing shadows of humans and nonhuman beings.

Also a graduate of the New Media Art department at China Academy of Art, the new media artist Feng Chen's installation W (2015) (Figure 2.17) is initially inspired by the mechanism of record player. Feng crafted a wood circle ring with its surface simulating ocean waves. A record player-inspired needle pointer, installed in the middle of the ring on a tripod, jump-spins on

FIGURE 2.16 *Deng Yuejun, O, installation, 2016. Installation view "Machines are not Alone: A Machinic Trilogy" Chronus Art Center, Shanghai, 2018. Courtesy of the artist.*

FIGURE 2.17 *Feng Cheng, W, installation, 2015. Installation view "Machines are not Alone: A Machinic Trilogy" Chronus Art Center, Shanghai, 2018. Courtesy of the artist.*

the circular surface, playing pink noise, the kind of noise used in testing and equalizing loudspeakers and used in helping concentration and productivity. The volume of the sound is adjusted by the height of the wave on the wood surface. The visual of the wave forms, rhythmically jumping needle pointer, and the sound of the pink noise mutually enhance each other to stimulate a meditative and calming experience. W interestingly contrasts with another installation titled *Ocean Wave* (2016) (Figure 2.18) by Shanghai-based artist Yin Yi. *Ocean Wave* consists forty-nine electric fans set in a matrix of seven. With mechanical sounds of fans' operation, mixed with winds coming from all directions, the audience experiences a tactile wave sound no matter where one stands. The fan is set to begin and stop at the same time at a five-minute operation and five-minute rest intervals, adding a dramatic and ritualistic feeling to the work.

Comparing with sound machines or installations that usually have a plastic form of a sculpture, Taiwanese artist Fujui Wang's sound installations, such as *Sound Watch* (2014) (Figure 2.19), *Noise Tube* (2014) (Figure 2.20), *Moving Sound Forest* (2015) (Figure 2.21) are often atmospheric. "I imagine the sound that changes over time as the clouds drifting in the sky, merging and separating, appearing and disappearing," Fujui Wang writes. These sound installations, including the hanging eye-shaped objects that make buzzing insects sound, the hanging vibrating chips installed in transparent

FIGURE 2.18 *Yin Yi*, Ocean Waves, 2016. *Installation view, The 11ᵗʰ Shanghai Biennale, Power Station of Art, Shanghai, 2016. Courtesy of the artist.*

FIGURE 2.19 *Fujui Wang*, Sound Watch, 2014. *Courtesy of the artist.*

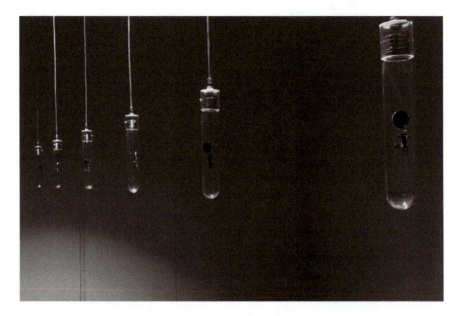

FIGURE 2.20 *Fujui Wang,* Noise Tube, 2014. *Courtesy of the artist.*

FIGURE 2.21 *Fujui Wang,* Sound Forest, 2015. *Courtesy of the artist.*

tubes that improvise mechanical noises through false computing, and up to 1000 sound dots that emit astral lights, generate an immersive, resonant acoustic ambient that is both mysterious and futuristic.

Fujui Wang (1965) plays an essential role in establishing the sound art scene in Taiwan. He founded the first experimental record label *Noise* in Taiwan in 1993 and he launched the *"BIAS" International Sound Art Exhibition* and *Sound Art Prize for the Digital Art Awards Taipei* in 2000. He also curated the *"TranSonic" Sound Art Festival* in 2008, 2009, 2010, and 2012 and *Digital Art Festival Taipei* from 2007 to 2009. He has been teaching digital art in Taipei National University of the Arts and cultivating new generations of sound artists and experimental musicians in Taiwan.

Public Sound Art

In 2005, Commissioned by the British Council's *Sound and the City* project, four British sound artists Peter Cusack, David Toop, Clive Bell, and Brian Eno were invited to explore sounds of Beijing in March and return in October to create site-specific sound works as a response to what they had found. The precursor of the project was the mayor of London's sound city strategy to realize the idea of city regeneration. The *Sound and the City* project encouraged "local people to think about their personal relationship with the city through sound" as such that it spoke to the general public and intervened in the everyday lives of the contemporary Chinese public (Yan and Gray 2007). David Toop and Brian Eno created site-specific sound installations in public parks. Clive Bell made an album *London Listens to Beijing Top Ten* to respond to his discovery of the "local pop music" as something that interacted with and defined the public soundscape of Beijing. Peter Cusack initiated an online competition calling for submissions of "your favorite sound of Beijing," which received a good number of creative responses from the public and drew much attention from the media. The label *Sub Jam* founded by Yan Jun also released a record titled *Favorite Beijing Sounds* (2007).

One year before the *Sound and the City* project, the Beijing-based new media artist He An (1971–) created a sound art piece, *Sound* (2004), dedicated to the city of Shanghai at the exhibition titled *Dial 62761232* at BizArt Art Center (September 10–20, 2004). He An asked several delivery men to sing their favorite songs and recorded their singing. Then he asked them to play the recording while riding their motorbikes at a fast speed through streets of Shanghai, playing their singing to the city. As the art statement reads, "The songs of these delivery men and the sound of the city mixed together, forcing a trace in the sky."

The British-Chinese artist and curator Colin Chinnery's (Chinese name Qin Siyuan) long-term project *Beijing Sound Museum* seems to be a

FIGURE 2.22 *Yin Yi*, A Farewell Party, *Photography, 2013. Courtesy of the artist.*

continuation of *Sound of the City* project, which he helped facilitate and organize, aiming to preserve sounds of Beijing that may disappear one day. Hundreds of sounds, including vendors peddling their wares on streets, ringing bells attached to running rickshaws, and whistles of flying pigeons, were recorded and digitalized to be accessed through a computer installed in Shijia Hutong Museum in Beijing since 2014. In 2018, Chinnery installed his public sound installation *Hawkers Refrain* at the Dashilan Commercial Street, a street of 800 years of history in Beijing. Eight speakers were installed underneath a long wooden park chair, playing recorded sounds of old Beijing at a scheduled interval from 10:00 a.m. to 8:00 p.m. everyday. A five-minute sound theater with the artist narrating through recorded sound of Beijing is played every hour through the sound system.

Sound has been an important element in constituting public life. It forms collective memory and solidifies a sense of belonging. The Shanghai-based sound artist Yin Yi also shows a genuine concern for public life of the everyday. His work *A Farewell Party* (2013) (Figures 2.22, 2.23) consists both photography and a sound installation with a set of fifteen sealed glass jars. In each jar is a raw speaker, playing off recorded chorus by elderly people performing in Lu Xun park in Shanghai. Yin Yi describes:

More than 300 people stood in a circle, singing together as a chorus. In the center of the circle stood an old man in his mid 60s, conducting the crowd with his sleeves rolled up and hands waving. Near him was a band, composed of erhu (Chinese instrument), bamboo flute, dulcimer, clarinet,

FIGURE 2.23 *Yin Yi,* A Farewell Party, *installation, 2013. Courtesy of the artist.*

violin, sand ball and plastic bucket as bass drum. Almost every singer held sheet music, while some also held microphones that connected to the portable sound box. The singers were mostly in their 60s. They sang songs that were popular in the 1950s that praised the motherland, the people, the People's Army, Chairman Mao, and rusticated youth during "down to the countryside movement" in late 1960s and early 1970s." (Yin 2017)

For Yin Yi, chorus singing in the park is this particular generation's way of claiming agency in a fast-developing city of Shanghai. Marginalized from the central productive force of the city, elderly people strive to make their voice in the public to be heard.

Experiencing and recording elderly people's collective singing in a public park led Yin Yi to further speculate on the nature of sound in public space in China. In his field recording-based sound installation *Traffic Light* (2010–2013), he invites listeners to attend to how sound signals used in traffic light systems vary culturally and nationally. In *Have You Heard the Ocean Sound?* (2016), he challenged the acoustic regulation of a shopping mall in Shanghai by inserting post-produced ocean sounds in the banal Chinese-pop music list looping the whole working hours in the mall. The artist later commented that only after going through a long and difficult negotiation process with the management team of the shopping mall did he realize the politics behind

FIGURE 2.24 *Yin Yi,* Gift, *installation, Comradery-A Rejuvenation Project, Shanghai, 2019. Courtesy of the artist.*

the seemingly innocent background music played in a commercial space. This investigation of "who decide what we hear in public space" continued in his another installation *Gift* (2016, 2019) (Figure 2.24). The work was inspired by his experience in Hamburger in Germany where he learnt that the local train station used classical music such as *The Four Seasons* to keep away tramps. In *Gift*, Yin Yi narrated both the story of Hamburger train station and the music history of the four violin concertos *The Four Seasons* by the Italian composer Antonio Vivaldi in the early eighteenth century. People were advised to play any music they want to share with the public by connecting their cellphones to the bluetooth sound system in the installation. When no one interrupted, the sound system played *The Four Seasons* on loop.

In the same spirit of interrupting institutionalized sound of public space, Yin Yi invited his friend, an economics professor Liang Jie to question the identity politics of Shanghai dialect. The younger generation born in Shanghai gradually lose their ability to speak in local dialect; this becomes a shared concern among local artists and scholars. Following Yin Yi's instruction, Liang Jie did a performance piece on the subway line 4 (the most important connecting line in Shanghai subway system). Every time after the Mandarin and English versions of stop announcement, Liang Jie played his prerecorded announcement in Shanghai dialect through a portable speaker. Yin Yi documented the performance, seventy-three-minute long, in his video

(Metro Broadcast in Shanghainese) The next stop is Pudong Avenue
（地铁广播上海话）下一站浦东大道

FIGURE 2.25 *Yin Yi,* A Trip in Shanghai, *Video Installation, 2017. Performer Liang Jie. Screen shot. Courtesy of the artist.*

installation *A Trip in Shanghai* (2017) (Figure 2.25). In this work, the artist questions the government's control over local language essential to Shanghai local culture in public spaces in Shanghai. For many Shanghai-born artists and scholars, it is important to keep local dialect to maintain the identity of Shanghai as a truly international and global city.

The politics of sound and listening is also a consistent theme in the Taiwanese artist Wang Hong-Kai's sound art works. Wang Hong-Kai employs performance to push people to think about tension of identities, ideologies, and knowledge emerged through narratives and collective listening. Adapted from Robert Ashley's opera *Ash* (1998), commissioned by the Taipei Women Rescue Foundation, Hong-Kai conceived the performance piece *Watching Dust* (2010) for the surviving Taiwanese "comfort women" during the Second World War. To avoid subjecting Taiwanese comfort women survivors to further gazes, Hong-Kai invited Taiwan artists to perform in an opera setting as fictional. Instead, Hong-Kai invited comfort women survivors to see the opera performance solely as audience. Collective listening was generated through watching the opera as a way to question, share, and cure personal pains. To continue her experimentation with collective listening, Hong-Kai applies the format of workshop in a series of her works to explore the transformative capacity of discussion and collective listening, as well as the potential politics in the process of collective listening, including *Workshop For How To Be Economically Powerful, Musically?* (2011), *A Composer Is That Without Which Something Would Not Have Happened* (2012), and *Conceptual Biography of Chris Mann* (2014).

FIGURE 2.26 *Zheng Bo, Sing For Her,* Tsim Sha Tsui, *Hong Kong, 2015. Courtesy of the artist.*

While collective listening can be transformative and therapeutic, so is collective singing. Beijing-born and Hong Kong-based artist Zheng Bo's *Sing For Her* (2015) (see Figure 2.26) was an interactive sound installation placed in the art square of *Tsim Sha Tsui* in Hong Kong. Shaped as a gigantic megaphone, the installation is only activated when one sings along with the karaoke system fixed on top of the megaphone. Different from commercial karaoke songs, Zheng Bo put in the karaoke system performances of collective singing he recorded from seven ethnic communities in Hong Kong, including Filipino domestic helpers, African asylum seekers, descendants of Gurkha soldiers, and new immigrants from China. Zheng Bo asked people from these communities to sing songs they were proud of at a location they usually gathered to hang out. Many of these communities are politically, economically, or culturally marginalized in Hong Kong. Zheng Bo prefers to call *Sing For Her* a "pedagogical encounter" to differentiate from participatory art (aka people's art) in Mao's era, which Zheng Bo criticized as a violently enforced art. Taking the friendly gesture of singing along and going through the span of the performance of a song, one experiences something beyond one's usual everyday routine that unconsciously limits one's knowledge of the surrounding world.

Zheng Bo's recent work moves to plants to investigate relations between plants and the political history of modern China that develops through

FIGURE 2.27 *Zheng Bo,* Weed Party: Kindred, *in the Group Exhibition* Precariat's Meeting, *Ming Contemporary Art Museum (McaM) in Shanghai, 2017. Courtesy of the artist.*

science and Marxism. For him, weed is similar to marginalized groups in urban cities, as something undesirable from the mainstream. In the series *Weed Party*, Zheng Mo creates *Weed Party: Kindred* in the group exhibition *Precariat's Meeting* (2017) (Figure 2.27) at Ming Contemporary Art Museum (McaM) in Shanghai. The work consists both a workshop and an installation. For the installation, Zheng Bo moved weed he found around the museum to the abandoned elevator sections in the museum that used to be the factory elevator of Shanghai Paper Machine Factory. Inside of each elevator, he placed a microphone connected to a speaker. During the workshop, Zheng Bo invited participants to write a letter to weed and asked them to read the letter out loud to the weed through the microphone. For Zheng Bo, even though the language used in the letters would not be understood by the weed, the vibration of the voice can nonetheless be vividly felt.

Sound and Net Art

As a representative artist in the new generation of net art in China, Wang Changcun makes sound net art works that enable a nonhuman sense of hearing. Majored in electronic engineering at Harbin Engineering University, Wang Changcun (aka Ayrtbh) made his first computer music piece, *Lunch Life* in 2002 using Cool Edit on his classmate's computer. *Lunch Life* was later collected in the double CD *China: The Sonic Avant-Garde*, and released in 2003 by Dajuin Yao's label Post-Concrete. Wang Changcun's first job was in a state-owned enterprise in the city of Daqing as a computer programmer from 2003 to 2004. Most jobs in state-owned enterprises by the time was not demanding and hence Wang Changcun had plenty of time to learn Max/MSP function by function. During an invited tour in Europe in October 2004, he purchased his first laptop. For Changcun, computer is never a tool to realize something but an art itself. In our interview, he commented, "If computer is only used to imitate sounds of a guitar or a piano, it loses its value in being an instrument. The unique thing about a computer is that it can be programmed. It can do real-time computing. If one really considers computer an instrument, one has to use it in a proper way."

Three windows in C Minor (2018) (see Figure 2.28) is a program Changcun writes that samples Bach's *C Minor Fugue* but plays through a new logic. Only when one of the three floating windows hits any side of the frame of the interface will the next note be played. The size of the screen frame, the moving speed of the three windows, and the chance of collision among the three windows replace factors such as notation and experience of the musician that would normally affect the performance of a classical music piece. Listening to Bach note by note following a computer logic is a nonhuman listening experience; human auditory perception never works that way. Similar nonhuman auditory sense can be found in *Aurum* (2018), in which Wang Changcun writes a program that compresses the top fifty hit songs on pop music billboards into one "super golden" song. In four minutes and fifty-five seconds, one can finish hearing fifty songs. The idea is

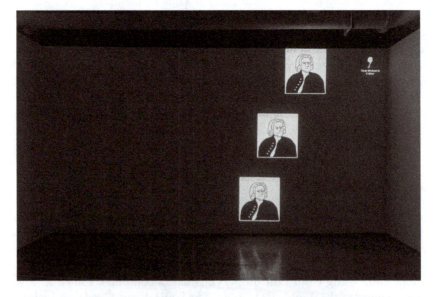

FIGURE 2.28 *Wang Changcun,* Three windows in C Minor. *Installation View OCAT Shanghai, 2018. Courtesy of the artist and OCAT Shanghai.*

that computer should never imitate the human, instead, the humans should try to sense in the way computer senses based on its algorithmic logic. Wang Changcun shares many net artists' dictum, once created, let free.

Songs of Anon (2018) is both a music album and a software. Wang Changcun uses Max/MSP to write a sequencer modulation algorithm to modulate the rhythm of the synthesizer/drum machine. Using his own music works as the reference for the modulation algorithm, the result is a subtle human-computer interactive music, the music is susceptibly played by the artist but at the same time full of alienation. Wang Changcun makes a free downloadable application under the same title *Songs of Anon.* Anyone who uses the application creates their own version of songs of anon.

Gao Jie's internet radio series *Faux Art History (2016.4.1-)* enacts another kind of programming; it reprograms art history by deconstructing famous art works, dissociated from its original historical background and recontextualized in another historical period. Gao Jie's heavy Fujian accent, which he never seems to hide, has made the radio program less authoritative and more individualized. As an informal student of Huang Yongping (1954–2019), the founder of Xiamen Dada in the '85 New Wave movement, Gao Jie has well inherited a Dadaist spirit, questioning canonical knowledge production. For the artist, only through an active reprogramming of information can one come to realize that information is not knowledge. *Faux Art History* alerts us of the rigid contemporary art knowledge and insists that only by its deconstruction will we be able to develop our own taste in contemporary art. Using knowledge of contemporary art to reconstruct contemporary art makes it a meta-art. The artist uploads *Faux Art History* onto one of China's largest mainstream podcast platform *Hymalaya*, among selections of other highly popular and authoritative art history podcast programs, such as Western Art History by the well-known Chinese art historian Fan Jingzhong.

Going back to the origin of China's contemporary art in the 1980s, on December 1, 1987, Huang Yongping washed two art history books in the washing machine at home for two minutes, *History of Chinese Painting* by Wang Bomin and *A Concise History of Modern Painting* by Herbert Read. The paper paste lumps were placed atop a plate of broken glass on a wooden box, on the cover of the wooden box was the handwritten description/title of the work, *The History of Chinese Painting and the History of Modern Western Art Washed in the Washing Machine for Two Minute. Faux Art History* resonates to Huang Yongping's two-minute washing cycle piece by extending the time of washing to an enduring event, a digitalized, immersive, portable acoustic monument.

It is a good time now to recall what Huang Yongping suggests in response to Wittgenstein's famous saying, "if there is nothing to say we keep quiet."

Huang says, "if there is nothing to say we make balderdash."[8]

---

[8]Huang Yongping's public talk at Fang Suo bookstore, Chengdu (2016.11.26), titled "保持沉默，或是乱说" (To Be Silent Or To Make Balderdash).

3

A Brief History of Electronic and Experimental Music in China

Writings on electronic and experimental music in China so far fall into two systems of historical narratives: the academic/official and nonacademic/ grassroots. The former is written by scholars mostly related to conservatories; the latter is primarily documented by nonacademic musicians or music critics of subcultures. In recent years, there is an increasing international attention to China's electronic music scene. Routledge has published two edited books that include articles on China's academic electronic music: *The Routledge Research Companion to Electronic Music: Reaching out with Technology* (2018) and *Electroacoustic Music in East Asia* (2019). Researches are mainly driven by questions of musical inspirations and cultural valence (Battier and Liao 2018; Landy 2018). It is worth mentioning that the musicologist and composer Leigh Landy, while focusing on Chinese conservatories in Beijing also attends to the grassroots, "the underground scene" as he calls it (2019). The revised edition of *Audio Culture: Readings in Modern Music* also includes a translated piece by the poet and experimental musician Yan Jun on the history of Chinese experimental music, with its focus on the nonacademic side (2017).

Building on published works, in this chapter, I steer my way through the archipelago of academic electronic music, nonacademic electronic experimental music, as well as a rarely mentioned and often neglected territory, electronic music instruments DIY culture. There is admittedly a discrepancy in my methods in approaching the three territories. My own ethnographic fieldwork has been with the nonacademic experimental music scene and hence I rely on more fieldwork materials. With Chinese academic electronic music and instrument inventions, my discussion is mainly based on published academic articles written in Chinese and English languages, archival journalist reports, and online forums. In addition, as much as I believe the fundamental importance of individual creativity, I want to stress the value of the curatorial mechanism that intrigues, supports, sustains, and reinforces individual experiments. Therefore, in this chapter I spend more time with curated events, thematic ideas, and interrelations between them.

Stories of electronic and experimental music in China were reported and discussed in public domains at least thirty years earlier than sound in contemporary art[1].

> I thought of another story about American "silent music." When it was played, it was even easier than this kind of "electronic music." The performer of this silent music, sometimes just need to place a few green beans in front of his/herself, and stare at them for ten minutes. Their theory is, "The world of music cannot be dependent on music itself, there has to be visual elements to make it more dramatic." This kind of theory, for ordinary music appreciators are unreasonable. However, this more thoroughly reveals the true bourgeois nature of western art.

The above words come from a report written by Wu Nanxing published on the Communist Party journal *Qian Xian* (*Frontline*) in 1961. The report introduced an "unsuccessful" electronic music theater performance from a Brazilian newspaper. The narrative was used as a more extreme example of the increasingly "absurd," "corrupted," "extremely boring and nihilist" Western art. What was mocked is suspiciously John Cage's known piece 4'33", although the story as we hear does not involve staring at green beans.

Another example comes from Fu Han on atonal music, translated from Soviet Union Encyclopedia, published in the academic journal *People's Music* in 1956. It reads like this:

> Atonality, is a formalist composition method which discards the tonality of music and changes harmony into a chaotic combination of noise. Atonality results in the loss of meaning in melody and thus leads music to a total collapse. Atonality represents the extreme formalist tendency in the decadent bourgeois music. This music has abandoned the basics of folk music and classical music. . . . In 1944, atonal music's disciples became the propagandists of imperialism, using the music structure to represent Napoleonicism and religiousism (for example, Schoenberg's Ode to Napoleon). . . . Atonality is the symbol of formalism; it leads to the death of the art of music.

---

[1]My attention to journal articles published before 1980s is inspired by the Chinese independent journalist, writer and music record collector Wang Mozhi's article published in Chinese in *The Paper*, titled "The Prehistory of China's Electronic Music: From *Dianziqin*" (2019). https://www.thepaper.cn/newsDetail_forward_3194834

In mainland China, before the economic reform which began in 1978, earlier knowledge of electronic music for the public was mainly published in official publications including *People's Music* (1950 till now), *Qian Xian* (*Avant-garde*) (1958 till now), *Musical Instrument Magazine* (1972 till now), and *Art of Music* (*Journal of the Shanghai Conservatory of Music*) (1979 till now). Many articles were translations from Russian and English sources, sometimes added with a brief commentary of the translators. Electronic music was in general considered a decadent Western bourgeois art practice. In 1955, there was an article titled "music of the atomic madman" translated from a book titled *Bourgeois Culture in Service for Imperialist Reactionaries* from Soviet Union, claiming that those kinds of music will not benefit people emotionally and mentally. Instead, they will depress listeners and empty their spiritual world.

> Some so called experimentalist musicians brings extraordinary insult to music in their pursuit of moving visual and audio effects . . . another music hooligan John Cage forms his band like this, a car horn, a pile of glass bottles, a piano with some bamboo sticks, metals and other things to the piano strings. Some American critics consider this composer the avant-garde pioneer in American new music thinking. (1955)

These writers will probably be appalled by the popularity and influence of John Cage in the art and music worlds and in popular culture today. Neither will they believe that the Chinese translation of John Cage's book *Silence* (2015) has been on the top list of recommended books in Chinese stylish bookstores in the twenty-first century.

Electronic and experimental music are not only musical practices but also resources for and medium of ideologies, cultures, technologies, and politics. In 2018, a group of young synthesizer fans (including new media artist Pei Feng, musician and synthesizer designer Meng Qi, and artist Ding Xin) went out to search for and eventually met and interviewed the pioneer Chinese electronic music instrument inventor Tian Jinqin, who was once nationally famous in the 1970s and 1980s. This further suggests that more than being a tool or an activity that divide people, music can be the reason for people to seek connections.

The Electronic Instrument Builders

Despite the ideological charge of new music forms in the mid-1950s and before the Cultural Revolution, Chinese people had earlier recognized the importance of inventing electronic instruments. According to articles published on *People's Music* in 1979, China's first synthesizer was invented in 1958 by Nanjing College of Posts and Telecommunications (*Nanjing*

Youdian Xueyuan) and Nanjing Instrument factory (*Nanjing Yueqichang*). In the same year, Nanjing College of Posts and Telecommunications published a small booklet on synthesizer (*dianziqin*) (Yi and Yan 1979). The same article also reports that in 1959, Northeastern Instrument Factory in the city of Yingkou trial-produced five sets of polyphonic triangle electronic organ and semiconductor polyphonic three-layer keyboard electronic organ, and had officially produced about fifty monophonic electronic organs. In 1960, Shanghai Guoguang Harmonica Factory produced polyphonic synthesizers. Taiyuan No. 2 Radio Factory in Shanxi Province began experimenting with synthesizers in 1964. These activities had to stop due to the ten-year-long Cultural Revolution. There is no further evidence of any actual synthesizer left from the 1950s and 1960s. During our personal communication, the independent journalist Wang Mozhi expressed his suspicion on the validity of claims of inventing those electronic instruments since the period between 1958 and 1962 was the Great Leap Forward era.

However, based on a recently published interview with the electronic music instrument inventor Tian Jinqin, we can see that during the late 1950s Tian began experimenting with adding electronic parts onto traditional instruments. It would not be too surprising if factories like Shanghai Piano Factory and Shanghai Harmonica Factory experimented with different models of synthesizers in the 1950s. Another evidence that may prove the existence of invention of electronic music instruments in the 1950s can be found in a small essay published in 1958 on *People's Music* (issue 1, p37), titled "Can performing art be replaced by machines?" The essay's author is Situ Huacheng (1927–1989), a known violinist in China.

> Our editorial department has received a few letters from our readers that they have designed many automatic instruments with design graphs. They subjectively believed that the automatic instruments can enhance music performance. Is this correct? . . . Some people even have the fantasy that they can use machines to replace difficult performing techniques, thus they invented some kind of an automatic performing machine.

Although this is a critique it nonetheless proves that experiments of making electronic music instruments existed in the 1950s.

In the late 1970s, synthesizer invention was listed as one of national science projects. After the Cultural Revolution from 1978, it witnessed a nationwide popularity in inventing electronic music instruments. According to reports on *People's Music* and *Musical Instrument Magazine* in 1979, more than twenty cities were involved in inventing electronic music instruments, including Beijing, Shanghai, Tianjin, Suzhou, Changzhou, Taiyuan, Haerbin, and Nanjing. An article on *People's Music* particularly mentioned an invention that did not exist in the West by the time, the XK-1 Ribbon-controlled analog synthesizer, invented by Taiyuan Radio factory (Han 1979).

This leads to one of the earliest and talented electronic instrument builders in the history of Chinese electronic music, Tian Jinqin.

XK-1 Ribbon-Controlled Analog Synthesizer 1978

The engineer Tian Jinqin from Shan Xi province invented China's first string-controlled synthesizer in 1978. Tian studied mechanical engineering and graduated in 1955. With a strong interest in physics, he self-taught radio electronics during leisure time after work. He preferred to read books of physics and electronics from Russia, because the writing was clear and practical. His earlier interest was to find ways to add more and richer timbres to traditional Chinese instruments. In 1958, he first added a pickup, electron tube amplifier, and electronic filter to a secondhand zither to get more variety of timbres. This focus on timbre can be explained by Tian's love for traditional Chinese string instruments which are known for being unique in its variety of timbre of every note. In the meantime, the lack of individual touch of electronic synthesizers had long been a problem that concerned Tian. To individualize and culturalize synthesizers, Tian focused on expanding the possibility of performance style.

For Tian, keyboard-based instruments lack the effects of traditional string instruments, which can be played with a variety of finger techniques including squeezing, pressing, trembling, and sliding. In order to create similar effects of string instruments on the keyboard, Tian added an upright fretless fingerboard with four wire wound resistance rod of thirty centimeters long to act as the resistor that determines the oscillation frequency in the oscillator and four metal strips on the side of the keyboard. Pressing the metal strips would cause a short circuit of the resistance wire. The more the short circuit, the smaller the resistance and the higher the frequency. The resistant-capacitor oscillator matches the law that the chord length is reduced by half the frequency by 8 degrees, so the same position change can achieve the effect of a traditional Chinese string instrument. While the four metal strips control frequency, Tian used four sliders to control volume and a row of buttons to control the filter to change timbres. The unique synthesizer not only simulates a variety of Chinese traditional instruments, but also generates natural (e.g., thunder, rain, birds' songs) and unnatural sounds (e.g., imagined animals' sounds), environment and machine sounds.

The year 1980 was an important one for Tian as he founded the Shanxi Taiyuan Electronic Musical Instrument Research Institute. The documentary film *Dianzi Qin* (电子琴, *Synthesizer*) produced by Shanghai Science and Technology Education Film Studio features Tian Jinqin performing his invention, the ribbon-controlled analog synthesizer (Figures 3.1.1, 3.1.2). In the same year, Tian performed his ribbon-controlled analog synthesizer at the small theater of People's Palace in Beijing. Tian wrote the book *Electronic*

FIGURE 3.1.1 *Screenshot one of Tian Jinqin Performing XK-1 ribbon-controlled Analog Synthesizer in the Documentary Film* Dianzi Qin *(Synthesizer) Produced by Shanghai Science and Technology Education Film Studio, 1980.*

FIGURE 3.1.2 *Screenshot two of Tian Jinqin performing XK-1 ribbon-controlled Analog Synthesizer in the Documentary Film* Dianzi Qin *(Synthesizer) Produced by Shanghai Science and Technology Education Film Studio, 1980.*

Synthesizer, which was edited by the known Chinese music scholar Huang Xiangpeng and published through Posts & Telecom Press Co., Ltd. in 1983.

In 1984, The Patent Law of the People's Republic of China was passed at the fourth Meeting of the Standing Committee of the Sixth National People's Congress on March 12. The Patent Law went into effect on April 1, 1985. On the exact day of April 1, four submissions of invention were electronic instruments, including "a multi-functional electronic percussion string instrument" by Gu Chengzhong associated with Shenyang Military Commission Political Work Department Song and Dance Troupe, "music toy bricks" by Wang Jing from Shanghai, "a programmed multi-functional signal generator" by Wang Xu associated with Northeastern Engineer Institute from Shenyang, and "cabinet electronic synthesizer" from Ye Guangzu in Beijing. There are also inventions of "music abacus" (1985.6.24), "dance synthesizer" (1985.8.14), "sound-controlled synthesizer" (1985.11.02), "ten thousand sound synthesizer" (1985.12.26) (Figures 3.2.1, 3.2.2, 3.2.3), "*suiyi* synthesizer (synthesizer at will)" (1986.1.13) (Figures 3.3.1, 3.3.2), "waving synthesizer" (1986.4.20), and "allotype synthesizer" (1987.8.5).

Tian patented "multiple dynamic sound effect and simple structured electronic instrument" in March 1986 (Figures 3.4.1, 3.4.2). In 1996, Tian retired from Taiyuan Electronic Instrument Institute and moved to Shenzhen. From articles he published, it can be guessed that he kept working

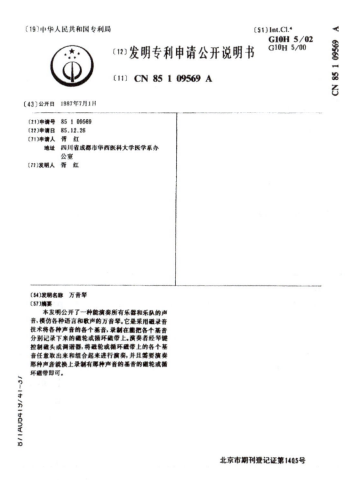

FIGURE 3.2.1 *Patent Cover Page of "Ten Thousand Sound Synthesizer" by Xu Hong, 1985.*

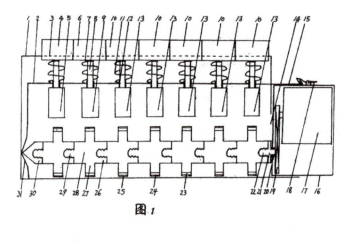

图.1

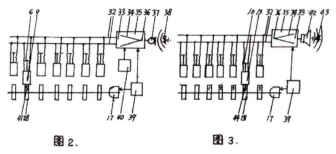

图 2.   图 3.

FIGURE 3.2.2 *Circuit Diagram 1 of "Ten Thousand Sound Synthesizer" by Xu Hong, 1985.*

in the field of electronic music. However, hardly any of his inventions were mentioned and advocated through public media.

In 1984, the first computer music lab was founded in Shanghai Jiaotong University, led by Professor Xu Shuzhong. Instead of building synthesizers, the lab focused on developing computer music hardware interface, electronic piano, and text to speech synthesis and analysis. The lab was active until Professor Xu retired in 1994. In 1986, Beijing University music acoustics and computer music research lab was founded (Huang 2008). In 1986, Composer Chen Yuanlin built the first computer music lab at the Central Conservatory of Music. In 1987, Liu Jian and Wu Yuebei founded computer music lab at Wuhan Conservatory of Music. In 1994, China modern electronic music center was founded in the Central Conservatory of Music, led by the composer Zhang Xiaofu. Series of conference and forums were organized by these music conservatories, with emphasis on learning how to use electronic synthesizers to compose and perform, rather than on making them.

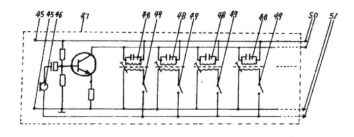

图 4.

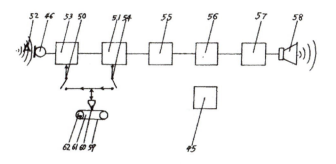

图 5.

FIGURE 3.2.3 *Circuit Diagram 2 of "Ten Thousand Sound Synthesizer" by Xu Hong, 1985.*

Inventions from the Grassroots

In the new millennium, more active electronic music instrument building scene was taken over by the grassroots. Internet has provided more opportunities for inventors to publish, share, and even sell their DIY synthesizers. Inventors began to communicate with musicians closely, and more often inventors themselves are musicians too. Also, there are more opportunities and venues to showcase one's inventions and performance of them.

In 2005, Nicolas Collins, the author of *Handmade Electronic Music: The Art of Hardware Hacking* and the professor of sound at the School of the Art Institute of Chicago, was invited to *Musicacoustica Beijing*, initiated by Zhang Xiaofu since 1994. Nicolas Collins collaborated with Peter Cusack to record sounds in the Central Conservatory of Music. In 2012, Nicolas Collins was invited to *Musicacoustica Beijing* for the second time. During

FIGURE 3.3.1 *Patent Page of "Suiyi Synthesizer" Chen Xuehuang, 1986.*

that trip, he not only participated in the official festival delivering a lecture titled "Music Production After Semiconductor-Transistor—Discussion of Software and Hardware Usage in Current Electronic Music Performances" but also engaged more with the grassroots. He performed with local noise and experimental musicians in Beijing organized by Yan Jun. On October 11, 2012, invited by Shanghai-based sound artist Yin Yi, Collins gave a hardware hacking workshop open to the public at BM space (founded by Yin Yi and Liu Yanan) in Shanghai, introducing CMOS oscillator, sensors (light, pressure, electrodes, potentiometers, etc.), Arduino, and DIY instrument (Figure 3.5).

In 2005, the music duo FM3 (Christiaan Virant and Zhang Jian) (also written as FM三) released the Buddha Machine, a small plastic music box that looped nine tracks of music created by the duo. Christiaan Virant was among the earliest generations of international students coming to China to study

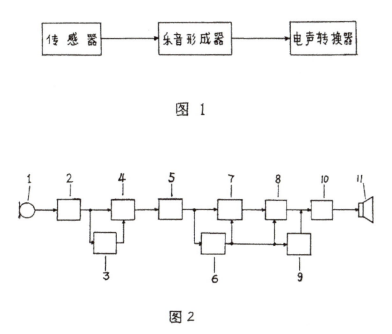

FIGURE 3.3.2 *Circuit Diagram of* "Suiyi *Synthesizer*" *Chen Xuehuang, 1986.*

after the opening-up policy. He met Zhang Jian and formed the duo FM3 in 1999 to make electronic music, focusing on making microsound music with a particular Chinese ambience. By chance, they came across the popular music device, referred to as the Buddha Machine, sold at every Chinese Buddhist temple. Buddhist followers wear these small music boxes to listen to Buddhist chanting whenever and where they want to. It occurred to them that they could put their own music in this little music box. It took them a while to finally find a factory that was willing to produce a small quantity, estimate of 300 units. The popularity of FM3's Buddha Machine in the global music circle was beyond their expectation. In the following years, they kept upgrading it, making the speed adjustable, changing the switch to pitch-shift knob, adding a Line Out, including loops of new tracks with the instrument of *guqin* and electronics. Buddha Machine has evolved from an interesting music player to a music game tool, a medium through which FM3 works with other musicians. And its sound is always dreamy, meditative, quiet, cool, and ambient.

Another talented, self-taught electronic musician and synthesizer designer is Meng Qi. Meng began to learn DIY synthesizer from 2007. He released "Voltage Memory" known as the first eurorack module from China in 2015 and has been teaching modular synthesis online and in different academic and nonacademic institutions. Now his synthesizers are widely used by electronic musicians around the world.

FIGURE 3.4.1 *Patent Page of "Multiple Dynamic Sound Effect and Simple Structured Electronic Instrument" by Tian Jinqin, 1986.*

An exhibition titled *Sound Bending* in 2012 had nicely showcased a developed scene in DIY electronic music instruments formed among nonacademic musicians. *Sound Bending* was curated by musician and sound artist Wang Changcun at the art space Imagokinetics in Hangzhou. It exhibited nine artists/musicians' inventions, including the noise musician Mei Zhiyong (Figure 3.11), the calligrapher Lu Dadong and new media artist Deng Yuejun (Figure 3.6), artist Xu Zhe (Figure 3.10), experimental musician and sound artist Xu Cheng (Figures 3.7, 3.8), cellist Wang Tian (Figure 3.9), artist Pan Chong, experimental musician Zhang Jianfu, and Meng Qi (Figure 3.12).

Academic Electronic Music: Inauguration

Right after the Cultural Revolution (1966–1976), the country resumed its college admission in 1977; the Central Conservatory of Music received

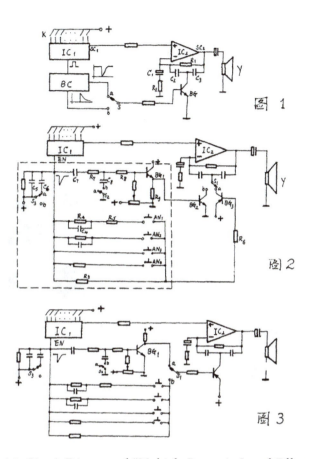

FIGURE 3.4.2 *Circuit Diagram of "Multiple Dynamic Sound Effect and Simple Structured Electronic Instrument" by Tian Jinqin, 1986.*

its first group of thirty students, later known as the famous "class of '78," including Tan Dun, Qu Xiaosong, Chen Qigang, Zhou Long, Guo Wenjing, Chen Yi, Liu Sola, Ma Jianping, Su Cong, Zhang Xiaofu, and Chen Yuanlin. It was students from this group who contributed to the first official electronic synthesizer concert in China in September 4, 1984. But we need to rewind back a bit to the year 1977.

Between 1977 and 1990

The first group of students of the Central Conservatory of Music were recruited in 1977 but School actually began in 1978, because the conservatory needed to renovate after destructions done by the Cultural Revolution. Notable composers Du Mingxin, Wu Zuqiang, and Zhu Jian'er returned to

FIGURE 3.5 *Nicolas Collins, Hardware Hacking Workshop, BM Space, Shanghai, 2012.*

the conservatory to teach composition, but their knowledge and materials on Western modern music were rather limited. They studied at Moscow State Tchaikovsky Conservatory in the mid and late 1950s, focusing mainly on nineteenth-century romanticism. Therefore, the conservatory invited a group of oversea composers and musicians to give talks to students and teachers on modern music, including contemporary classical music composer Chou Wen-Chung (student and friend of Edward Varèse) in 1977 (Chang 2006), the British composer Alexander Goehr (student of Arnold Schoenberg) in 1980 (Kouwenhoven 1990).

Chou Wen-Chung went to the United States in 1946 to first pursue architectural studies on a scholarship at Yale University, but he soon decided to learn music and went to study composition with Nicholas Slonimsky at the New England Conservatory of Music. Chou moved to New York after graduation and there he met Edward Varèse and became his protégé in 1949. In 1972, after US president Nixon's visit to China, the US-China communication was finally restored. Chou visited China in 1972 when the

FIGURE 3.6 *Lu Dadong, Deng Yuejun,* Che Zhen (Bicycle Lineup), *2012. Installation View,* Sound Bending, *Imagokinetics, Hangzhou, 2012. Photo courtesy of Imagokinetics.*

FIGURE 3.7 *Xu Cheng,* Dusty apc, *2011, based on Steptone Generator Circuit of Forrest M. Mims III,* Sound Bending, *Imagokinetics, Hangzhou, 2012. Photo courtesy of Imagokinetics.*

country was experiencing the Cultural Revolution and his plan to promote cultural exchange between the two countries fell apart (Chang 2006). In 1977, right after the Cultural Revolution, Chou visited the Central Conservatory of Music in Beijing, gave lectures on contemporary music in the West and brought with him scores and recordings of composers including Bartok, Hindmith, Varèse, Babbitt, Davidovsky, Hovhanes, Shapey, Luening,

FIGURE 3.8 *Xu Cheng, Bear567∞, Based on Christian P. Hemmo's Noise567 Circuit,* Sound Bending, *Imagokinetics, Hangzhou, 2012. Photo courtesy of Imagokinetics.*

Ussachevsky, Crumb, Tokemitsu, and his own work (Chang 40). In 1978, Chou established the center for the US/China Arts Exchange at Columbia University. Through this program, he brought the American conductor David Gilbert, violinist Isaac Stern, and playwright Arthur Miller to Beijing.

Among the invited international speakers to China, one person drew more public attention beyond the conservatory, the French electronic musician Jean Michel Jarre. An anonymous diplomat brought Jarre's hit music album *Oxygène* to China and introduced it to his Chinese friends. The music was then played through China national radio foreign music program. According to Wang Mozhi, in May 1980, Jean Michel was officially invited to Beijing to give a lecture at Central Conservatory of Music on synthesizer and electronic music. He gave the conservatory an AKS synthesizer made in England as a gift. Students formed an electronic music study group to learn how to use this synthesizer. The year after, in 1981, Jarre held public concerts in Beijing (October 21, 22) and Shanghai (October 26, 27, 29), making the record of being the first foreign musician's public concert in China in the post-Mao era. The third concert in Shanghai was added after the show on the 27th, with a news released on the *Liberation Daily* that tickets for an extra performance would be sold in seven places from 1:00 p.m. on the 27th, with two tickets maximum per person. All tickets were quickly sold out. In 1983, Jarre performed in Capital Indoor Stadium in Beijing.

If Alexander Goehr and Chou Wen-Chung's lectures attracted over a thousand students and teachers inside of the conservatory's lecture hall,

FIGURE 3.9 *Wang Tian*, Waterphone, Sound Bending, *Imagokinetics, Hangzhou, 2012. Photo courtesy of Imagokinetics.*

Jarre's public concerts, as described in the documentary titled *Jean-Michel Jarre—China Concerts 1981* made by Andrew Piddington for Central Television in the UK, drew over a two-hundred-thousand audience all together. This may also explain why published accounts of the history of academic electronic music often began with Jarre's visit to the conservatory in 1980, instead of Chou Wen-Chung's visit in 1977 or Alexander Goehr's visit in 1980 or any other composers who were invited around the year of 1980 but with hardly any records and reports.

Back to the electronic synthesizer concert in 1984 at Central Conservatory of Music, the equipment used in the concert mainly included a Roland

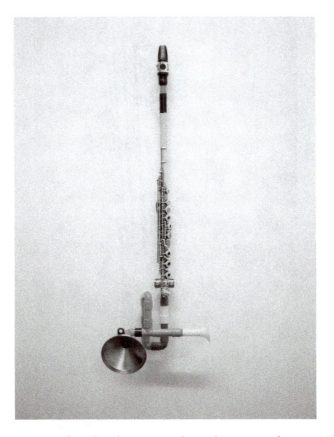

FIGURE 3.10 *Xu Zhe,* Plaxphone, Sound Bending, *Imagokinetics, Hangzhou, 2012. Photo courtesy of Imagokinetics.*

Jupiter 8 synthesizer, a variety of vocoders, and effects. Eight pieces of compositions were created all by graduates of the music conservatory, including Chen Yuanlin, Tan Dun, Chen Yi, and Zhou Long. Zhou Long's *Yuzhou Zhiguang* (*The Light of Cosmos*), Tan Dun's *You Yuan Jing Meng* (*Dream in A Garden*), and Chen Yuanlin's *Nv Wa Bu Tian* (*Nvwa mends the Heavens*) had won much praise. The one that captured most attention was Tan Dun's *You Yuan Jing Meng.* Tan Dun described the process of making the piece in an interview that he went to a radio factory to gather all kinds of electronic devices that make sounds, recreating the acoustic scenes by fusing electronic music and traditional Kun opera. According to the scholar Wang Cichao, what makes Tan Dun's piece unique is that he combines the vocal music and spoken parts of Kun opera with electronic sound effects of the twentieth century to generate the theatrical ambience for the narrative (1984). This concert was officially considered the beginning of China's

FIGURE 3.11 *Mei Zhiyong,* Tape DJ Fuzzy, *2010, Sound Bending, Imagokinetics, Hangzhou, 2012. Photo courtesy of Imagokinetics.*

FIGURE 3.12 *Meng Qi, Musical Instruments Workshop, Sound Bending, Imagokinetics, Hangzhou, 2012. Photo courtesy of Imagokinetics.*

electronic music, a milestone that symbolized the beginning of the history of academic electronic music in China to be exact.

In 1985, through the introduction and support of Chou Wen-Chung, Zhou Long, Chen Yi, and Tan Dun were offered scholarship to study composition at Columbia University in the United States. Chang writes, "one of Chou's lasting contributions to Columbia was to transform the old electronic music center into the present computer music center in the early 1980s" (2006, 39). Chou's teaching and his own composition emphasizes the aesthetic and philosophical dimension of contemporary music and the synthesis of the Eastern and Western cultures. Through Varèse's conception of sound, Chou rediscovered Chinese calligraphy as both technical and conceptual inspiration for his music making. While the majority academic electronic music pedagogy seems to be centered around technology, Chou's emphasis on the aesthetics and philosophical aspect of composition in his teaching and music works proves to be particularly valuable.

As a graduate of the class of 1978, Chen Yuanlin was hired back to found the very first computer music lab at Central Conservatory of Music in 1986. In 1991, Chen went to pursue further education in computer and electronic music at SUNY at Stony Brook in the United States with Professor Daria Semegen and Daniel Weymouth. Other than United States, Germany and France were also favorite options for young Chinese composers. Most of them returned to China after graduation. Composer Yang Liqing (1942–2013) studied at the Musikhochschule in Hannover in Germany in 1981 and returned to Shanghai to teach at Shanghai Conservatory of Music. Zhang Xiaofu studied in Paris and returned to Beijing to found CEMC-Center for Electronic Music of China at Central Conservatory of Music.

CEMC and Zhang Xiaofu

Zhang Xiaofu plays an important role in founding and promoting the academic electronic music scene in China. Zhang studied with the Chinese composer Wu Zuqiang at Central Conservatory of Music. After graduation in 1983, Zhang was offered a faculty position in the Department of Composition. Jarre's concerts were the first time Zhang experienced electronic music. When a chance to study in France came up with a grant from the Chinese Ministry of Culture in 1988, Zhang decided that he needed to learn electronic music in France. Zhang then studied with Yoshihisa Taira, Ivo Malec, and Jean Schwarz at the Ecole Normale de Musique de Paris, and he also attended classes of Boulze, Stockhausen, and Denisov. In 1994, Zhang Xiaofu returned to Beijing and founded CEMC and initiated a series of events and official music associations, including Beijing International Electronic Music Week, Beijing International Electronic Music Composition Competition, Asia Electronic Music Forum, and Electronic Music Association of China in the following years.

The official history of electronic music in China, according to Zhang Xiaofu, consists of three time marks and three stages. The first time mark is 1984 when the electronic synthesizer concert took place at Central Conservatory of Music. The second is the founding of CEMC in 1994 and the first Beijing Electronic Music Week held at Central Conservatory of Music in the same year. Both were organized by Zhang Xiaofu. The third is when Beijing Electronic Music Week changed to *Musicacoustica Beijing* Festival in 2004. The first stage (1984–1993) was the recognition of the fledgling electronic music in China, the second stage (1994–2003) was the expansion and accumulation, and the third one (2004–2012) was innovation and development in all aspects (Zhang 2012).

Leigh Landy summarizes three commonalities/paths shared by mainly academic composers based on case studies of Zhang Xiaofu and three of his former students, (1) sampling, (2) the use of Chinese instruments and/or musical approaches, (3) inspirations from Chinese culture (e.g., Buddhism, Taoism, poetry, philosophy) (2019, 77–95). Landy observes that Zhang Xiaofu has a strong tendency to promote the Chineseness in his music composition. This tendency is later clearly elaborated in articles written by Zhang Xiaofu himself and two of his doctoral students, unanimously stressing an effort in building a Chinese model in the process of developing electroacoustic music (Zhang 2019; Li 2019; Wang 2019). Specifically, Zhang Xiaofu strongly advocates building an "electroacoustic music with Chinese characteristics" by incorporating "the cultural heritage" from "Chinese traditional folk songs, traditional instrumental music, traditional Chinese parlé-chanté, traditional operas" (2019).

Up to 2008, three academic institutes formed the backbone of academic electronic music in China: Central Conservatory of Music, Shanghai Conservatory of Music, and Wuhan Conservatory of Music (Huang 2008). Each conservatory hosts a music festival: Musicacoustica Beijing, Electronic Music Week (Shanghai), Wuhan International New Music Festival (Wu Han). It is worth mentioning that academic composers and professors in Shanghai Conservatory of Music He Xuntian and Cheng Bi'an are both uniquely different from Zhang Xiaofu's composition tradition. Neither do they particularly emphasize on building electronic music platforms in the academic domain. Both deserve a separate space for a fuller exploration of their electronic music compositions, but to avoid digression from current narrative, I will not elaborate on the two composers here.

While tracing the history of electronic music in China, Zhang Xiaofu has clearly stated his criteria in what would be taken account of as legitimate in this history, that is, officially approved concerts, works released by official publishers, compositions or performances that won national or international awards, articles published on academic journals or presented in academic conferences. Works or writings that were not officially released or approved would not be considered in his account of the history of electronic music in China (Zhang 2012). This attitude and criteria unfortunately has created an invisible wall between academic music practice and nonacademic/grassroots music activities.

Despite the exclusion of nonacademic activities from the official history, interestingly, conservatories in China seem to always encourage their students and teachers to collaborate with popular and commercial cultures. The world known composer Tan Dun's commercial success as a composer began quite early when he was still a student at CCoM. He later composed music for movies and for popular music singers. The Shanghai-based composer He Xuntian works closely with popular music too. Zhang Xiaofu also works with commercial shows. Additionally, for academic electronic music composers, the national or local music competitions organized by official institutes are the major way for them to showcase new music works. Wining these competitions also means official recognition, promotion, and probably commercial opportunities.

Nonacademic Electronic and Experimental Music

Most nonacademic electronic and experimental music developed out of the rock music culture in mainland China in the 1990s in the sense that most electronic and experimental musicians played rock music before they explored more alternative and extreme form of music expressions, including noise, free improvisation, electroacoustic, field recording, ambient, and drone metal. Compared with academic electronic musicians' resources of labs, international symposiums, forums, and professional concert halls, nonacademic or grassroots musicians need to constantly deal with unstable and ever-changing resources. In recent years, as music venues face increasing difficulties in hosting experimental music due to financial and sometimes political reasons, musicians keep exploring all kinds of creative spaces for sharing their music experiments, including space underneath the bridge of highways, someone's living rooms, independent bookstores, caves in rural mountains, or live streaming. From the year 2012, in terms of curatorial formats, there has been a tendency of transitioning from publicly promoted events/festivals to private gatherings.

Rock Music and Spring of New Music, 1998

The nonacademic electronic and experimental music scene has its own minor history, coming out of the underground rock music and even jazz music culture in the context of post-Mao neoliberal China. The very first documented rock music band was a student band from The Beijing International Studies University called Wan Li Ma Wang (1979–1985). In 1979, the band debuted their public performance of songs by Beatles and Rolling Stones at the school's playground. Their performance took the audience by surprise and caused excitement. The band thus was considered the very first rock music band in China. The leading member of the band Wang Xinbo (1954) grew up in the community of Central Academy of Fine Art in Beijing. He became interested in electronics and radio technology when he was ten years old. In 1971, he got an album of the Beatles. Without understanding the lyrics, he immediately felt for its rhythm, melody and way of singing which was uniquely different from revolutionary operas and red songs during the cultural revolutionary time. In mid-1970s, Wang Xinbo joined Beijing Toy Research center to experiment with making simple acoustic toys. He self-designed synthesizers and effects in his spare time. After the disintegration of the band in 1985, Wang Xinbo devoted to music production and recording technology and has produced Cui Jian and Xie Tianxiao, both of whom became soul figures of Chinese rock music.

In 1993, the first non-state run modern popular music school Beijing Midi School of Music was founded. In the same year, Udo Hoffmann, a German sinologist, initiated *Beijing Jazz Festival*. With limited sources, the first festival only invited four foreign jazz bands and a local band led by Beijing-born jazz musician Liu Yuan. In the second year of 1994, Hoffmann was able to find more investment and invited up to eleven bands, among whom were the Japanese experimental musician Otomo Yoshihide, the Australian jazz violinist, and free improvisor Jon Rose. This was probably the earliest live experimental and improvisational music performance in mainland China. In 1995, with the help of the artist and independent curator Ou Ning, the Hong Kong musician Dickson Dee (Li Chin Sung) toured cities of Shenzhen, Fo Shan, and Beijing with the American avant-garde musician John Zorn and the Japanese noise musician Yamantaka Eye. Dickson Dee was also an organizer of music events, running several independent music labels, including *Sound Factory*, *Sonic Factory*, and *Noise Asia*. He was perhaps the first person to introduce new trends of Western experimental music to mainland China.

As rock music gradually became commercialized and centralized in Beijing, some rock musicians chose to go underground to experiment with alternative music forms. In its early stage, China's underground music was predominantly consisted of punk, gothic rock, heavy-metal, and avant-rock music. Musicians mainly imitated bands from the West. Experimental music was to a large extent only an idea and a music style introduced and discussed in underground music journals and forums, and was rarely practiced. This situation made the Lanzhou-born musician Wang Fan's music album *Dharma's Crossing* significant and groundbreaking (see more discussion on Wang Fan's music in Chapter 5). In 1998, Wang Fan was invited as a special guest to the public concert Spring of New Music, 1998 in Lanzhou organized by Yan Jun, dedicated to the American poet Allen Ginsberg. The concert was to feature China's non-Beijing-based underground bands for the first time. Within the circle, it was called "China's Woodstock" and it would symbolize the "Independence day of Underground Rock." Preparation for the show took over half a year, but the concert never occurred. However, this unrealized event proved to be crucial for the emergence of China's sound art and experimental music scene.

To memorialize this attempted concert, Yan Jun made a fanzine and titled it *Sub Jam*. Yan Jun explained, the word "sub" refers to subcultures and emerging things and "jam" means to make noise together. Printed on the front cover of the booklet is a quote from Ginsberg. On the back, is the Chinese translation of Ginsberg's poem "Howl." In addition to snapshots of underground music scenes in various cities in writing, the booklet also features essays by influential music critics and artists in the independent music and contemporary art scene, describing the general condition of the underground culture or delving into theoretical and critical analysis of Western rock music. In these articles, names like John Cage, Gilles Deleuze, and Michel Foucault and concepts like postmodernity and consumerism appeared frequently. This self-publication was a rarity as these subjects barely appeared, let alone were analyzed in other music magazines in China at that time. The last article was written by Yan Jun; resembling a manifesto, it expressed his resolution to draw a clear line between new music and the Beijing rock music scene,

It is time that we get together, looking for a new path against the current music industry, against the rotten Beijing rock music scene. We must take advantage of this advancing new age and unite our hot-blooded comrades, putting our diehard creative desires, pure music attitudes, and independent critical life views into action.

FIGURE 3.13 *The Front (left) and Back (right) Covers of* Sub Jam *fanzine.*

In 2002, Yan Jun established the independent label *Sub Jam* (撒把芥末) named after his fanzine to release China's independent films, music, literature, and poetry.

The first half of the year 2003 was special when SARS erupted in China and no public events were allowed. Musicians and fans stayed indoors to experiment with new ways of music making, producing records, and listening to music. Yan Jun began to experiment with making sound during this period of time as well. SARS was finally under control in May 2003. By the end of 2003, Yao organized Sounding Beijing (also known as Beijing Sonart) at Cangku Art Space (see more in Chapter 2).

Grassroots Experimental Music Concerts and Festivals

Immediately after 2003, there was an eruption of monthly and annual public experimental music, sound art concerts, and festivals in cities of Beijing, Shanghai, Hangzhou, Chengdu, Guangzhou, and Shenzhen, organized by musicians themselves with little external funding. Through these public events, more varieties of audience were drawn to this new form of music beyond the underground music and contemporary art circles.

2pi (Music) Festival (2003–2007), Hangzhou

On November 29, 2003, immediately after Sounding Beijing 2003, another music festival 2pi Music Festival (changed to 2pi Festival in 2006), curated by the experimental music couple, the free improvising musician Li Jianhong and the laptop noise and improvisation musician Weiwei (aka Vavabond), was launched in the city of Hangzhou. Li Jianhong, identified by Zbigniew Karkowski as "China's best noise music artist," started his noise music band 2pi (the second skin) in 1999 and subsequently founded the independent music label 2pi Records in 2003. The first 2pi Music Festival was only a small-scale local festival that took place over one day, with three local groups and three groups from its neighboring city Shanghai. Although the music critic Li Ruyi made a comment that musicians within this festival were making experimental music in a rock music way, it nevertheless created a space for experimentation, as well as communication among people with similar acoustic aesthetics and listening sensibilities.

2pi Music Festival was held annually on the last weekend in November from 2003 to 2007. The first three 2pi Music Festivals (2003–2005) were held at No. 31 bar and the following two (2006–2007) were moved to Loft 49, No. 12 Warehouse, owned by Common International Cultural Institution. The next four were extended to a two-day festival due to the increasing number of musicians from other cities and countries who were invited to perform. The fourth festival in 2006 was the most reported and documented one and was also recognized as a watershed, emblematic for the development of China's experimental music and sound art scene. It was this year that the word *music* was taken away from the title, and it became 2pi Sound Festival. In fact, in previous 2pi Music Festivals, there were already sound artists who did not consider themselves to be musicians. The change of the title could be seen as an adjustment made to better incorporate all participants. It indicated a recognition of the limitation of the category "music." The night after the festival, some of the musicians met and had a four-hour-long discussion reflecting on their own performances, the identity of Chinese experimental musicians, their future directions, and the need for changes and new blood. The last 2pi festival was held in 2007. Despite its increasing scale and recognition among sound artists and musicians from abroad, the festival never received any commercial, government or institutional funding during its five-year run. The festival could only afford board and lodging for performers. Artists and musicians paid for their own trips. As the only large-scale annual experimental music festival in southern China at the time, the closure of the festival was a big loss for both fans and musicians. But Li Jianhong and Weiwei displayed a positive attitude when I asked them why they stopped organizing the festival, "Money was a problem but we felt that 2pi Festival had done its job in opening up and establishing the scene."

WaterLand Kwanyin (2005–2010), Sub Jam Monthly Concert at UCCA (2010), Beijing

Beginning in 2004, Yan Jun began to collaborate with the musician and painter Wu Quan and the duo FM3. It marked the beginning of a group activity active till 2007, with two cofounded music labels: WaterLand Kwanyin and Kwanyin and a miscellaneous music event series titled WaterLand Kwanyin, featuring spiritual sounds, field recordings, noise, video art, body performance, experimental, avant-garde, improvisational, and electronic music, along with independent film screenings. This free event occurred weekly at the 2 Kolegas Bar in a drive-in movie theater in Chaoyang District in Beijing. In 2008, the schedule was changed to twice a month, and the organizers began to charge admission. With its frequent performances and openness for participation, WaterLand Kwanyin soon became an important venue in China for both domestic and international experimental, noise and electronic musicians, and sound artists.

Over the course of five years, WaterLand Kwanyin gradually evolved into a gathering place for artists and musicians. Other than foreign artists, there were fewer new faces joining; people came to the event more for meeting old friends, instead of listening to new sound works. For the organizer Yan Jun, this closed sense of community built around WaterLand Kwanyin was a serious problem, an obstacle that stifled creativity and the production of good sound works. By the end of 2009, Yan Jun began looking for new performance spaces and stopped WaterLand Kwanyin series. Beginning in 2010, he collaborated with the contemporary art institution UCCA located at 798 Art District to organize another series, a monthly performance titled Sub Jam Monthly Concert at UCCA.

Although the new project was still music-oriented, it differed from the WaterLand Kwanyin series at 2 Kolegas Bar in significant ways. The art space itself has given the event a new context, more contemporary art-oriented. The time of the show changed from 9:00 p.m. to 2:00 p.m. The new project was also relatively less selective of its audience. There were new groups of visitors who included regular art gallery visitors, foreign artists, tourists, art students, and families who would go to 798 during weekends. The gallery space also provided a better listening environment for sound installation and participatory sound art.

Mini Midi Experimental Music Festival (2005–2010)

In 2005, four months after the opening of the first WaterLand Kwanyin event, Yan Jun curated another annual festival, the Mini Midi Festival, as the experimental stage of the larger annual event known as the Midi

FIGURE 3.14 *Poster of Mini Midi 2008, outside of 2 Kolegas Bar. Courtesy of Yan Jun.*

Festival, the earliest and largest outdoor rock music festival in China, which began in 2000. The Mini Midi Festival offered free admission. The first three Mini Midi Festivals were held at Beijing Haidian Park. The fourth one was a three-day event (May 1–3, 2008) at 2 Kolegas Bar. It featured forums, outdoor and indoor performances, lectures, and exhibitions (Figure 3.14). The fifth Mini Midi Festival began in May 2010. This year, it changed to a tour across five cities in southern China, including Shanghai, Fuzhou, Quanzhou, Xiamen, Wuhan, and Changsha. The tour has unveiled small fan bases for noise, experimental, and improvising music in southern cities.

Frightened by Dog Live (2005, 2007), Tongzhou, Beijing

Frightened by Dog Live was another outdoor music festival in Beijing, organized by a unique group of anarchist musicians widely known as Raying Temple (Xiao Leiying) (Wang 2015). Compared with the Mini Midi Festival and 2pi Festival, it was less formal and less strictly experimental. The organizers were rock musicians from other provinces, mainly Shandong province, living in Sun village in Tongzhou, an inexpensive area nearly one hour away by subway from the center of the capital city. One afternoon in the fall of 2004, Li Yangyang (drum), Zhang Zhongshu (vocal/bass), and Xiao Guang (guitar) met and recorded an improvisational CD in Sun Zhuang. There were often wild dogs in Sun village and the musicians sometimes were frightened by them. They named the group *Bei Gou Jing Xia ing* (Frightened by Dog) and titled the CD with the same name.

In 2005, Li Yangyang organized the first Frightened by Dog Live Festival. The idea was as simple as telling musicians and music fans to take their own instruments and devices out and play together in an open area in Sun village. The festival was free and even provided with free beer. It featured bands including Mafeisan, 4xfangge, Defect, Xiuchang Guatou, thx, Ju, and Liu Er. The groups were diverse in musical styles such as grunge, punk, hardcore, improvisational noise, post rock, and laptop noise. Although the festival was loosely organized, the openness of the festival created a rare meeting place for musicians of all levels. These included those without any formal musical training, without much experience with instruments, and those who were simply interested in music but did not necessarily know how to play.

Organizers of these grassroots experimental music festivals like 2pi, WaterLand Kwanyin, Sub Jam Monthly Concert at UCCA, Mini Midi, and Frightened by Dog Live, were musicians themselves. There are also nonmusician organizer who were promoters for radical and alternative forms of music making, for example, Sally Can't Dance China Avant-garde Music Festival and (((Sunday Listening @ 798))).

(((Sunday Listening @ 798))) (2008–2010), Beijing

Sugar Jar, an Independent Culture Transmission Studio and an independent music store located at 798 Art District, was originally a distributor of China's experimental, noise, and sound art works. Yang Licai, more commonly known as Lao Yang, opened Sugar Jar in June 2003, illegally selling music works made by his musician friends in Beijing in a four-square meter room near the west gate of Qinghua University. In October 2005, Lao Yang rented a small space about 15 square meters at 798 Art District, and applied for an Industry and Commerce Business License for the studio and left its underground status. In our interview Lao Yang revealed, "after 2006, the money earned through selling independent music works could cover the rent, basic office expenses and salaries for two of my assistants and myself." Their salary was very low, around 1000 RMB (US$158) per month. Before 2006, Lao Yang had to sell handmade things to earn money to keep the studio alive and meet his basic needs in Beijing. From 2008, Lao Yang began to host a public and free event called (((Sunday Listening @ 798))), open to experimental/noise musicians and sound artists. As of June 2010, Sugar Jar moved to Xiao Bao village in Song Zhuang (an artist village in Beijing). Lao

FIGURE 3.15 *"Sunday Listening @798" Performance by Vavabond and Thee, Stranded Horse, July 20, 2008. Photo by author.*

Yang later left Beijing and moved to Yunnan. *Sunday Listening* lasted for three years, with a temporary gap after its 42 series at 798.

Sally Can't Dance China Avant-Garde Music Festival in Beijing (2008 till now)

Sally Can't Dance China Avant-Garde Music Festival is the longest-running avant-garde music festival in China so far. The festival was sponsored by Michael Pettis, a professor of finance at Peking University, the owner of D-22 music club (2006–2012) featuring punk, Indi-rock, and experimental music and, the founder of now one of the most important Chinese Indie music labels *Maybe Mars* Record Label (2007–).

Established in 2008, the first three years of the Sally Can't Dance China Avant-Garde Music Festival were held in D-22 every March with an invited curator every year, featuring different forms of sound experiments in noise music, experimental music, improvisation, experimental play, free improvising for silent film, and interactive installations. The first festival (March 1–17, 2008) was curated by the experimental saxophonist Li Tieqiao. The second one (March 21–22, 2009) was curated by independent music critic and producer Zhang Xiaozhou. The third one (March 27–28, 2010) was curated by Yan Jun. The third one was special for local musicians because the British free improvising guitarist Fred Frith was invited to the festival to perform. Fred Frith and Derek Bailey have been major influences for Chinese free improvising musicians. The fourth one occurred two years later, curated by Josh Feola (the founder of Beijing independent music website *Pangbianr*, a music writer and reporter) and Zhu Wenbo (the organizer of Zoomin' Night featuring experimental music by younger generations). Both are experimental musicians as well. The intension of bringing together experimental musicians primarily from both Beijing and Shanghai was explicit. The fifth one was still curated by Josh Feola and Zhu Wenbo at School live bar, but with a refreshing curatorial theme. Instead of featuring musicians, they invited composers to submit compositions to be performed by musicians. More like curating artworks, the organizers arrange music compositions rather than lining up musicians. In a way, the festival has reinforced the identity of a composer, an identity that has nonetheless been a tradition in Western academic experimental music but has been missing in the early stage of experimental music practices in China.

Other than Beijing and Hangzhou being the major two cities where experimental music and sound art originated and developed rapidly between 2003 and 2012, there were also stable experimental music events happening in Shanghai and Shenzhen. NOIShanghai was organized by Cao Junjun (aka Junky) in Shanghai from 2004 to feature harsh noise, HNW (harsh noise wall), power electronics, and grind noise. Inspired by Japanese Noise legends Incapacitants and Hijokaidan and the self-published Zine *Noise* founded by

Fujui Wang in Taiwan, Junky abandoned rock music and formed the noise group Torturing Nurse in Shanghai, which later became the representative group in the category of harsh noise in mainland China. NOIShanghai continues its activity till today, the longest noise event series in China so far.

In the city of Shenzhen, China's first special economic zone in 1980, a city long being considered a cultural desert, the artist Zen Lu curated an annual experimental music festival ChoP (2006–2016) together with the Polish artist Grzegorz Bojanek. Zen Lu studied finance in college and self-taught playing electronic and experimental music. In early 2007, Zen Lu founded the independent label "We Play! Records" and organized sound events in Shenzhen. Through the funding of the Polish Ministry of Culture and National Heritage and the Art and Technology Foundation, and various venues supports from China, ChoP continued for ten years, bringing independent musicians and artists from Poland and China together to give concerts, lectures, and workshops in southern China.

From Festivals to Semi-Private and Semi-Public Events

Finding a stable public performance venue, gathering enough funding and audience to organize festivals has always been challenging for grassroots organizers. While experimental and improvising music still have a space in large-scale non-mainstream music festivals, for instance, Tomorrow Festival (2014–) in Shenzhen organized by Teng Fei and Tu Fei, there has been an increasing tendency for smaller and more private music events as workshops, with an emphasis on learning, sharing, experimentation, and communication rather than giving public shows.

Since 2012, the number of small music collectives has increased. Impro Committee of Beijing and Free Music Collective of Shanghai were both formed in 2012, responding to the call of the Japanese musician Otomo Yoshihide's project "DOMMUNE FUKUSHIMA!," asking artists to think about how to interpret and deal with one's living reality through art/culture power.

Behind the changing models of platforms from public festivals to smaller private gatherings are factors including censorship and more specialized needs and supports from the audience and musicians. If large-scale festivals of experimental music still embodies a romanticism's passion for liberating and guiding a large body of audience, pockets of private events present a more reflexive and relaxed attitude in creating something interesting together or just listening together.

Yan Jun's individual sound series Living Room Tour, which began in 2011, can be seen as the prelude for a later more widely shared model of organizing events. The protocol for Living Room Tour is simple: anyone can invite the musician to his/her living room for a private concert. There is no invitation fee charged, but the artist's transportation has to be paid for. Yan brings his feedback noise set and supplements it with whatever is available in the inviter's house. The tour is an ongoing project and has been conducted in several cities, including Beijing, Shanghai, and Montreal.

Windowless Scenery (2015.6–2017.1), Shanghai

Windowless Scenery was organized by Shanghai-based artist and free improvising musician Jun-Y Chao and experimental musician Maimai. Jun-Y Chao received his art education from Germany as a visual artist and during his time in Germany he self-taught playing clarinet. Maimai studied playwright at Shanghai Theater Academy and is a professional playwright who has written a few popular Chinese mainstream TV drama series. He has self-taught making experimental music and experimental films. They write in introducing *Windowless Scenery*, "We need to find a proper space to perform, a space without smoking and decoration, a space with fairness and experimentality."

The series emphasize inward looking and listening. It is less of a show but more of an in-depth exploration of individual artists' own experimentation. There are altogether eight events, each lasting two days with one day of performance and another day of discussion. It was like an individual research project, sharing with the public what one is working on, thinking about, and experimenting with. It is a process of experimentation in its real sense.

The eight series include Jun-Y Chao's exploration of all possible variables of a performance space, Maimai's feedback study in combination with the music of the *Dream of the Red Chamber* TV series made in 1987, Yan Yulong's attempt to make music for the shape of rectangle space, Zhuwenbo's action score aiming to disenchant participating audience members of the classical Western instrument the clarinet, Xu Cheng's field recording-based research on the city soundscape in pipelines between 2006 and 2016, Liu Xinyu's electroacoustic improvisation inspired by Japanese sculpture Tomio Miki and his ear-related sculptures, and the Kazakhstan musician Anuar's exploration of the Kazakhstanian music concept *küy*, explained by the musician as "a supreme sensational concentration achieved through sound, an impromptu based on the emotions of the surrounding, an autonomous derivative and development motivated in energy accumulation."[2] The Beijing-based violinist, artist, and experimental musician Sheng Jie (also known as GogoJ), one of the few female experimental musicians in China, explored the concept of the French word *duo* (meaning duet and confrontation) between different timbres (one electric cello, one traditional cello), genders (Sheng Jie as the female performer, A Ming as the

---

[2]http://www.amspacesh.com/eng/newsdetail.asp?newsid=83

FIGURE 3.16 *Sheng Jie,* Duo, *Audiovisual Art Performance with A Ming (right),* Windowless Scenery, *AM Art Space, Shanghai 2015.12. Courtesy of the artist.*

male performer), breathing rhythms, and emotional reactions at the moment in the same space (Figure 3.16). The performance space remained dark, with light sources coming from headlights wore by the two performers and projected video images captured by a camera in real time. Sheng Jie added a delay to the real-time video projection, experimenting with an audiovisual time duet.

Read/Aloud (2018–)

After *Windowless Scenery,* Jun-Y Chao and Xu Cheng organized another event series Read/Aloud, a project cosponsored by Mingshi Bookstore and the independent label founded by Jun-Y Chao named *Where is the Zeitgeise?* The project program reads:

> Mingshi Bookstore is a semi-public private space on Shaoxing road for many years. It is small, but packed with books, the food storage for bookworms. Shaoxing road in the past is known for its bookstores. Although it is no longer like the past and has become more permeated by everyday life and popular culture, book is always a theme for the road. What connects *Mingshi bookstore* and *Where is the Zeitgeise?* is a mutual purpose, that is, to try to stay away from the noisy outer environment, to build an inward going spiritual communication. Inward does not mean closed, but an emphasis on small scale practices. This time, our project is to ask, how to perform in piles of books and what to perform.

Listening resembles reading in that both require quietness as a prerequisite state of mind. Bookstore is a special venue not only because of its unusual spatial acoustics but more uniquely because of the *qi*/life force of the space. Maybe people who still enjoy reading are the kind of listeners both organizers look for.

Read/Aloud consisted of film screening including *Blue for a Moment* by director Antoine Prum tracing the artistic career of the Berlin-based Swedish free improvising percussionist Sven-Åke Johansson, short experimental film *Dream Enclosure* by Ding Xin, who teaches film and video art at Central Academy of Fine Art after studying experimental film at CalArt, *Palmania* by Gao Yanqin, *Sunrise* by Li Huihui, five silent films of insects by Maimai, *Out of Focus/end of Century* by the group The Mustangs In Social Modulator (Xu Cheng and Huang Lei), *The Man Holding a Camera* by Xu Cheng, *Plaxophone* by Xu Zhe, and *The Metaphysics of Pure Language* by Jun-Y Chao. Performances were normally quiet improvizations. Some were intentionally related to text and words, and sampling sounds related to texts.

The term *yaji* was applied again after it was used twice in events organized by Sub Jam in 2008. To borrow the definition of *yaji* from Sub Jam, it reads,

> Ya: elegant, gentle, refined Ji: meeting, party, gathering
>
> Ya Ji: a gentle meeting of music, art and intellect

Spaces of "Nowhere"

In recent years, when venues for experimental music and independent music in Beijing were closed one after another due to pressures including increasing rents and cultural, political censorship, experimental musicians began to look for alternative places, mostly public (deserted) space to perform. Zoomin' Night was a sound, noise, and experimental music series taking place in the underpass near Sanyuan bridge in Beijing since 2015 (Figures 3.17.1, 3.17.2). "Tonight at 10 pm, underpath of the sanyuan bridge. Bring your own instruments. Pair up freely." The organizer Zhu Wenbo wrote on his WeChat. Zhu began organizing *Zoomin' Night* weekly at D-22 in 2009. The owner Michael Pettis closed D-22 in 2012 and opened another club *XP* a few months after to focus on promoting more experimental and avant-garde music. *Zoomin' Night* continued in XP until 2015.

By accident, Zhu discovered Sanyuan bridge near his apartment and decided to organize *Zoomin' Night* there, "There's a park next to it, and the steps leading up to it resemble the step-seating of an amphitheater. It's not that far from the city center, but it's just far enough removed from residential buildings to avoid noise complaints," he told Josh Feola in an interview.[3] The particularity of the space makes it more challenging to find musicians. "There are really

---

[3]http://joshfeola.com/blog/notes-from-the-underpass/

FIGURE 3.17.1 *Zoomin' Night, March 21, 2019. Courtesy of Zhu Wenbo.*

few performances that are suitable for this space." Zhu wrote on the official WeChat account of Zoomin' Night, where he sends out simple reminders to followers of upcoming shows. Zoomin' Night later broke its regularity and merged with miji concert organized by Yan Jun, taking places at multiple spaces, including Meridian Space, Fruityspace, or someone's living room.

Nowhere Festival (*Huang Yin Ji*) is organized by the saxophone improviser Wang Ziheng and the independent documentary director Fu Xiuliang, taking place even further away from the city of Beijing in the mountains on the outskirts[4] (Figure 3.18). Almost written as a manifesto, Wang Ziheng published on his WeChat,

Not the kind of enclosed space of a livehouse. We prepare the wildness and mountains for noise. Everyone can play instruments wandering through mountains with the wind under the sky and immersed in noise. As long as you have an ear, you can listen to the sun and the creeks . . . this is the series four of *Huangyinji*. As the founder, I do not want to define what it is. The more important question is, under such high-handed policy and silent violence, what *Huangyinji* will become.

---

[4]An edited clip of Nowhere Festival can be seen on YouTube https://www.youtube.com/watch?v=YyTd19l-qzU

FIGURE 3.17.2 *Zoomin' Night, Performers (from left to right) Ake, Xu Shaoyang, Zhu Wenbo, Liu Lu. March 21, 2019. Courtesy of Zhu Wenbo.*

FIGURE 3.18 *Nowhere Festival, Wang Ziheng performing Prepared Saxophone, Qian Geng Performing Body Calligraphy, 2018. Screenshot of YouTube video.*

Either it is the underpass of a highway bridge or in the wild mountains, there is no sound system supports, no stage lightening. Everything needs to be rebuilt from scratch for every performance. But at the same time, there are no longer demands for regularity or pressure of the size of the audience. The raw creative life energy that was once felt at the beginning years of the new millennium returns.

Conclusion

In his essay "An audience of six in Chengdu," Yan Jun wrote about a live concert organized by Chengdu-based musician and artist Sun Wei. Sun Wei initiated *Audible Area* in 2016, to host public events of listening, sound art, improvised music, sound installations, experimental music, and workshops. Sun Wei works with ultrasonic recordings of nature, underwater frequencies, and field recordings of the everyday. The event took place at the venue NU space in Chengdu featuring performances and screening. The space has a capacity for 400 to 500 people. With only an audience of six, as Yan Jun worries, the cost for hiring the technicians and staff must have been higher than the door money shared by the venue. "I appreciate this open spirit, but I'm not sure how long it can continue" (Yan 2019).

Censorship comes not only from political ideological control, but also from the music and art market, from real estate companies, fans, peers, and universities. As I argued somewhere else, to speak of China's electronic and experimental music, one needs to be cautious of holding the crystal shoes of the canonical experimental practice of the global North as a measure (Wang 2016). I want to add to this caution. Domestically, there is also no need to seek a unification of academic and nonacademic electronic and experimental music practices. It is more necessary to have "a sonorous archipelago" to borrow François J. Bonnet's expression, to allow highly creative and original collectives (both unprofessional and professional) to have a chance to grow freely and even wildly.

In this account of the history of academic electronic music, nonacademic experimental music, and electronic instrument building, my choice of taking account of event-as-platforms and my focus on musicians who are also organizers is at the expense of missing discussions on talented individual artists and musicians including but not limited to the duo Soviet Pop (Li Qing, Li Weisi), Walnut Room (Feng Hao, Li Zenghui), 33, Ake, Dou Wei, Huan Qing, Gao Jiafeng, Gooooose (Han Han), Lao Dan, Liang Yiyuan, Mei Zhiyong, Sun Wei, Vavabond (Weiwei), Wang Changcun, Wang Ziheng, Xiao He, Yan Yulong, Zhao Cong, Zhang Shouwang, Zhou Risheng, as well as academic composers He Xuntian, Chen Bi'an from Shanghai Conservatory of Music.

4

Shanshui-Thought in Experimental Music Practices

Notions of nature, landscape, and its descendant term soundscape, become the center of creative attention of sound art and experimental music practices in the West from the middle of twentieth century. Through *4'33"*, first performed in 1952, John Cage brought sounds of the environment into the concert hall in both conceptual and practical senses, extending the concert hall to the outside streets. In early 1960s, La Monte Young created a series of performance-based compositions, incorporating nature in his conceptual art, such as "Piano Piece for David Tudor #3" which reads "most of them, were very old grasshoppers" (1960). In 1964, Young conceived his most known piano improvisation piece "The Well-Tuned Piano," which extensively makes use of natural resonance of piano strings and the surroundings. Young's friend, the American artist Walter De Marina created two music works "Cricket Music" (1964) and "Ocean Music" (1968), which marked an important transition in the artist's career from sculpture to land art, an art movement in the 1960s and 1970s advocating making art directly in the landscape using natural materials from the site. These sound works were created under the spirit prevalent among avant-garde and experimental artists around 1960s, given force by a variety of intellectual influences that include cybernetics and Eastern philosophies, or revolting against the visual-centric art world and the history of classical composition tradition.

In recent decades, partly informed and inspired by notions of Anthropocene, hyperobjects (Morton 2013), Gaia (Latour 2017), Chthulucene (Haraway 2016) advanced by contemporary philosophers, theorist, and scientists, global ecological crisis has become a unanimous curatorial concern in the art world. For example, Taipei Biennial themed its 2018 exhibition "The Post-Nature—A Museum as an Ecosystem." In the same year, the nomadic art biennial Manifesta 12 took place at the botanical garden of Palermo titled "The Planetary Garden, Cultivating Coexistence." In 2019, the first ecology and environment-related exhibition in Russia, "The Coming World: Ecology as the New Politics 2030–2100," invited over fifty artists to address humanities' relation with nature. The sound community share similar concerns. Ecoacoustic music as practiced by the composer and ecoacoustician Matthew Burtner, as well as the video-audio installation project "The Great Animal Orchestra," led by the soundscape ecologist Bernie Krause, provides knowledge about the ongoing ecological crisis in the world we live in today. Both projects continue and expand the acoustic ecological concerns raised by the Canadian composer Murray Schafer in his "World Soundscape Project" from the late 1960s.

But by making music with or in the environment, artists can embody a different intellectual sensibility.

The experimental musician and improvising guitarist Li Jianhong developed environment improvisation out of his habit of playing guitar in natural environments. "It is not a dialogue between me and the environment" as he would often emphasize. It is something in between that is generated in the improvising process that allows only him to dwell in. Listening to insects has been a popular culture practice in China since Tang dynasty; observing singing insects has taught the Shanghai-based artist and musician Jun-Y Chao to play wind instruments. Shen Piji, a *guqin* (古琴)player, held series of concerts called *Frog Jam* in his courtyard with his musician friends, as well as a few singing frogs. These frogs are not home-raised or trained. They are self-invited "guests" and would play along when they feel like it. In live performances of The Tea Rockers Quintet, four musicians with different instruments improvise with a tea master. The kind of tea served in the performance affects the sound and dynamics of the collective improvisation.

Unfortunately, abstract notions of different thinking modes are among those that are most difficult to translate. For instance, the notion of *shanshui* (山水), which is often seen translated as landscape in English, suggests a rather different thinking mode from the notion of landscape. Landscape suggests a bird-view perspective; it is something to be perceived. *Shanshui*, instead, literally translated as mountains-waters, is organic and correlational; *shanshui* perceives. Landscape, as the Chinese scholar Zhao Tingyang argues, is a modern invention; *shanshui* is mistakenly understood as landscape while nature is disenchanted by science and commerce (Zhao 2019, 71). In his book on the Chinese notion of *shanshui*, *Living Off Landscape: Or, the Unthought-of in Reason*, the French philosopher François Jullien summarizes three biases in the landscape-thought developed in European landscape painting. First, it was conceived in the shadow of the part-whole relation; secondly, it was ascribed to the primacy of visual perception; finally, it ended up folding into subject-object coupling (Jullien 2018a, 5). Chinese *shanshui*-thought, according to Jullien, presents a whole other approach distinct from the cutoff gesture that divides between subject and object, part and whole, entailed in European landscape-thought, "In China we are thinking no longer of a portion of the land offered up to an observer's eye but of a correlation of opposites: 'mountains' and 'waters'" (Jullien 2018a, 13).

An exploration of *Shanshui*-thought in experimental music may at first appear counterintuitive, since historically *shanshui* painting is considered the de facto artistic manifestation of *shanshui*-thought. The task in this chapter hence is twofold: first, to discover the acoustic nature of *shanshui*-thought in relation to *qi*-philosophy, and second, to examine how contemporary experimental music in China embodies and accentuates the classical wisdom of *shanshui*-thought. While my initial motivation is to find an adequate way to describe and understand certain experimental music practices in China, as the writing develops, it seems possible that *Shanshui*-thought may provide a new set of vocabularies for current experimental music practices at large to test, experiment, and evolve with.

Shanshui-Thought: An Overview

The term *shanshui* (consisting of two characters, *shan* (山) as mountain and *shui* (水) as water), as one joint expression, had its earliest appearance in *Mozi* (墨子)(ca. 478–392 BC) as *shanshui guishen* (山水鬼神), meaning the ghost and spirit of mountains and waters (Berque 2013, 29–30). In his search of landscape thinking, Augustin Berque discovers that the birth of *shanshui*-thought in China was in the painter and musician Zong Bing's text, titled *Hua Shanshui Xu* (*Preface to Landscape Painting*) around 440 in the South Song Dynasty (31). Influenced by Daoism and *Xuanxue* (玄学)(metaphysics), Zong Bing believes that *shanshui* presents *dao* (道)(understood here as cosmological principles of myriad things, including mountains and waters) through its form. As an object of aesthetic appreciation, *Shanshui* painting needs to be concrete in form and texture and at the same time spiritually alive and interesting. The function of *shanshui* painting is to "free the spirit" (*chang shen*)(畅神), very similar to the Daoist Zhuangzi's idea of free and easy wandering (*xiaoyaoyou*)(逍遥游).

The notion of *shanshui* as a manifestation of *dao* is shared by Shi Tao (ca.1642–1707), an artist of late Ming and early Qing Dynasties, who converted to a Buddhist monk known as Daoji at very young age and converted to Daoism in his later years. In his famously profound and difficult essay *Huayu lu* (画语录)(*Comments on Painting*), Shi Tao developed notions of *yinyun*(氤氲) (diffusive with thick clouds of *qi*) and *huwei tuotai* (互为脱胎) (mutual birth). Shi Tao applies the term *yinyun* to describe all possible conditions of the ink when saturated in the brush at the moment before one paints. Once the brush dips into the ink, water in the brush and the ink immediately mix up. It is an essential technique for *shanshui* painter to master how to act swiftly to different conditions of the saturation. The state of *yinyun*, before the tip of the brush touch the rice paper, is *hundun* (chaos)(混沌); it requires wisdom to release the ink from the brush to the paper, to break the chaos. During the process of painting, the painter needs to always bear the state of *yinyun* in mind and body.

For Shi Tao, the process of painting is a process of *huwei tuotai*, mutual birth: "*Shanshui* is born in me, I am born in *shanshui*." The form, intensity, depth, vastness, rhythm in mountains, and waters are seen as the embodiment of the changing intensities and forms of the cosmos. Mountains and waters have their own agency; *shanshui* selects its own painter. Shi Tao wrote, "Mountains and waters enable me to announce their secret." This notion of mutual birth inspires Francios Jullien who translates the term as *coenfantement*. "After all, what gives rise to landscape is precisely the following: it is not that I, the autonomous subject, the subject with initiative (the knowing subject), have the landscape at my disposal but, rather, that the landscape has *me* at *its disposal* in equal measure. Each of the two, 'self' and 'landscape,' *brings the other into the world* (*tuo tai*, 脱胎)" (2018a, 116). The process of *huwei tuotai* helps to better understand Jun-Y's music work *Learning from Insects*. That is, he does not imitate insects singing to play wind instruments; they give birth to each other, or in Jun-Y's words as written in the liner notes, it is to cultivate his own nature that parallels the insects.

Although most contemporary discussions of *shanshui*-thought develop through the visual and the literary, there is an inherent acoustic nature in both *shanshui* painting and *shanshui*-thought. As the art historian Susan Nelson argues (1998/1999), Chinese *shanshui* paintings in the eleventh century presents an increasing interest in depicting in its pictorial themes including listening looks, pine trees, and waterfalls as evidence of sound or listening. Commenting on Shi Tao's painting *Pure Tones of Mountain and Water*, as one of the best examples of what she calls listening painting, Nelson nicely renders the painting audible. "The whole landscape reverberates throughout with throbbing contours and vibrating dots, the 'pure tone' of the piping of the earth" (Nelson: 50). Picturing sonic vibrations of *shanshui*, as Nelson convincingly argues, is to evoke sonic sensations or ideas in the viewers' own mind and body. More importantly, as Nelson points out and I very much concur, what ultimately matters in *shanshui* painting is *qi* (气).

Shanshui-thought derives from *qi*-philosophy. Depicting dynamic gestures of pine trees is a way to depict wind, which is, according to *qi*-cosmology and later *qi*-philosophy, a metaphor and manifestation of *qi*. According to the Chinese philosopher Zhang Zai (known as the philosopher of *qi*), *qi* is not just a concrete entity but has a real existence that is capable of mutation, a translucent and empty capacity for resonance. As Jung-Yeup Kim interpreted in his study of Zhang Zai's *qi*-philosophy, "to say that 'x is *qi* and y is *qi*' is to say that 'x' and 'y' are correlative polarities mutually resonating, interpenetrating, and forming an organic unity with one another" (2015, 34). Sound is produced when *qi* that possesses *shi* (the advantage of position or force) changes and consequently, sound conveys and also affects conditions of *qi*. The notion *yinyun* used by Shi Tao in *shanshui* painting originally describes a particular condition of *qi*: the state of intermingling and fusing. In Zhuangzi, as Kim points out, *yinyun* describes the state of organism mutually breathing life into one another, a wildly shimmering heat (2015, 64).

Similar to *shanshui* painting, guqin music is also a practice of directing and cultivating *qi*. In fact, "Waiting for *qi*" (气候)(*qi hou*) is one of the most important qualities in *guqin* music, also known as scholar music. For *guqin* players, music has its own *qi*, reflected in its intensity, volume, rhythm, and speed. One has to detect it, connect to it, and internalize it into one's own living *qi*. Only when *qi* is alive and in motion can one know where and how to wait for it. Similar to *shanshui* painting, to play guqin music, one has to first of all detect the dynamic principle of the cosmos. Developed out of the philosophy of *qi*, *Shanshui*-thought as practiced through painting and music can be understood as ways to access the transcendental *dao*. It is often the case when looking at paintings of Zhuang Feng's "Listening to a waterfall by a rocky cliff," one cannot help "hearing" guqin music *High Mountain and Flowing Waters*. Listening to Li Jianhong's environment improvisation in *Empty Mountain* (2010) reminds one of the Ming Dynasty painter Shen Zhou's (1427–1509) water-ink paining *Night Vigil* (1492) created when Shen sat in his study situated in a sound saturated dark night.

Shanshui as a concept, functions as the connective plane between the transcendental and the practical (Zhao 2019), between the invisible upper stream and its sensible manifestation in the lower stream (Jullien 2018a, 116). *Shanshui* is the perceptible transcendental, as Zhao Tingyang succinctly puts it (2019, 61). Compared to the ocean, which is also often used as a transcendental reference, Zhao argues that *Shanshui* is more habitable for humans, and hence has developed a more direct reference to civilization and social life (61–69).

In "Against Soundscape," the anthropologist Tim Ingold expresses an insight similar to *shanshui*-thought but still with some essential differences. Ingold argues that landscape, the light, sound, and wind are not object of perception, but that which we live in and experience with. "We do not touch the wind, but touch in it; we do not see sunshine, but see in it; we do not hear rain, but hear in it. Thus wind, sunshine and rain, experienced as feelings, light and sound, underwrite our capacities, respectively, to touch, to see and to hear" (Ingold 2007). *Shanshui*-thought and *qi*-philosophy which informs *shanshui*-thought, does not distinguish the thing and the medium in which the thing transforms. *Qi* is both the material and the medium through which the material functions. Therefore, we both touch the wind and touch in it;

we both hear rain and hear in it. *Shanshui* is both the object of perception and the medium through which one perceive *shanshui*. It is also a result of creative practice.

Shanshui: The Existential and the Epistemological

Shanshui-thought rewires our sensibility through which we perceive and live in the world. According to Michel Serres, landscape now as an object of protection was once a world that threatens in ancient times and a target of human subjugation since the Industrial Revolution (1995). Through *shanshui*-thought, however, landscape is always conceived as secret and nurturing. It cultivates an existential gesture of following, rather than obeying, mastering or conquering. It suggests a sense of becoming, dwelling, and a moral way of knowing.

Jian: Li Jianhong and Environment Improvisation

Born in the southern Chinese city of Fenghua, the experimental musician Li Jianhong develops an innate intimacy with natural environment of the South, trees of hundreds of years old, ferns and wild grass, and damp weather. His topophilia with the South manifests in his music and photography works. While still living in Hangzhou, a southern city known for its mountains, the West Lake and Buddhist temples, Li Jianhong liked to hike and enjoyed the five-yuan (less than a dollar) vegetarian lunch at *Faxi* temple. During one of his trips to Faxi temple in 2004, he encountered a sudden rainfall. Not being able to go anywhere, he waited at the Mahavira Palace and fell asleep. Later he wrote down this experience in his journal, which was printed in the liner notes of the album *Twelve Moods* (2011).

> I did not expect to listen to the rain under the roof of the cloister. After a long time till now, I still remembered the rain—watching it marching towards my direction from the other side of the mountain, then hearing the rain washing over the trees, sensing the smell from the summer earth. The smoke from the burning incense in front of Mahavira Palace was not psychedelic, but when it met and mixed with the rain vapor, it started some visual and aural chemical actions. I heard the chanting sounds from inside of the palace covering the entire temple and mountains. I could not feel the contour of my ears. It became everywhere—suspended above the mountains and the temple wrapped by the rain and chanting sounds. The ear listened with joy and ease. Facing the scene, I thought the best thing to do is to sleep. In fact, I did not consider there was a choice. I

fell asleep. I know it was in fact very normal to encounter such a rain in the mountain. The rain, originally that of the universe, became my rain, because I existed that day. After that, I had a thought to make music with rain. . . .

Compared to the experience four years ago, the rain this winter sounded quite realistic. The sounds of each raindrop falling onto the ground, the leaves, and the roof were clear and powerful. It seemed that each raindrop, each sound had their individual identity. At night, I could not see the raindrops. But I could vividly feel them right beside my hand. The realistic feeling assured me that this was the best moment to make music with them.[1]

The creation myth of Li Jianhong begs a question: where is he when he listens to the rain? And further, where are we when we listen to Li Jianhong's environment improvisation?

As discussed in Chapter 1, this strange existential question posed by the philosopher Peter Sloterdijk is rehearsed in the ethnomusicologist Veit Erlmann's discussion in *Reason and Resonance* (2010). Heidegger and Sloterdijk conceive music as the "acoustic uterus," where the primal sympathetic resonance is regained (Erlmann 2010, 337). For Heidegger, we are in resonance when we listen (Erlmann 2010, 337–338). For Anders, according to Erlmann, being in music is extraterritorial and hence when we listen to music we are in music (2010, 25). As Erlman understood, Heidegger and Anders seek answers beginning with the personal or the psychological, operating through a cut from the world. Sloterdijk is no exception. While developing the notion of sonosphere or phonotope, Sloterdijk suggests a return to the genesis of the human ear. However, neither the existential reference of the uterus, nor music as the extraterritorial seems to apply to Li Jianhong's case. Li Jianhong listens in and to the cosmos of the myriad things: the monks' chanting, the rain, the smoke from the burning incense, and the rain vapor. It is essentially a *shanshui* mode of being, cosmic before psychological, diffusive, and impregnating. "The rain, originally that of the universe, became my rain, because I existed that day" (Li 2010).

Where did he exist when he listened to the rain?

To answer to this question, *Shanshui*-thought, as the perceptible transcendental, points us to a unique and contingent space known as *jian*. Classical Chinese character of *jian* is written as 閒, a door with a moon inside. It can be interpreted as moonlight coming through a door. The later simplified Chinese character 间 replaces the moon with the sun. The

---

[1] A blog entry by Li Jianhong on November 22, 2010, titled *Written before Shi'er Jing [Twelve Moods]*. The tracks of *Twelve Moods* are available for listening at https://cfimusic.bandcamp.com/album/twelve-moods.

FIGURE 4.1 *Album Cover of* Empty Mountain *by Li Jianhong, Released through CFI (Chinese Free Improvisation), 2010.*

Japanese architect and artist Masayuki Kurokawa notes, *jian* is a kind of space created by *qi*. Once a thing gets separated, there arises *qi* (life energy/ aura) around the parts. The attraction between *qi* of separate parts create *jian*. Masayuki Kurokawa describes *Jian* as one of the eight most essential Japanese aesthetic concepts. Artists, designers, and architects design an object not for the sake of the object, but for the sake of the space of *jian* created by the object (2014, 68–82). One creates light for the shadow; one creates separation for obtaining connective life power. To create *jian*, is to enter a game of *qi*. As Jullien also confirms, "European thinking prioritize seeing which is set out to identify and represent. *Shanshui*-thought instead, drawing largely from the philosophy of *qi*, prioritize breathing, which is to connect" (2018b, 188). Breathing keeps the tension of regeneration in *jian*, or in Jullien's French translation *entre*.

Jian is a space to let pass and to let connect. Think of opening the door to reveal a crack, creating the crack is *jian*. Jullien describes *jian (entre)* as *non-lieu*; It does not have *en-soi*, no definition, no belongings, no intrinsic nature, no properties (2018b, 184–9). *Jian* cannot be understood as "in the middle of," because it is itself a kind of terminal. *Jian* is a space only when it is understood as that where every arrival unfolds. Breathing is a kind of *jian*. It lets air in; the arrival of one's physicality regenerates and unfolds. It is through breathing that one keeps a vitality that never dries up. Musicking is another example, when the vibration of one string causes the vibration of medium around, vibrations feed back and regenerate rounds of reverberations. *Jian* invites indwelling to emerge. It implies sources of energy, just like Deleuze and Guattari's notion of annex milieu, "defined by the capture of energy sources (respiration in the most general sense), by the discernment of materials, the sensing of their presence or absence (perception), and by the fabrication of nonfabrication of the corresponding compounds (response, reaction)" (Deleuze and Guattari 1987, 51). *Jian* does not pre-exist. It is generated when one enters a certain relation with *shanshui*.

As Li Jianhong reflects, the environment he improvises with is not the environment the other would see in reality. One can only improvise with an environment that one has established a certain affective relation with.[2] Between the musician and *shanshui*, what most matters is not equality or individual happiness so much as the emergence of a felt-new life, a felt vital life force. Environment improvisation does not require the presence of audience. It is private and even secret. A good piece of environment improvisation happens when a kind of connection develops in the process of improvising, a coexistence of mutual birth. In environment improvisation, there is no subject or object. There is no dialogue between the improvisor and the environment. This means that sounds of the wind and rain are not going to respond to the musician. One's attention is in the environment, rather than in music.

While the uterus functions as a physical reference for the existential function of music for Sloterdjik and Heidegger, the existential notion *jian* also has its physical reference, the Chinese traditional architecture— *ting* (pavilion). As I wrote in another article on acoustic milieus (2018), a Chinese pavilion is usually built in private literati gardens or temples or public areas, with names like "wind listening pavilion" or "pavilion of wind in the pines" or "pavilion of the drunken old man." A pavilion suggests a pause for travelers or walkers, rendering a moment of rest and play. In private literati gardens, the site where the pavilion was built was selected according to directions of wind, surroundings of trees, plants, architectures and paths to reach the most perfect kind of harmony. For the Chinese literati, living space and spiritual space are not separate; they interchange and convert into

---

[2]Artist talk at "Savaka: Asia Experimental Music Currents" at Rockbund Art Museum in Shanghai, curated by Yin Yi and Wang Jing (the author), 2014.1.19.

each other all the time. Curiously, the Chinese pavilion appears in several experimental music works, such as Li Jianhong's "stringless pavilion" in his free improvising album *Bird* (2007), the Beijing-based musician Feng Hao's self-released album titled *Pavilion without Words* (2016), and the bamboo fulist and improviser Lao Dan's "pavilion" in *Going after Clouds and Dreams* (2018). Titles of these works do not signify; like *shanshui*-thought, they are allusive in nature.

This leads us to the particular way of knowing in *shanshui*-thought, also inherent in everyday practices of breathing, walking and musicking, known as *moqi* (tacit resonance).

Moqi, the Cosmic Mind, and Improvising

"We agreed before the performance that the piece will be thirty minutes long and that everyone performs on his or her own. One should not listen to other people's sounds, neither should one intentionally collaborate with each other. But, there is a deeper sense of collaboration, that is *moqi* (默契),"[3] Yan Jun wrote in his blog reflecting on the concert series "This is not a Music Concert (Musiklos)," which he cocurated with Goethe Institute Beijing beginning from April 2018 (Figure 4.2).

Improvising, as a "method," describes the moment when everyone began playing instinctually without prescribed notations or instructions. It is widely used in classical music, jazz, blues, rock, electronic music, and so on. Since the 1960s, improvisation itself is considered a music genre when paired with another equally important yet abstract concept, free. The significance of free improvisation often goes beyond its technique and aesthetics and extends to social and ethical realms. Improvisers often make particular rules as a performance collective, either banning any musical familiarities including harmony or tonal system (e.g., the Gruppo di Improvvisazione Nuova Consonanza in Rome), or restraining from communication about performances (e.g., AMM) (Gottschalk 2016, 192–3). The social significance of free improvising music derives from its non-structural thus non-hierarchical nature and hence often considered a musical model for democracy. Of course, not every contemporary musician or composer advocates improvisation. John Cage, for example, expresses his intention to avoid improvisation, because he feels people who improvise often fall back to their habits and memories (Darter 1982). To circumvent this, Cage uses indeterminacy as his major composition method. It seems that creating the unknown becomes the de facto goal of improvising experimental music; anything traditional or habitual is intentionally avoided.

---

[3]http://subjam.org/blog/462#more-462

FIGURE 4.2 *Beijing Impro Committee with International Nothing (Kai Fagaschinski, Michael Thieke),* This is not a Music Concert 3 (Musiklos 3), *Goethe Institute Beijing, 2019.9.22. photo by Gao Xiaotao. Courtesy of Yan Jun.*

Improvising is also an important technique and aesthetic principle of Chinese art, including *shanshui* painting, calligraphy, and *guqin* music. The function of improvising is not so much knowledge production as *qi*-cultivation which requires a cosmic mind to conceive and perceive the *qi* of the cosmic. Objective knowing will not work in the process of waiting for, following, and cultivating *qi*; it requires what Michael Polanyi suggests as the tacit dimension of knowing, "It is not by looking at things, but by dwelling in them, that we understand their joint meaning." Or as Tim Ingold (2000) suggests in his notion of sentient ecology that listening to our sound environment belongs to a sensual, experiential way of knowing (e.g., how to sail; how to fly a kite). In *shanshui*-thought, this tacit dimension of knowing or sensual way of knowing is called *moqi* (tacit resonance), achieving understanding through nonlinguistic ways.

In experimental music that requires improvisation, informed by *shanshui*-thought, the effort is spent in mastering how to resonate, to enter a relation of *moqi*. Jullien translates *moqi* as connivance, "The Latin *connivere* means to come to an understanding 'with a wink'" (2018a, 106). For Jullien, "Connivance stakes a rightful claim opposite knowledge. It recovers what knowledge has ended up repressing, though not quite abolishing, and from this opposite position demonstrates the coherence of what has been repressed" (2018a, 105–6). When one winks at another person or walks in the woods, one finds that one is anchored to a connection in an elementary and expansive way.

To achieve connivance with either a person, a living or nonliving being, one does not control and grasp (knowledge would require these gestures). Instead, one waits, detects and carefully initiates the link. In fact, one of the major characteristics of guqin is following; "following means nurturing the Right Essence of balanced harmony" (Van Gulik, 49). *Shanshui* unravels and overflows. One waits for the *qi* of *shanshui*, follows it, links to it, and becomes an element in it. *Moqi* fails to happen when one of the parties withdraws. In Shen Piji's case, the singing frogs very often stay quiet in their improvising concerts.

The *guqin* player and experimental musician Shen Piji lives in Shenzhen since 2015, China's leading city for technology and industry, linking Hong Kong to mainland China. Shen rents his studio in an urban village of Shenzhen in 2015. In his front yard, Shen placed five ceramic jars of different sizes in a self-made pond. The jars attracted a group of music frogs (Hylarana daunchina, endemic to China) and they stayed afterward. From 2015, Shen initiated a series called *Frog Jam* and invited musicians and artists nearby to participate. The first event occurred in July 11, 2015 (Figure 4.3). He invited musician friends from his hometown Chaozhou (a city in Guangdong province) to perform Chaozhou opera together with these frogs. To use a hometown music meant something special for Shen as a new immigrant to the city of Shenzhen. On July 18, 2015, for the second

FIGURE 4.3 Frog Jam Experimental Concert, *2015.7.11, Wutong Mountain, Shenzhen. photo courtesy of Shen Piji.*

concert, Shen Piji invited his neighbor, a Japanese new media artist Macoto Cuhara, as well as Hong Kong-based sound artist Pal Pal aka (Paul Yip). Macoto programmed an infrared sensor installation to interact with the frogs. Once the frogs croak, the sensor would make beeping sounds and emit cross infrared ray at the same time. There are altogether five sensors set to correspond to each pottery jars.[4]

Moqi or tacit resonance connects one to the interiority of the life power of the other. In the case of collective music improvising, one needs to know each other as a full person, their tempers, characters, spirits, and values. The music group FEN (Far East Network) consists of Otomo Yoshihide from Japan, Yan Jun from China, Yuen Cheewai from Singapore, Ryu Hankil from Korea, taking its form in 2008. They are significant individuals in their respective cultural scenes, organizing events and festivals, performing as artists, musicians, and curators. They seldom discuss music when they were together. Staying together, eating, drinking, and traveling helps them to establish *moqi*. Listening and improvising give this growing tacit resonance an ever-changing acoustic form. The affective bond formed in life feeds back to musical communication which further nurtures the well-being of the collective and the individuals.

Waiting and following characterize the kind of improvising experimental music which develops *moqi and jian*. Live performances of such often sound quiet and restraint but still with dynamic, tension, and a degree of chaos.

Making *Shanshui*-Thought Audible: Two Aesthetic Qualities

During his lecture invited by Alvin Lucier, in his concluding remarks Christian Wolff gave a passing comment on two ideas in experimental music, described as operations of renunciation or restriction, as a kind of "ascetic minimalism."

> One is the notion of musical poverty, of an avoidance of rhetoric, of the presence of silence or spaciousness, of sparseness of the irreducibility of material, one might think of music of Satie, Webern, Feldman, Lucier, Cage, for example. The other notion is of what Adorno refers to as "the ideal of darkness," which does not simply match what he feels to be the darkness of the times, of social reality, but "does no more and no less than postulate that art properly understood finds happiness in nothing except

---

[4]For a video recording of the second concert, see https://www.youtube.com/watch?v=cGP_DnV_q08

its ability to stand its ground. This happiness," he continues, "illuminates the sensuous phenomenon from the inside . . . blackness [darkness]—the antithesis of the fraudulent sensuality of culture's facade—has a sensual appeal." This notion, of poverty and darkness, would function, so to speak, to keep us honest; and Adorno adds the point that in that very function their music achieves its particular beauty. (2017, 30)

These two notions of poverty and darkness as Wolff identifies and advocates in music making resonate well with two aesthetic (also moral) qualities in classical Chinese *guqin* music and in today's experimental music practice in China. That is, the quality of *dan* (quiet and bland) and *you* (inward expandedness).

Dan (Quiet, Bland): The Taste of Wisdom

Informed by the organic and relational *qi*-philosophy, ancient Chinese aesthetic qualities are often at the same time cosmic and moral qualities; the aesthetic, cosmic and moral are mutually dependent and penetrable. *Dan*(淡) is related to the virtue of neutrality (*zhong*)(中), which applies to both the Heaven and Sage. "There is no other basis in reality apart from this value of the neutral: not leaning in one direction more than in another, not characterized more by one quality than by another, but preserving, perfectly whole within itself, its capacity for action. From this neutrality derives, in the eyes of Confucians, all true efficacy. And to the neutral we owe, of course, the ineluctable blandness that is the mark of the Sage" (Jullien, 49).

Neutrality means harmony, which means music needs to balance with social, moral, and natural conditions. The sound of neutrality corresponds to *gong*, the first tone of Chinese musical scale. *Gong* corresponds to the organ of spleen. It also refers to the emperor and the humming thunder of fall. Spatially, gong means the middle. As an aesthetic category, *dan*, meaning mild, vast, or bland, challenges most European or American individuals who would consider *dan* boring and the opposite of aesthetic stimulation. However, *dan* is a highly valued sound quality in classical Chinese aesthetics, particularly in *guqin* music. According to the Chinese scholar Cai Zhongde (2003), one can trace the idea of *dan* in music to Ruan Ji's (210–263AD) article "On Music (*Yue Lun*)," and find a more developed aesthetic theory of *dan* in the text *Xishan Qinkuang* by Xu Shangying (1582–1662). Informed by Daoism, Ruan Ji suggests that music embodies the nature and spirit of the earth, the heaven and every organic and inorganic thing. Taoism suggests that one has to be desire-less to achieve peacefulness. Music accordingly has to be quiet and bland to accommodate this moral need.

In *Xishan Qinkuang*, the motif of *dan* corresponds to two Chinese characters that are pronounced the same as *Dan*, one is 澹 and the other is 淡. Dan is first of all a state to be acquired by guqin players. As Xu Shangying describes, "clear spring, white stone, bright moon and slight breeze, freely exist. The listener sets free their mind to reach the state of *xuanmiao* (metaphysical subtly), the desire for entertainment will disappear as well."[5] The character used by Xu is 澹, somehow neglected by Jullien in his book *In Praise of Blandness* (2004). The two characters, 澹 and 淡, are often used interchangeably, but there are still some differences. 澹 tends to mean quiet, peaceful, and slow, while 淡 refers to blandness in taste. Quiet and bland sound leads to the flow of the spiritual *qi*, referred to the state of *tian* (恬). Xu Shangying explains the relation between *dan* and *tian*, "one achieves *dan* when one reaches subtlety, when *dan* reaches *miao* one creates *tian*, when *tian* reaches *miao*, one's music will be even more *dan* but never makes one feel tired of."[6]

Dan is a sensual category but it is too simple and unappealing to the senses that it requires the intellect to engage with. François Jullien speaks highly of *dan* as a concept to grasp the depth of Chinese thinking. Blandness is the most basic and authentic of all flavors: that of the "root" of things (Jullien 2004, 52–3). *Dan* is a quality shared on ethical, aesthetic, relational, psychological, and metaphysical levels practiced through classical paintings, music, social codes, individual characters, literature, ideology, and taste. Jullien identifies several variations of *dan*: the stone sculpture of Buddha in Datong grottos showing very little curves on the face, the painter Ni Zan's water-ink painting, the aesthetic value of lingering tone in music. *Dan* is the color of the whole, as it appears to the eyes of those who look farthest into the distance; it makes us experience the world and existence itself beyond the narrow confines of the individual's point of view. What is missing in the sensual will be reacquired in the intellect. Therefore, *Dan* is the taste of wisdom.

You (Inward Expandedness)

Bland sound, as Jullien describes (2004), is "an attenuated sound that retreats from the ear and is allowed to simply die out over the longest possible time. We hear it still, but just barely; and as it diminishes, it makes all the more audible that soundless beyond into which it is about to extinguish itself" (79). Here Jullien is actually talking about the dimension of *you* (inward

---

[5]"qinquan baishi, haoyue shufeng, xiaoxiao zide, shi tingzhizhe yousi piaomiao, yule zhixin buzhi hequ—si zhi wei dan"(清泉白石，皓月疏风，翛翛自得，使听之者游思飘渺，娱乐之心不知何去—斯之谓澹) from Xishan Qinkuang (溪山琴况) by Xu Shangying (徐上瀛).

[6]"wei cao zhi miao lai, ze ke dan; dan zhi miao lai, ze sheng tian; tian zhi miao lai, ze yu dan er bu mie"(唯操至妙来，则可澹；澹至妙来，则生恬；恬至妙来，则愈澹而不厌) from Xishan Qinkuang (溪山琴况) by Xu Shangying (徐上瀛).

expandedness)(幽), related to *dan* but itself a separate quality in guqin music appearing in both *Xishan Qinkuang* and Leng Qian's *Sixteen Rules for the Tones of the Lute*. Originated from *Laozi*, the notion of *you* means deep, hidden, and secret. In *The Lore of the Chinese Lute*, Robert Van Gulik (1969) translates *you* from the text of *Sixteen Rules for the Tones of the Lute*, as the profound touch.

> The quality of music depends upon the personality of the player; thus profundity comes from within. Therefore, when a high-minded and cultivated scholar executes a tune, then the resonance is profound . . . the music will be broad and generous like the wind, and unstained by earthly dust . . . when one hears his music one shall know the personality of the player. Such as the wonderful qualities of the profound touch. (112)

You is often seen paired up with another character *xuan*(玄), which means empty, dark, and unclear. *Youxuan* (幽玄) means deep and mysterious. *Youxuan* refers to those unspoken beauty, secrets, a kind of state beyond logic and language. It is an idea influenced by Chan Buddhism. The quality of inward expandedness brought a sense of subtly and lightness. It exists not in the body of music, but in the fading sound when music ends, as well as in the music player's personality. When used to describe a person as *youxuan*, it means that the person is elegant and refined.

The notion of *youxuan* originates in China, but was developed further in Japan. According to the Chinese scholar Zhou Jianping, the idea of *youxuan* as a philosophical term, was introduced to Japan from China and soon became an essential concept and value in Japanese aesthetics. *Youxuan* was developed first in medieval poetics in Japan (2015, 190). It was extended from the field of singing to poetry, literature and Noh, gradually becoming the top aesthetic concept in Japanese aesthetics. *Youxuan* describes a personality that is aloof, morally lofty, or describes a performance that insinuates. Among different derivations of *youxuan* developed by Japanese poets and art theorists, the Haiko master Matsuo Basho particularly values *youxuan* as an aesthetic quality generated through sound. It refers to the remaining rhythm after sound has died out, a high art form that is silent, sad, solemn, and meditative. To give an example of his famous poem,

> The old pond;
> A frog jumps in
> The sound of the water.

The sound of *dan* and *you* does not seduce or incite. It, however, leads to the most profound quietness of both the inner world and the cosmos. Music that bears the qualities of *dan* and *you*, resembles guqin music in that it is not to be performed on stage; it should be listened to as having a private dialogue with oneself or a few friends. Examples include the Japanese experimental music genre known as *onkyô,* feedback music by Yan Jun, stone music by Christian Wolff, and certain experimental music works that operate on the border of audibility.

The Tea Rockers Quintet

The Tea Rockers Quintet includes Yan Jun (feedback system), Wu Na (guqin), Xiaohe (guitar, voice, laptop), Li Daiguo (voice and multi-instruments). Formed in Berne in October 2010, when they performed at the same music festival, the collective combines traditional instruments such as guqin and pipa with contemporary electronic instruments. Besides these instruments, there is a nonmusical presence: a tea ceremony performed by Lao Gu, now replaced by his disciple Xi Jian. The kind of tea they drink during the concert determines the tenor of their performance (Figures 4.4.1, 4.4.2). The group so far has only released two albums, *Ceremony* (2012) and *Fictions* (2017).

In their album *Ceremony,* we can sometimes hear sounds of tea making and the clicking of cups. The entire performance creates a poetic space in which one begins to feel that it is not so much a simple musical event as a casual gathering of like-minded friends. The small, high-frequency, and nonhuman feedback noise constitute the opposing dimension of sounds of *guqin*, *pipa*, cello, guitar, voice, and tea making, opening up a world of ceaseless reinvigoration of intimacy and well-being mixed with a sense of mystery and aloofness. The aroma of the tea does not give structure to the

FIGURE 4.4.1 *Tea Rockers Quintet (left), Live Performance, 2012. Courtesy of Yan Jun.*

FIGURE 4.4.2 *Tea Rockers Quintet (right), Live Performance, 2012. Courtesy of Yan Jun.*

music performance, rather it creates the non-existent sound that interestingly generates an attractive space of *jian*, with individual sounds reach tacit resonance with tea making. Sound and tea may or may not have anything to do with each other; they can just be in parallel existence in the same time-space, just as the cloud, trees, and cats.

Conclusion

Experimental music informed by *shanshui*-thought is paradoxically quotidian and elite. It belongs to the amateurs and it should stay so. Just like guqin music being practiced by amateur scholars from the literati class in Chinese history, professionality or musical virtuosity is not preferred because neither guqin music nor experimental music is meant to be played to entertain the public. The Chinese experimental musician Yan Jun speaks of minimizing techniques in his music practices. He speaks openly about his lack of professional musical training and never intends to master a musical instrument. He makes subtle gestures with his body over his DIY feedback sound system. He even sleeps in his performance set. Yan Jun organizes the Beijing Impro Committee, consisting of experimental, improvising music performers of little professional training in music. They are programmers, housewives, vendors, designers, painters, or self-taught musicians. In their performances, they decide not to intentionally collaborate with each other in order to make space for *moqi* (tacit resonance) to develop.

When we hear music that appears quiet, bland, dark, or restraint and when we feel that the music is not actually performed for us but for musicians themselves, we may, before making any quick judgment, rewire our sensibility through *shanshui*-thought. It might be true that *shanshui*-thought-informed music fails to excite or entertain the public or fails to produce objective knowledge. It does not even seem to be a useful artistic medium to directly address pressing social, cultural, political, and ecological issues. However, experimental music driven by *shanshui*-thought embodies a care for the cosmic well-being, a no less political way of being and becoming.

5

In Praise of Strange Sounds
of the Shamanistic

In the exhibition titled *Holographia: 2018 International Intermedia Art Festival* at Times Museum in Beijing, an inconspicuous piece stood out for me among other VR, AI, laser-based installation art pieces. It was Xu Cheng's sound-visual installation *Soul Summoning Device* (Fig.5.1), hanging at one end of a dark long narrow insulated room. It was made of iron sheet and shaped almost like a small boat, with a small contact mic attached to the lower bottom of the inner surface of the device. Abstract light images are projected on to the metallic surface, creating a phantasmagoric atmosphere. When the audience makes sounds or speaks through the contact mic, the device echoes back.

As the artist explains in the work's statement, the idea of making a soul summoning device was inspired by a soul summoning ritual practiced by fishermen in Zhoushan, a seashore city in Zhejiang province. In old times, when fishermen disappeared during shipwreck, their relatives would practice a soul summon ritual if they failed to find the bodies. They carried straw-men on their backs along the sea and stroke a gong. It was called striking a cold gong. At the same time, they called names of the dead in local dialect and shouted out "the sea is cold. The soul should come home quickly." The ritual was to reckon the soul of the dead for a proper burial. After the ritual, the relatives buried the straw-men in the dead's clothes. For Xu Cheng, the voice that summons the soul in this ritual is considered a medium that exceeds the normal role it plays in delivering words and meanings. The voice becomes a self-therapeutic psychic medium that helps to deal with issues that goes beyond one's control.

Meanwhile in Shanghai, the 12th Shanghai Biennale was taking place at the contemporary art museum Power Station of Art, with the theme "Proregress: Art in an Age of Historical Ambivalence" (2018.11–2019.3).

FIGURE 5.1 *Xu Cheng,* Soul Summoning Device. *Installation View,* Holographia: 2018 International Intermedia Art Festival *at Times Museum in Beijing, 2018. Photo by author.*

According to the curatorial statement, the English title "proregress" comes from E. E. Cummings, meaning condensation of progress and regress, as a critique of the progressivism held by Western enlightenment movement. Intriguingly, In Chinese, the phrase *Yubu* (禹步)(the walk of *Yu*) was selected to correspond to the English term proregress. *Yubu* is explained as "the basic mystic dance step of Daoist ritual in ancient China." According to the chief curator Cuauhtémoc Medina as quoted in the curatorial statement, this vigorous dance steps "imply values of artworks and inspirations for mankind" and "these works illustrate a commitment to transforming our sensibilities into new ways of living, mimicking the manner with which contemporary art and culture confront the complexities of our time."

Most Chinese audience has to learn the meaning of *yubu,* which is supposed to be a native Chinese knowledge. The term *Yubu* is as esoteric to most Chinese in contemporary time as to non-Chinese speaking individuals. While literally translated as the walk of Yu, the emperor of Xia dynasty, also a master shaman, there are several versions of how this way of walking was developed. In one version, Emperor Yu severely hurt his legs after soaking them in water so long in controlling the ongoing flood. Out of respect, people of Xia named his way of walking as *yubu*. Another version attributes the walk to a mythical bird Yu once encountered in deep mountains. Yu saw this bird with magical power controlling demons, monsters and ghosts. Hoping to acquire the same magical power, Yu imitated the way the bird walks in his shamanic ritual. *Yubu* was later incorporated into Daoist ritual and was further refined as a walking performance following the nine stars of the big dipper as a way to resonate with the cosmic power. The English title "proregress" and Chinese title "*yubu*," while both suggest a certain choreographic walk, embody two stances. "Proregress" launches a critique of modernization and its related ideology of progress; "*yubu*" expresses an unconcealed celebration of mythical Daoism and its relation to contemporary artworks as selected.

Interestingly, while shamanistic ritual practices together with Daoism in folk culture has been deemed largely as superstition in China since the beginning of the twentieth century, this so-called minor tradition seems to have a return in contemporary culture, particularly in contemporary art and music practices.

The 12th Shanghai Biennale has further revealed the global nature of this shamanistic reference already prevalent in contemporary art world at large. Influential contemporary artists like Joseph Beuys or Matthew Barney have long been known as the shaman-artist. In the music world, categories of world music, new age, dark ambience, industrial noise, drone metal are all more or less associated with mysticism and shamanism (Coggins 2018). David Toop, improvising musician and a renowned writer of sound and culture, in both his book *Ocean of Sound* (2001) and his field recording *Lost Shadows: In Defence of the Soul—Yanomami Shamanism, Songs, Ritual, 1978* released through Sub Rasa (2015), has directed the sound art world to the marginal, spiritual, and disappearing sound of the shamanistic.

Interlacing intellectual-cultural-economic forces give rise to this shamanistic retrieval in various cultural practices and we can identify a few here: the 1960s counterculture's embrace of Eastern spirituality (Pickering 2010), the ethnographic turn in the arts from 1970s (Foster 1995; Kosuth 1975), the popularization of quantum mechanics in the arts and its connection to shamanic visions, and the growing global spiritual marketplace (Carrette and King 2005).

Other than being a phenomenon that is contingent on historical development and cultural variations, the shamanistic is understood as a universal human nature. Through the perspective of the psychiatrist Carl Jung, the shaman archetype is a kind of psychic organ, a collective unconsciousness, an inherited structure of the soul, present in all humankind (Jung 1980). Or as the media theorist Marshall McLuhan interpreted, the reappraisal of the archetype of the shamanistic is a retrieved cliché for new inventions, a "retrieval from the rag-and-bone shop of past experience" (McLuhan and Watson 1970).

China cannot easily escape influences of the above forces in today's highly globalized art and music world. Admittedly, contemporary shamanistic return is a complex subject and in this chapter I set a small goal. I focus on how China's own shamanic cultural past registers in Chinese contemporary sound art and electronic, experimental music practices. To put in other words, I aim to understand how the mythical tradition of ancient Shamanism, Daoism, and Buddhism in Chinese history works as productive forces in contemporary creative works of sound. This local interpretation hopeful will add some diversity to the global celebration of the shamanistic. Specifically, through works by Tan Dun, Xu Cheng, Wang Fan, Lin Chi-Wei, and Sheng Jie, I identify two tendencies in contemporary praise of sounds of the shamanistic that oscillate between appropriation and participation, between inheritance and alliance. One treats shamanism as a cultural gene or a national treasure. The other one is driven more by the sensual and intellectual sensibility known as *huanghu* first suggested by the ancient shamanistic and later rationalized into Daoism and Buddhism. These two tendencies, if closely investigated, are nothing completely new but have existed far back in ancient Chinese history.

The Minor Tradition in Ancient Chinese Culture: Shamanism and *Chimei Wangliang*

Daoism and Confucianism are two known Chinese thinking systems, often interpreted as two opposing and at the same time, complementary schools of thoughts. As the known Chinese historian Li Zehou points out during the later stage of his scholarship, both Confucianism and Daoism derive from the same origin, ancient shamanism, and the shamanic ritual ceremony (1999, 2015/2018).

The Cultivated Gentleman versus the Folk Shaman Spiritual Man

This is the greatest secret of the history of ancient Chinese thought: the fundamental qualities of shamanism were directly rationalized from the path of the integration of shaman and king, or political governance and religion, to become the basic characteristics of the mainstream tradition of Chinese thought. In China's mainstream tradition, the characteristics of shamanism have been firmly preserved and carried forward in rationalized form, and have become the key to understanding Chinese thought and culture. (2018, 19)

As Li postulates, during shamanic ritual ceremony the shamans exhibited ecstatic psychology, which was later rationalized and ethicalized by Confucius to create ideal humanness (仁)(2018, 42). Particularly, the psychological emotions of awe, fear, and admiration of the divines during the shamanic ritual ceremony was further developed as reverence(敬). Together with ritual (礼), reverence constitutes virtue (德) to "denote the behavior and character of a king, ultimately coming to refer to the morality of individual psychology" (32).

What Confucius insisted while rationalizing mystical shamanism was to introduce the psychological emotion of shamanism into everyday mundane life and human relations. That is, to make human relations sacred. During his time, Confucius lamented that rituals were becoming superficial languages, gestures, and appearances; ritual lost its internal emotional psychology of awe, respect, devotion, and sincerity. At the same time, Confucius asked not to speak of topics the master did not speak of, which was prodigies, force, disorder, and gods (怪力乱神, *guai li luan shen*). Confucius also discouraged discussions of death and ghost, "Without knowing life, how can one know death?" "Without serving for the livings, how does one serve ghosts?" These teachings, as Li interpreted, suggest the origin of differences between the mainstream and the minor traditions that persist till today.

as I see it Confucius's statement here refers precisely to the two paths along which shamanism developed, the mainstream and marginal traditions. Confucius was admonishing the scholars of his time against becoming the shaman spiritual men of popular folk culture (inferior men), and encouraging them instead to become the protectors and inheritors of the ritual institutions of the "sage," as was more befitting of worthy men. (40)

Like Confucius, Li does not spend much time in discussing marginalized shamanic practices in folk cultures. As Li explains, "Confucius promotes being a scholar after the style of the gentleman, and not after that of the lesser man. The cultivated gentleman refers to the inheritor of the Duke of Zhou's ritual institutions, the lesser person refers to the folk shaman" (129). For Li, the more important thing is to recognize the shamanistic spirit in China's mainstream tradition, instead of sweeping shamanism entirely under the fold of these lesser traditions. Li's argument is valuable in pointing out the intellectual weight of shamanism in the history of Chinese thoughts, but it also confirms Confucius' denunciation of the lesser tradition that nonetheless keeps the mythical dimension alive. In Confucian's rationalization of shamanism as Li explains, there seems to be a question that remains unsettling for me: can the inner psychological emotions of ancient shamans be disassociated from shamans' relation to the mythical others and remain the same while being transplanted into human relations? Li does not seem to see a problem in this transplantation.

Laozi, in comparison to Confucius, as Li points out, preserved the mythical vision, the wisdom of early shamanism, and further rationalized it into Daoism and Daoist mythical practices. Most importantly, the ecstatic psychology of the practicing shaman, which was rationalized to become humaneness by Confucius, became the inspiration of *Dao* for Laozi. As Li explains, *Dao* is *wu* (none-presence)(无) pronounced the same as *wu* (shamanism)(巫), as well as *wu* (dance)(舞). "*It is the divinity that emerged through primeval shamanistic dance*. In shamanic dance, the divine descended from heaven, but 'through sight it is unseen' and 'through listening it is unheard.' Yet, through efficacious virtue it arises of itself" (49). Although Li does not explicitly say so, but it seems that he is referring to a chapter in *Daodejing*, where *dao* is also defined as *huanghu* (elusive, evasive, vague, and indistinct)(恍惚),

> Looked at, but cannot be seen. That is called the Invisible (*yi*). Listened to, but cannot be heard. That is called the Inaudible (*hsi*). Grasped at, but cannot be touched. That is called the Intangible (*wei*). These three elude our inquiries and hence blend and become One. Not by its rising, is there light, nor by its sinking, is there darkness. Unceasing, continuous, it cannot be defined, and reverts again to the realm of nothingness. That is why it is called the Form of the Formless, the Image of Nothingness. That is why it is called the Elusive: Meet it and you do not see its face; Follow it and you do not see its back.[1] (chapter fourteen, *Daodejing*, translation by Lin Yutang)

If Confucianism is shamanism further rationalized and moralized, it can be said that Daoism is shamanism rationalized and mystified. Despite the dominance of Confucianism in the mainstream official Chinese culture, the minor culture or the lesser tradition continues quietly in the periphery. *Huanghu*, a notion through which Daoism relates to the ancient shamanic ritual practices, has later informed aesthetic sensibilities in literature, painting, music, and poetry. The last section of this chapter will explore the notion of *huanghu* in more details.

Chimei Wangliang: The Lesser, Minor, Strange Dimension of Chinese Culture

It is after all difficult not to think of death, ghosts, and the afterlife, which prove to be full of life forces for the living. In the *Classic of Mountains and*

---

[1]视之不见，名曰夷；听之不闻，名曰希；搏之不得，名曰微。此三者不可致诘，故混而为一。其上不皦，其下不昧，绳绳兮不可名，复归于无物。是谓无状之状，无物之象，是谓惚恍。迎之不见其首，随之不见其后。执古之道，以御今之有。能知古始，是谓道纪。

Sea, written in pre-*qin* period (2100 BC–221 BC), monsters and demons are referred to as *chimei wangliang* (Chimimōryō in Japanese). The term is believed to be coined in the classics *Zuo Zhuan* during the fourth century BC. *Chimei wangliang* refers to two kinds of monsters, *chimei* and *wangliang.* *Chimei* are monsters made of the eerie *qi* of mountains, with human face and animal bodies. *Wangliang* refers to monsters from water, taking the form of three-year-old baby, with red eyes, long ears, and shining hair. *Wangliang* is also used to describe the outer layer of a shadow, generating a feeling of desperate loneliness. All four characters of *chimei wangliang* (魑魅魍魎) contain the same radical, *gui* (鬼)(ghost). Interestingly, the Chinese character for ghost is pronounced the same as the word "return," the euphemism for death. According to *qi*-cosmology, the condensation of *qi* is life, its diffusion death. This may explain why the dispersed *qi* of deep mountains is called *chimei.* Following *qi*-cosmology, there is no essential difference between the living and the dead, only different modes and states of *qi*.

Tracing examples of classical, modern, and contemporary literatures, from writers including Qu Yuan (343–278BC), Gan Bao (286–336), Li He (790–816), Su Dongpo (1037–1101), Pu Songling (1640–1715), Ji Yun (1724–1805), Yuan Mei (1716–1798), Lu Xun (1881–1936) and Mo Yan (1955–), the Chinese historian Leo Ou-fan Lee (1942–) convincingly suggest that a persistent alternative, minor, and hidden tradition of *chimei wangliang* constitutes an essential dimension of Chinese culture (2016).

Neither Leo Ou-fan Lee nor Li Zehou discuss the acoustic aspect of this minor tradition. As in Western mythologies, in Chinese mythologies sound is often given special powers, destructive, transformative, prophetic, and interspecies. Monsters recorded in the *Classic of Mountains and Sea* are believed to make infants' sounds to lure and kill humans. Ear is often considered an extraordinary organ that symbolizes longevity and wisdom. Big ears symbolize longevity and even immortality. From the *Classic of Mountains and Sea*, we read about people with gigantic ears living in an island-kingdom called *Nie Er.* They have to hold their ears when they walk. Ear is also considered connected to one's inner spirit. In *Strange Tales from a Chinese Studio* by Pu Songling in Qing Dynasty (1636–1912), we read a story of a scholar named Tan Jinxuan going mad when seeing a tiny fiendish looking person jumping out of his ear during his Daoist breathing practice. Insanity in ancient China has never been considered as a terrible disease; educated people in ancient times would even secretly want to admit to themselves. Moreover, instruments, especially *guqin*, made of wood from trees in high mountains and preferably trees stuck by lightening accompanies with thunder, were believed to have life of their own; like ancient mythical weapon, instruments chose their own masters.

Contrary to Li's argument that "lesser traditions carry forward shamanistic 'forms' (outer appearances and ceremonies) while mainstream tradition has inherited shamanism's spirit (substantiality and characteristics)" (129), I would argue in this chapter, based on analysis of varied artworks, that what the current mainstream inherited from shamanism is its form, while the lesser or minor culture carries forward the shamanism's spirit.

Acoustic Cultural Heritage and Nationalism

In the new millennium, the arrival of the cultural industry in China (Keane 2016), the state government's call for cultural preservation (beginning in 2006), Western and domestic academic studies of shamanism, all together constitute major external factors of legitimizing shamanism in the minor tradition of folk cultures. But as the musicologist of shaman music Xiao Mei remarks, most academic studies decontextualize shaman music to focus on the change of musical and performative styles in tonal structures. The whole belief system behind the shaman music is largely ignored (Liao and Xiao 2008). This critique can be extended to the first tendency I have identified in the praise of sounds of the shamanistic, that is, the artistic appropriation of the shamanic as a resource or cultural gene, as an identity forming strategy.

The electronic music composer Zhang Xiaofu, as discussed in Chapter 3, has been strongly advocating for building a Chinese model in electroacoustic music composition and one of his main strategies is sampling. For example, as Zhang reveals in writing, "In composing *Nuo Rilang* (1996), I took unique Tibetan Lama chanting vocals as the core material that formed and represented symbols of Tibetan culture. These short chanting vocals constituted a looped leading motif that was deep and full of mystery" (Zhang 2019). The percussion part of the piece, as he revealed to Leigh Landy in their interview, was inspired by Chinese thought through the choice of materials used: bronze, leather, wood, and stone (87). Studying Zhang's composition, Landy identifies Zhang's signature composition strategy as "techniques of acousmatic gestural music are applied using Chinese material" (2018). Like Zhang Xiaofu, his former classmate, now world-renowned composer Tan Dun also extensively uses materials from his culture origin, with even stronger and more explicit identification with shamanism from Chinese culture.

Tan Dun and Shamanic References

Tan Dun is known for his fusion of ancient Chinese cultural elements with classical music, contemporary avant-garde music and popular music in his composition. Tan often refers back to his childhood memory of growing up in a rural Hunan village saturated in a shamanic folk culture to explain the strong shamanic reference prevalent throughout his compositions, including *Daoji* (1985) composed particularly for his grandmother when she passed away, the ritualistic opera *Nine Songs(1989)* based on the Chinese poet Qu Yuan's (ca.340–278 BC) poem *Nine Songs* addressed to nine deities through the voice of a shaman, the music theater ritual piece *Ghost Opera* (1994) composed for the Kronos Quartet and the Chinese traditional instrument pipa, as well as the orchestra theater *O* (2002) in search for the origin of the primitive sacrifice ritual performance of *Nuo* opera. In his multimedia orchestra theater, *The Map* (2012), Tan intends to present minority music culture in China, placing ancient shamanic ritual *ba gua* stone drumming, minority tongue singing, cry singing, into dialogue with the contemporary urban avant-garde.

The Hong Kong-based sound artist and scholar Samson Young in his detailed analysis of *The Map* criticizes, "Tradition for Tan Dun is specially defined as a frozen cultural moment in time that is preserved and idealized in the collective psyche of the Chinese people, and such a precious cultural moment is not to progress with time" (2009, 86). Young detected similar treatment of Chinese folk cultural materials in Tan Dun's *Ghost Opera* (2007). "Ghost Opera promises a world in which Bach, Chinese, Shakespeare and Monks are not East or West, but simply human. Yet as we listen to how the folk materials are being consistently singled out as out of context by dissonant key relationships, while with subsequent reappearance the Bach quotation remains largely intact and firmly in C-sharp, we are confronted with a different picture. Bach, his legacy and the importance of harmony and counterpoint are firmly centralized" (2007, 613).

Despite existing critiques, Tan Dun's music works remain highly popular among the mainstream culture and Chinese official culture. Tan is both resourceful and mindful in orchestrating Chinese cultural heritage as acoustic treasures. After a research on the secret language system invented and used exclusively among women in Jiangyong County in Hunan province, Tan produced *Nv Shu: The Secret Songs of Women* (2013). He also spent weeks inside of the Dunhuang Mogao Caves with mural paintings and worked with scholars on lost musical manuscripts and composed the oratorio *Buddha Passion* (2018).

During his time at Columbia University back in late 1980s, Tan Dun encountered John Cage whom as Tan reflected has marked a turning point in his way of composing. After meeting Cage, Tan began to use nonmusical instruments in his composition and composed *Water Concerto for Water Percussion and Orchestra* (1998). This influence is now best showcased as a permanent architecture-instrument at one of the historical water towns Zhujiajiao in Shanghai. Together with the Japanese architects of Isozaki Studio, Tan Dun renovated a Ming Dynasty style house into what he named Water Heaven, with an auditorium called Water Music Hall. Tan Dun said in an interview, "My ultimate goal for Water Heaven is to create a space where the architecture is an instrument that can be heard and played." Water Heaven locates on the river bank, facing an ancient Buddhist Temple

Yuanjing Temple. The organic concert "Water Heavens" at Water Heaven Hall is designed to begin at the exact same time when monks begin their evening chanting across the river. The music performance continues Tan Dun's music composition strategy, fusing nonmusical instruments percussion with string quartet of Bach, rock and roll, rap, and water splashing and dripping.

What is at stake in the goal of cultural heritage preservation? It asks one to play the role of the guardian, the inheritor, as well as the spokesman of the past. The past is easily reduced to an object without the ability to change and is subject to appropriation. Without making a space for alternative belief systems and cosmic worldviews to develop their own vitality, the spokesman or the inheritor's revitalizing project is simply capitalizing and consuming the past.

Chang Xiao (Transcendental Whistling, Chanting, Roaring)

Chang Xiao (长啸) is a way of making sound with the mouth without using the vocal cords, words, or beats, a vocal practice existing as early as in pre-*qin* era (2100–221 BC). According to *Shuowen Jiezi*, *Xiao* tends to be long rather than short and hence is called *chang* (long) *xiao*. The Taiwanese scholar of Daoist religion Li Fengmao (1997, 2010) notes, during the Han Dynasty, *Xiao* was a kind of incantation practiced by shamans; *xiao* summons and commands souls, ghosts, birds, beasts, cloud, wind, thunder, and rains. *Xiao* was also practiced by women as a way of expressing their emotions. In Weijin era, *xiao* was developed into a technique related to the fetal respiration technique in Taoist *qi*-cultivation, a method of achieving longevity. Xiao became a popular practice among reclusive literati in Weijin era, who were known for their rebellious and wild characters. Not saying any words but making sounds expressed their defiant attitude, a more negative refusal.

In 2016, *xiao* was registered as a provincial immaterial cultural heritage in Henan province. Henan is known as the birth place of Ruan Ji, a known *xiao* artist and literati in Weijin era. Efforts are made to promote *xiao* to become a national culture heritage but this effort seems to go right against the defiant and elusive spirit of *xiao*.

The age of globalization has been a primary reason for nation-states to seek and reinforce national identities by reaching back to and at the same time constructing cultural heritages. Investment in cultural heritages is beneficial for local economy, but it can also be a way of governance. It is the innate nature of any centralized entity to control those threatening and unruly elements that endanger its stability. As Deleuze and Guattari notes, "For societies, even primitive societies, have always appropriated these becomings in order to break them, reduce them to relations of totemic or symbolic correspondence" (248). Therefore, to provide government stipend to shaman cultures, to keep them as a cultural heritage, can be a process of domestication. The state has to appropriate the anormonous shamanic impulse to maintain its dominant ideology. Allowing the shamanic to exist in artistic, academic, or tourist practice can be a form of kettling, just like permitting graffiti on prepared walls inside of an art district. It is a noise reduction operation with the right amount of manufactured white noise to conceal violence.

If treating ancient and traditional shamanic rituals as a cultural gene implies identification, another kind is, to borrow from Deleuze and Guattari, "unnatural participation" (242). Only through unnatural participation can transformation/becoming happen.

Huanghu and Its Two Aesthetic Operations: Resonance and Withdrawal

Instead of being an inheritor of the past and being identified as the virtuous sages or worthy men, one takes alliance with the mythical periphery. Rather than representing the shaman, one enters the process of becoming-shaman, to borrow from how Deleuze and Guattari describes sorcerers. "Sorcerers have always held the anomalous position, at the edge of the fields or woods. They haunt the fringes" (246).

> What exactly is the nature of the anomalous? . . . The anomalous is neither an individual nor a species; it has only affects, it has neither familiar or subjectified feelings, nor specific or significant characteristics. . . . it is a phenomenon, but a phenomenon of bordering . . . it is evident that the Anomalous, the Outsider, has several functions: not only does it border each multiplicity, of which it determines the temporary or local stability (with the highest number of dimensions possible under the circumstances), not only is it the precondition for the alliance necessary to becoming, but it also carries the transformations of becoming or crossings of multiplies always farther down the line of flight." (Deleuze and Guattari, 244–50)

For Deleuze and Guattari, composers like Olivier Messiane, Edgar Varèse, Karlheinz Stockhausen, Steve Reich, Philip Glass, and Arvo Pärt, painters like Cézanne, Paul Klee, and Kandinsky, and writers like Henry Miller, Franz Kafka, and Virginia Woolf share the anomolous position and bordering quality of sorcerers. Artists operate over transversal lines that cross and unite human and nonhuman, organic and inorganic, natural and cultural domains (Ramey 2012; Deleuze and Guattari 1987).

Huanghu: The Dim, Evasive, Noisy

The notion of the anomolous suggests a conceptual sensibility that is essential to the notion of *huanghu* (恍惚)(elusive, evasive) in Daoism. Other than appearing in chapter fourteen, the notion of *huanghu* can be also found in chapter twenty-one of *Daodejing*.

> The thing that is called Dao is elusive, evasive.
> Evasive, elusive, yet latent in it are forms.
> Elusive, evasive, yet latent in it are objects.
> Dark and dim, yet latent in it is the life-force.[2]

One interpretation of the origin of *huanghu*, as mentioned in the beginning, comes from the ecstatic psychological state of the practicing shaman to connect to the heaven, the deceased, the nonhuman elements during the shamanic ritual ceremony. The other interpretation relates Daoism to moon worship in ancient times. Du Erwei (1977) and Wang Bo (1993) argues, the way Laozi describe *huanghu* and *dao* is the same as describing the changing of lunar phases, including crescent, full, new, and dark (*xian wang shuo hui*) (弦望朔晦). Wang Bo suggests, "Evasive, elusive, yet latent in it are forms" in *Daodejing* refers to phases from dark moon to new moon; "Elusive, evasive, yet latent in it are objects" refers to phases from new moon to dark moon (1993, 164). The relation between *huanghu* and the moon also makes Laozi's use of the term *youming* (dark and dim) more sensible. Comparing with the essential role, the metaphor of light plays in Western religions, moonlight is more valued in Daoism, suggesting dim and dark background, instead of spotlighted foreground. Therefore, we can say that *huanghu* concerns more with the background where things just emerge from or withdraw into.

Both its relation to the moon worship and to the ecstatic psychology of the practicing shaman should be considered together to understand the notion *Huanghu* as describing a particular inner state, a strange space, a mode of sensual perception, and a mystified spiritual state.

Huanghu is Dao. At the same time, it is the method to achieve *dao*. Specifically, *Huanghu* is the way to experience the mysterious *dao*, to lose focus, to not see, to not hear, and to not grasp. The goal is not to know *dao*, but to resonate with *dao*, and ultimately, to become unison with *dao*. As a Daoist concept often used in cultivation practice, *huanghu* refers to a dissolution of division of senses—visual, aural, smell, taste, and touch—to return to the sense of resonance, to remain in what is now called synesthesia state. Spiritually, it requires *xu* (to nullify one's ego) to cancel directivity of

---

[2]道之为物，惟恍惟惚。惚兮恍兮，其中有象。恍兮惚兮，其中有物。窈兮冥兮，其中有情。《道德经》

one's spirit, to return to a primeval state. Through *huanghu*, one resonates with the myriad things and with the heaven and the cosmos.

Through *huanghu* appears the spectral world of *chimei wangliang*, the eerie *qi* of mountains and water, the outer layer of shadows, a world of becoming, full of transformation, reincarnation, interspecies relations, in which anything from a vase, a candle holder to a tree or an animal, can transform, mix up, and disintegrate. Nothing has a set value. There is no longer sovereign relation; nothing owns anything forever. There is also no longer set relations, only profound isolation and solidarity. This is the charm of the world of the strange. It suggests an organic cosmology. It synthesizes a sensibility, both aesthetically and morally, toward the evasive and allusive. The notion of *huanghu* is not limited to Daoism, but can be identified in other system of thoughts.

François Jullien relates *huanghu* to the Greek term *pneuma divin*, the breath of life, and considers *huanghu* a crucial notion through which Western ontological thinking that demands essence and fixation can be circumvented, that is, "to think about the productivity of the inassignability of the evasive" (Jullien 2018b, 148). To be evasive is to dissolve oppositions, to express the indeterminate and the unfathomable. With the example of Chinese painting, Jullien suggests, "to render it evasiveness, we will have to evoke things, not in the objectifying plenitude of their presence, which fills the gaze with their distinctive traits, but on the edge of their invisibility, on the threshold of their emergence or resorption. The only way to characterize the fundamental haziness will be to work against characterization and de-characterize, the only way to paint a picture is to de-pict" (Jullien 2009, 32).

To de-pict, borrowing from the Chinese philosopher Feng Youlan, is to use "the negative method" as in *hongyun tuoyue* (烘云托月)(to bring moon to the fore by depicting clouds). It means if the painter wants to draw the moon, instead of directly drawing the moon, he/she draws clouds on paper to leave a blank space to insinuate the moon. By "the negative method," Feng Youlan originally refers to that which is opposed to the positive method of logics. Resonating with Wittgenstein's dictum, "That whereof we cannot speak, thereof we must remain silent," Feng suggests that only through negative method can one achieve wisdom. Feng does not oppose positive method, instead he proposes the two methods as both important; one needs to use positive method of reasoning to develop intellect and then one negates reason to get to the Daoist "realm of non-distinction and undifferentiableness," which is "crossing the boundary" (Feng 1948). By "crossing the boundary," one is absorbed in the "realm of non-distinction and undifferentiableness." The practical effect of crossing the boundary in Chinese tradition, according to Feng, is the improvement of life by elevation through man's spheres of living. For Feng, there are four spheres of living, the innocent sphere, the utilitarian sphere, the moral sphere, and the transcendent sphere (1948).

Feng Youlan's discussion of negative method, based on Daoism and Chan Buddhism, prepares us to understand *huanghu* as a negative aesthetic method (not limited to Daoism and Chan Buddhism) in art making, which relies on aesthetic strategies of withdrawal and resonance with the impure and strange.

What does *huanghu* sound like?

The sound of evasiveness and elusiveness that borders on the verge of inaudibility, too loud or too weak to hear, hard to put in a category, and hence referred to as strange, is what now called noise. Noise is sound that does not carry information, that disrupts clear acoustic communication, or that may be annoying to some and comforting for others. The sound of the evasive and elusive, or noise if you like, takes the listener to the realm of undifferentiableness. Different from modern conception of noise, noise in ancient China refers mostly to sounds of defiant and free-spirited roaring, long whistling, and chanting. The Chinese character for noise is *zao* (噪), originally meaning birds or insects singing together on a tree. It is later used to describe the singing of cicadas as *chan zao* (蝉噪). *Chan* is a very special insect in traditional Chinese culture and is often used as a symbol of immortality. It is believed that cicadas never die and is a sacred insect that can connects to the spirits. In ancient funeral rituals, a jade cicada was placed in the mouth of the dead to suggest reincarnation. Also, the Chinese pronunciation of cicadas is *Chan*, which is the same as Chan Buddhism. Therefore, *chan zao* (noise of cicadas) could even be a desirable sound. In the book *Xiao Zhi,* cicada-whistling is one of the thirteen kinds of *xiao,* titled "Cicada on a Tall Willow."

> The "Cicada on a Tall Willow" was heard by a fine whistler of olden times, and written down while listening. Floating idly and rising high, it eddies and permeates. The beginning of the sound Chiieh is not clear; it is high but harsh; thin but stressed; it ceases suddenly at times, then resumes. It suggests flowering forests, with bamboos overhead. (Edwards 1957)

Xiao, evolving from shamanic incantation, to Daoist *qi*-cultivation, to singing art, is probably the earliest anti-language and interspecies sound making in Chinese history, the ancient Chinese version of twentieth-century Dadaist sound poetry. Other than making *xiao* a national immaterial heritage, we can continue its defiant, elusive, and free spirit by treading down the path of the twenty-first-century interspecies/cyborgian noise making. It is, as I would like to show, what artists and musicians like Xu Cheng, Wang Fan, Sheng Jie, and Lin Chi-Wei are seeking to do. Their inspirations come from that of *chimei wangliang*, mythical Daoism, or esoteric Buddhism.

Withdrawal

Withdrawal to the background, to the inner world, to eliminate oneself from the center, or to go the reverse direction to advance, is one way, though a negative one, to create an acoustic world of *huanghu*. It is what the Chinese expression *mixiang pangtong* (secret sounding leads to omniscience) suggests.

Instead of representing the soul summing ritual practiced by fishermen in Zhoushan, Xu Cheng creates a *soul summoning service*, through which every audience who is willing to make a sound to the device becomes a "summoner." After emitting a sound, one waits, listens carefully, expects, and imagines in a dark space with shimmering abstract visual effects and echo of sounds. The work incubates an immersive experience with weak audiovisual stimulant, which nonetheless triggers a great degree of inner expansiveness.

Wang Fan and the Sound of Awakening

Wang Fan is a master of creating sounds of inner expansiveness. In his own words, what he looks for in making music is the sound of awakening. For the underground music circle, Wang Fan is considered the first experimental musician for his creative ways of experimenting mixing sounds to produce mythical and otherworldly listening experience.

As an autodidactic musician, Wang Fan began to play music while he was still in the army service around the age of eighteen. During the 1980s, the Army in China still took care of the resettlement of retired army cadres; Wang Fan got a job as a factory electrician in the heavy industrial city of Lanzhou in Northwestern China. At the same time, he formed his own rock band and sang in local music clubs during night times. That was when Wang Fan met Yan Jun who was still a college student majored in Chinese Language and Literature in Northwest Normal University in Lanzhou. Although the economic reform in the 1990s has brought Western cultural products into China, compared to cities of Beijing, Shanghai, and Guangzhou, Lanzhou was relatively behind in getting access to musical and art products due to its geographical location and slow provincial economic development. Wang Fan knew little about Western avant-garde and experimental music. His musical influences were primarily Chinese popular music from the 1970s and 1980s, particularly singers like Deng Lijun from Taiwan and Zhang Qiang from Beijing. Michael Jackson was the only Western musician that he listened to extensively. His early music and live performance, a style mixing folk, rock, and punk music, had quickly drawn him a crowd of followers in Lanzhou. Around 1996 when he moved to Beijing, he began experimenting with new ways of making music. Reflecting on his musical transitions, he responded in our interview,

At a certain point, I started to feel that the kind of music and sound I really want was not like that [rock and punk music], and the way in which I knew the world was not as conveyed in those music. I believe there is a sound in this world that can wake people up. It wakes you up from inside. So, I began to work towards that direction with my music.

This mythical vision of sound was an influence from his childhood when his mother, a Tibetan Buddhist, helped raising a candidate boy of the reincarnation lama in their family. Without being a Buddhist himself, Wang Fan holds a strong esoteric and mythical way of thinking that manifests in his way of making and interpreting music. "The most important thing for a good musician is not his tool or technology, but his/her personal state, including the physical health, mental and spiritual state, and how he/she understands the world. Experimental music is a process of exploration of the self and the world through sound."

Dharma Crossing (2000) was a highly original music work that defined Wang Fan's later style, mixing samples of baby crying, uncanny laughing, folk singing by himself, rhythmic Chinese temple block percussion, and Buddhist chanting. In our interview, Wang Fan explained:

Dharma is the interior that contains everything and travels everywhere. The interior is the axis, and the axis is the only passage to enlightenment and transcendence. The axis is beyond good and evil. One should go outside of the world and go back inside and then go outside, and keep crossing. Only through Dharma's crossing, one gains gnosis.

In this music album, Wang Fan for the first time articulated his idea of "universal breathing (宙吸)," a term he coined to describe "the breathing state of the cosmos and breathing in the state of cosmos." Using the method of universal breathing, one could produce a kind of sub-bass sound, creating illusions for its listeners. Wang Fan wrote on the sleeve notes, "Universal breathing is the ultimate passage in which the cosmos and the living beings connect. In this passage, all the living things and their innermost beings awake simultaneously in the movement of revolving. At the same time, the innermost beings undergo a process of merging and splitting." This concept and method of universal breathing resonates with Indian Nãda-Yoga, a rarely known yoga practice outside of India, brought to my attention during my interview with Wang Fan. According to Guy Beck, a musician and a historian of religions, Nãda is "a loud sound, roaring, bellowing, crying; any sound or tone; (in the Yoga) the nasal sound represented by a semicircle and used as an abbreviation in mystical words" (1993, 81). Nãda comes from Nãda-Brahman, an Indian word for sacred sound, including both the concept of linguistic word, nonlinguistic, nonverbal sound as in music, and female sonic power of a god in Hinduism (Beck 1993). Nāda-Yoga gives central importance to meditation on sound, claiming it to be the simplest and most original method for attaining liberation (Mangalwadi 1977, 114).

After making *Dharma's Crossing*, Wang Fan bought Roland VS-880 digital studio workstation, a self-contained recording system with recorder, editor, digital mixer, and effects, with the prepaid money by the Chinese record label *Modern Sky*. With this new tool, Wang Fan made the album *Sound of Meditation within the Body*, and self-released through his own label *Adopin* and Yan Jun's label *Sub Jam* in 2001. The CD contains two pieces, each around thirty minutes long. The first track of *Sound of Meditation within the Body* begins with a low drone sound, followed by a slow and weak irregular beat, with the droning sound becoming louder and harsher and developing into increasingly engulfing sound swirls. Abrupt and quickly, the overwhelmingly swirling sound falls into fragments and particles. There is a vague sound of human murmuring and chanting. The first track, later collected in the label *Sub Rosa*'s collection *An Anthology of Chinese Experimental Music 1992-2008*, is in a way still calming. Sounds in the second track are noisier, drier and more intrusive, with occasional piercing sounds and consistent loud droning sound. After the climax of all sounds leashing out, vibrating, trembling, arising, all sounds stop without any hint. On the liner notes printed eight phrases: black hole, filtering into the core, pilgrimages each on their own, the original chanting in chaos, touching the dust-covered path, helpless predestination, an inward journey through birth, aging, suffering, death, and nirvana in the small hours of the morning. Without dividing the sound work into eight pieces corresponding to the eight titles, or assigning two titles to the two sound tracks, Wang Fan seems to suggest that sound reveals sensations and thinking in flow, languages are in nature fragmented, and there is no direct correspondence between the two.

The mystical Buddhist thinking provides the primary source for Wang Fan's intuitive music experimentation. All tools and methods, regardless of their cultural origins, are simply materials for him to continue creating and searching for the sound of awakening. However, Wang Fan's pursuit of awakening sound is constantly accompanied by a sense of failure. While a naturalist's search for waking up to the natural world suggests human-nature connection (recalling John Cage), Wang Fan's awakening sound relates to a sense of isolation from the outside by withdrawing deep to the interior world. Never satisfied with any music he has created, he keeps searching and experimenting. Wang Fan stopped making music after severely breaking his legs during a trip in Indian, jumping off a moving train to catch a thief. Only until recent, he began collaborating with contemporary artist Zhang Ding, experimenting with Zhang Ding's monumental speaker-installations (see more in Chapter 6).

If Wang Fan's sound making suggests an inward-listening inspired by Buddhist mysticism, the Taiwanese artist Lin Chi-Wei's artworks embody a sense of nihilistic mysticism influenced by more varieties of factors, which include Dada movement, industrial art, and Daoist ritual practices. Lin's advocate for non-modern ritual practices coming more out of a conscious intellectual criticism against modernism.

Lin Chi-Wei, Tape Music-Sound Intestines *and Cybernetic Music*

Lin Chi-Wei's performance piece *Tape Music-Sound Intestines* was originally created as a reaction and a challenge to computer-based electronic music. In 2004, Lin Chi-Wei was invited to perform at Taipei Sonar-International Festival of Art+Technology. When he found out that he was scheduled to perform between two computer music pioneers, Carl Stone and Francisco Lopez, he decided to give up using computer or electronic music instruments and conceived something more radical. He invited audience members to pronounce handwritten syllables on a long tape passed in front of them. The work turned the sounding crowd into a magnetic tape machine, generating a hesitant mixture of vocal noise that gradually became rhythmic chanting. The debut performance was not well accepted among the audience, but it somehow fit Lin Chi-Wei in multiple dimensions. *Tape Music*, as Lin reveals, was inspired by Dadaists' early sound poems, the French artist and poet Jean-Jacques Lebel's polyphonix. As a reaction to electronic and digital music, *Tape Music* returns to the form of analog, using the body as sound sources. One does not need to use consciousness to make sounds, but making sounds (together) generates a certain kind of consciousness that is communicative and self-healing. *Tape Music* becomes the signature art piece of Lin Chi-Wei; the tape itself was upgraded to become a finely made fabric on a spinning wheel and the work has been performed in various venues all over the world (Figure 5.2). The most recent one was given at the center Pompidou in Paris in 2019 at the exhibition *Cosmopolis #2 Repenser L'Humain* (Figure 5.3).

In the early 1990s, right after the Wild Lily students protest in March 1990 in Taipei, together with Liu Xingyi and Chen Jiaqiang (Steve), Lin Chi-Wei founded Taiwan's first noise group Zero and Sound Liberation Organization (ZSLO). Noise was a weapon for the group to intervene mainstream cultural control. The group's first public performance took place during International Community Radio Taipei (ICRT) Student Singing Show. Lin and Liu dressed up in hospital gowns and slippers. Steve the singer painted his face all white and wore funeral gowns. They performed with an untuned guitar, drum, and voice. When the host asked what

FIGURE 5.2 *Lin Chi-Wei,* Calligraphy *(graphic score tape), 2018. Courtesy of the artist.*

they wanted express, they responded, "I don't know. I don't know. I don't know."

The early 1990s, when he was in his early twenties, proves to be a crucial period of time for Lin. He describes his experience in an interview with independent curators Zhen Huihua and Luo Yuequan,[3]

> During that period of time, I have listened to a considerable number of lectures, watched a considerable number of performances, and participated in a variety of above-ground, underground, public and private activities. It was an exceptional era, full of energy, exciting and interesting. Everyone was questioning, everyone was involved in some movement, everyone was creating a scene. When you read the headline of the *Union New*s, you read about events by your friend. A situationist would come to the stage when a heterosexual person is giving a speech. A stupid performance would be subverted by the audience, or an academic speaker will deconstruct the speech by himself. It was an incredible time, almost like a fiction, but it made me feel like experiencing what happened in the 1960s Taiwan once only can be my imagination. At the same time, I met a whole group of free thinkers, activists, artists, and cultural workers.

[3]For more on Taiwan's sound culture see *Zao Yin Fan Tu: Zhan Hou Taiwan Sheng Xiang Wen Hua De Tan Suo (Altering Nativism: Sound Cultures in Post-War Taiwan)* (噪音翻土:战后台湾声响文化的探索), edited by He Donghong, Zheng Huihua, Luo Yuequan. Yuanzu Wenhua (Book Republic), 2015.

FIGURE 5.3 *Lin Chi-Wei,* Tape Music, *Performance at* Cosmopolis #2 Repenser L'Humain, *Centre Pompidou, Paris. 2019.*

> This wonderful group of friends opened my mind. Between the ages of 18 and 22, I grew in this state of inexplicable restlessness days and nights. This also prompted me to face the limitations of creation.[4]

During 1993 and 1995, Lin studied traditional folk culture in Taiwan, conducting fieldworks in religious temples and aboriginal cultures. Witnessing an entire Daoist shaman ritual over two days was an extraordinary experience for Lin. In his later artist practices, he continued his research in all kinds of shamanic and cult rituals from different cultures, which form the backbone of his critique of modernism. As Lin explained in the interview, for him, noise music functions not as a composition but as invocation and emancipation through forming a temporary collective sounding ritual.

In making *Tape Music-Sound Intestines*, Lin Chi-Wei finds a way to control the piece by designing the sounding system on the one hand while withdrawing from the work on the other, giving the audience the power to shape the process.

Curiously, despite the drastic difference in how their works sound, this operation reminds us of Brian Eno's cybernetic music system in which he coined the name "ambient music" in the sense that the musician sets up the system of the music and lets the dynamic of the system drive the piece on

---

[4]http://praxis.tw/archive/interview-with-lin.php

its own. The musician withdraws. Eno's interest in cybernetics can be traced back to his time as an art school student at Ipswich between 1964 and 1966. Particularly, the book by Standford Beer titled *Brain of the Firm* inspired him to take a cybernetic approach to music, creating a music system that unfolds in unpredicted ways (Pickering 2010). As the artist Peter Schmidt, a lecturer at Ipswich and a friend and collaborator of Eno, writes, "Systems, nevertheless, dispense neither with intuition nor mystery. Intuition is instrumental in the design of the system and mystery always remains in the final result" (Dayal 2009).

Inspired by cybernetic music, particularly that of the German musician Roland Kayn, Xu Cheng built a software module synthesizer. With this self-build system, Xu made a series of sound works, all titled *Cries of Wind*. *Cries of Wind* was first the name of a set of installations by the duo the Mustangs In Social Modulator (TMISM) exhibited at the independent art space Between Art Lab in Shanghai in 2016. TMISM is a group Xu Cheng formed with the visual artist and musician Huang Lei in 2011. The duo gave their debut performance during Nicolas Collins's workshop on hardware hacking in Shanghai (see more in Chapter 3). *Cries of Wind* was also the name of a sound recording released in 2019 through the music label *Playrec* run by Xu Cheng and Wang Changcun. Xu Cheng tells the story behind the recording as follows:

> I began to interest in Roland Kayn's music and his Cybernetic system on 2015. I tried to build a similar system in Analog Box—a software module synthesizer. Then I was experimenting the system on an abandoned man-made mountain. (a hill built by garbage dump in the city, once used as a shooting ground, then occupied by many scavengers, and now semi-closed.) The synthesized sound is played by gongs and cymbals hanging from trees. (Similar to the effect of Ondes-Martenot D3 resonator) It's amazing that the subtle electronic sound mixes with the noise of the city and the sound of natural wind.
>
> My group the Mustangs in Social Modulator (Xu Cheng/Huang Lei) held a solo exhibition in Shanghai Between Art Lab on 2016. We decided to make a better version of it. Huang Lei and I founded four huge scraps of abandoned boilers at the garbage station near the gallery. The scrap iron is used as new resonators. Each of our sound systems use two resonators around the space. After the opening ceremony, we decide to meet and record "cries of the wind" as a sound piece. Huang Lei did not appear that day for some reason, so I recorded three takes by myself with my own system.[5]

---

[5]https://playreclabel.bandcamp.com/album/cries-of-wind

Resonance, with the Impure and Strange

The selection of a garbage dump hill with a history of being a shooting ground and occupied by many scavengers, as well as abandoned boilers at the garbage station, suggests an aesthetic preference for the dark, the impure, the old, the deserted, the abandoned. This sense of impurity is prevalent in Xu Cheng's sound works, spanning from noise, electroacoustic, ambience, music concrete, to DIY sound objects and sound installations. Xu's music recording *Wild Fox Chants* (2008) is a free improvised piece with a handmade antique guitar Xu bought by chance. According to Xu, the guitar might be made from the period of the Republic of China (1919–1949). Before playing with it, he changed a few strings with thin springs and loosened up the rest. The performance style was inspired by the free improvising music of Derek Bailey and Keith Rowe, as well as Li Jianhong's album *Bird* (2007). The name "wild fox chants," as Xu Cheng explains, was inspired by the ancient Chinese, who named their *guqin* piece "wind chants" or "dragon chants." It felt appropriate to name music made using a broken guitar after a fox's call.

In the book *In Praise of Shadows*, the Japanese writer Junichiro Tanizaki describes the ancient Chinese value of impurity, "the sheen of antiquity," "the glow of grime" as a particular aesthetic taste (1977, 11). "In both Chinese and Japanese the words denoting this glow describe a polish that comes of being touched over and over again, a sheen produced by the oils that naturally permeate an object over long years of handling—which is to say grime. If indeed 'elegance is frigid,' it can as well be described as filthy." He confides, "living in these old houses among these old objects is some mysterious way a source of peace and repose" (11–12). Longing for the impure, hidden and mythical, paradoxically suggests the purity of human morality. This is a Daoist wisdom; the wise man always appears ugly and tardy. Wisdom in the dung. Qualities of being impure, shadowy, ugly and tardy dispel social relations but is considered the way to expand spirituality. Imbedded in these qualities is also reverence for mysterious forces. If modernization is a process of purification and normalization, the taste for impurity can be understood as anti-modern. Anti-modern is not primordial. It is simultaneously with, pre-, and post- the modern. Behind the praise for impurity is the wisdom of *huanghu*.

For the Beijing-based musician and artist Sheng Jie, this particular state of *huanghu* is the most essential in art-making. She describes the state as *mi* (迷), an almost spiritual state of extreme focus, a trance. Born into a renowned musical family, Sheng Jie studies piano and violin at a very young age. Never fully satisfied with classical music, in 2000, Shen Jie went to study art at Ecole Superieure Des Aat Decoratifs de Strasbourg in France, working with video, sound, and performance. Listening and watching become her two primary perceptual focuses to explore deep into notions of space and perception. The inspiration for her album *Oviparity* (2020) came from dream-yoga and Tibetan indigenous religion known as Bon. For Sheng Jie, sound is more about space than time. Listening is not a temporal experience, but a spatial one; it is "to walk through spaces of sound." Using an electric cello and effects of delay, reverb and RAT (an edgy, jagged distortion sound effect), in *Oviparity* Sheng Jie creates an acoustic cosmos of Bon, a world of only space derivations and transformations. Using only one instrument, cello, is an intentional choice. "I always feel that the cello is a kind of instrument that is full of sorrow and narration, like an aged intoning the past repeatedly and sadly alone," Shen Jie writes in the sleeve notes, "cello, which is particular but unitary for me, can express a kind of true emotion which is very 'clumsy,' because true emotions always seem to be clumsy by being direct and parched."

Oviparity's relation to Bon religion is not that of appropriation or quotation. They are structurally and conceptually resonant, in the sense that they share similar way of perceiving the world. Sheng Jie writes in our correspondence:

> Bon religion . . . describes the formation of the world as bulk space of passivity. This is very similar to the structure of music. Music is not linear although a piece of music can be marked in a linear timeline as waves. Music is a fermentation of scattering and derivative spatial bulks. This is why it is always difficult to accurately describe how we feel about a piece of music. The spaces created by music are distributed in different parts of the heart-soul. One's thought move through these spaces as if taking an adventure.

Sheng Jie's resonance with religious thoughts of Bon is both sensual and intellectual. The same can be said of Xu Cheng's work after 2013. The live performance of *Hhum* in New York in 2013 was a turning point for Xu Cheng. It was around the time when Xu became interested in Esoteric and Vajrayana Buddhism. Using the bassline from the American soul singer Melba Moore's song *Underlove*, sound sampled from the recording of a live performance of TMISM in 2012, post-processed through a self-remodeled Alesis drum machine, the sound of the piece reminded Xu in search for a Buddhist deity. He felt a connection between the dharmapala deity Rāgarāja and the direction in which the piece was going. *Hhum* is one of the variations of the basic syllable *ong*. The use of the bassline of *Underlove* coincides with one of the symbolic meanings of Rāgarāja. The original use of waterphone in TMISM's live performance provides a metaphor for water in the piece. The end of the piece is a long droning sound for about eight minutes, meant to simulate the state of mediation. The piece *Hhum* is almost an acoustic version of Rāgarāja.

Such mythical resonance was reenacted in another work by Xu Cheng, a composition titled *Counterpoint* written for the art event *Crazy Music* in 2018, organized by Jun-Y Chao for the American composer and Fluxus artist Philip Corner when he was invited to Shanghai. Following Fluxus' tradition, every participant Chinese musician prepared action scores to perform at the event. The score for *Counterpoint* is as follow,

> Performer: two performers with healthy hearing and of similar height
> Instrument: use sirenphone made by the composer, or use any
>   instrument easy to carry around during performance. A metronome
>   can be used if needed, and the rhythm is fixed at 110BPM.
> Inside a symmetrical room. The two performers close their eyes
>   throughout the performance and stand back to back in the center
>   of the room. Both started playing musical instruments at the same
>   time, and walked straight ahead to the edge of the room. Judge
>   the position of the other party through hearing and follow it with
>   mirror-symmetrical movement. Follow each other and imitate each
>   other's performance, changes of timbre and subtle movements. When
>   the two performers come into physical contact again in the space,
>   they immediately stop playing. Playing time is unlimited.

Counterpoint in Western music composition follows the symmetrical principle that is mathematical. While it may appear the same, Xu Cheng's composition of counterpoint abides by the rule of resonance that is sentient, cosmic and moral. Such resonance with things, events, moments, humans and nonhumans, can be understood through a classical aesthetic category in Chinese art, *wu gan* (resonance with things), underlaid by the ancient philosophical principle of resonance between human and heaven tracing back to *Yijing (the Book of Change)*, known as *tianren ganying(天人感应)*. *Wu gan* is an essential principle through which music is interpreted and used. For example, *Yue Ji* (The Record of Music) opens with the principle of *wu gan*:

> All notes arise from the heart of humans, and humans' hearts are affected by external things. Human hearts are touched and hence moved when affected and hence give shape to sounds. Sounds resonate with each other and hence give birth to change; change in sound forms pattern and pattern is called note. Compose notes and accompany them with martial dance using shields and axes and with literati dance using feathers and pennants, this is called music."[6]

---

[6]凡音之起，由人心生也。人心之动，物使之然也。感于物而动，故形于声。声相应，故生变；变成方，谓之音；比音而乐之，及干戚羽旄，谓之乐。《乐记》

FIGURE 5.4 *Xu Cheng,* Counterpoint, *Performers Zhao Shinuan (aka Xiao Bai Neng) (left), Li Huihui (right). 2018. Photo by author.*

Relations develop from external things to human hearts to sounds and eventually to music; they all follow the principle of resonance. The word things (物) in *Yue Ji* in particular and in *wu gan* is general, refer to not only objects, but phenomenon, humans, events and even the imaginary. *Wugan* was developed into a mature aesthetic category during the six dynasties period (220–589), exemplified in the literary scholar Liu Xie's (ca. 465–521) classical work during the fifth century, *The Literary Mind and the Carving of Dragons*, in which Liu Xie introduced the idea of *mixiang pangtong*, which means the writer does not hold accuracy and directness as the creation principle and instead the writer insinuates continuously just like a mythical sounding. For Sheng Jie, this mythical sounding is *Oviparity*, for Xu Cheng, *Hhum*, for Wang Fan, *Sound of Meditation within the Body*, for Lin Chi-Wei, the sound of embodied noise.

Conclusion

Neither the acoustic cultural inheritors nor the mythical musicians have anything to do with the reality of the life of practicing Chinese shamans. Their praise of the sound of the shamanistic suggests two tendencies, which can be related back to the ancient time when ancient shaman ritual practices were rationalized, moralized, or mystified.

The shamanistic works as a productive force in art and music making, either as a cultural gene, a treasured museum of antiquity to enhance and solidify individual or nation-state identity, or as a source of acquiring alternative visions, to perceive, capture and create a world of specter that helps to cross external and internal boundaries, to enter a different sphere of life world of *huanghu*. The difference can be understood in Wang Guowei's discussion on two notions of veiled (*ge*, 隔) and unveiled (*buge*, 不隔). For Wang Guowei, as Wang Keping explains, "The veiled poetic state is weak in scenic description and leads us to approach some poems as if we were viewing flowers through a mist" (2002). Wang Guowei recommends unveiled poetry, that is, using words that directly describe real feelings and scenes. Musicians like Tan Dun is applying the method of unveiling, of communication, to map the harmonious past to make today richer and stronger. While following the notion of *Huangpu*, musicians and artists like Wang Fan, Xu Cheng, Sheng Jie, and Lin Chi-Wei resort to the method of veiling, withdrawing, to map the dissonant past to make what is claimed as reality blurring, suspicious, and porous. As Sheng Jie so nicely reflected in our correspondence, what makes art more interesting is exactly the strange, the unknown, and the magical.

6

Ubiquitous Control

From Cosmic Bell, Loudspeakers to Immanent Humming

Humming, that accompanies movements of vocal cords, bodies, machines, winds, waves, and many more unknowable flows of qi, have connected the cosmic, the military, the economic, the aesthetic, and the urban mundane. Like air, sunlight or moonlight, humming passes through us, constituting the very condition of our sensual experience, without drawing much attention. The ambient only becomes a focus of attention, a conscious sensual experience, when it lacks a sudden cutoff of electricity, virus-free air, or a sudden silence in an anechoic room.

Underneath the seemingly innocent and easy-to-be-romanticized humming sound, lurks power and violence. The ancient Chinese qi-cosmology has always been attentive to diffusive forms of violence. As recorded in *The Art of War* (*Sunzi Bing Fa*) (fifth century BC), the shaman-diviner in ancient China listened to the humming of his tubes to decipher the collective qi of the enemy army to further predict the intensity of their fighting power. Unfortunately, while shamanic techniques were largely abandoned as pseudoscience in the process of modernization, the wisdom behind those were forgotten too. Now we have entered a new epoch that is largely shaped by the ambient—ambient advertising, ambient music, ambient art, ambient interface, ambient warfare, ambient subjectivation, and ambient humanities (McCullough 2013; Mowitt 2015; Prendergast 2000; Roquet 2016). It becomes urgent to regain an ambient literacy. Sound, as produced by moving-qi and a manifestation of qi, proves to be an appropriate medium to turn to.

Steve Goodman, also known as DJ Kode9, in his book *Sonic Warfare* reminds, "Every nexus of sonic experience is immersed in a wider field of power" (2010, 190). From the humming drones issuing from loudspeakers and cameras swirling above residential communities during the coronavirus outbreak in China, to the anonymous masked woman sitting on her Wuhan apartment balcony striking a homemade gong for help, to the whistling of volunteers memorializing the death of the whistleblower doctor Li Wenliang, to the unanimous collective singing heard from windows of apartment buildings in Wuhan during the quarantine period, to the continuous humming of refrigerators, air conditioners, and purifiers inside an apartment powered through the national electric grid, to the low rumbling sound of seismic and microseismic activities—all these together indicate the interlacing and contradictory nexus of power weaving together the cosmic, the technical, the bureaucratic, the civic, the disempowered, and the subversive.

The use of drones in tracking individual routines become apparent in China during the 2020 coronavirus public health crisis. The immediate application and emergence of the drone on a national scale also reminded many of us once again of the potential violence of an increasingly invisible yet ubiquitous surveillance system—the visual-based project "The Skynet" and the quiet construction of a national voiceprints database through voice recognition technology—shadowing every individual. Yet, the operation of such surveillance is global. "The piezobeeps of ubiquitous surveillance," as Holger Schulz calls it, "every Beep represents large sets of data gathered. Beep! Your existence being tracked and incorporated into this experialist nanopolitics" (166).

As a complimentary notion to macro- and micro-politics, nanopolitics offers a revelatory analytic to understand the politicizing of ambience, that is, of the diffusive, immersive, and peripherally present. As Schulz describes it, nanopolitics is "neither present in the foreground nor intensely discussed. They enter everyday lives by way of all the micro-decisions one makes, by way of sensory preferences and routines, by way of inclinations and aversions you and I might tend to follow" (164). The notion of nanopolitics, popularized by a London-based art group that calls itself "The Nanopolitics group," founded in 2010, specifies a politics through and with the body. "With nanopolitics, we talk about how what occurs at the level of the group, the world, the institution or the social comes to exist under our skin, in our guts, through our voice, in our touch and in the way we feel" (2012). The gaseous quality of sound makes it an immediate and convenient subject of nanopolitics. Brandon LaBelle poses, "If sound art is essentially a careful configuration of molecules, a sculpting of the air, a base for aesthetical listening, can we follow it as a proposition for a nanopolitics, that is, a platform for challenging precisely what is always already at work, those discourses, technologies, and social systems that impress themselves upon, within, and around my body?" (2015, 326).

It is in such techno-political context, sound works of Zhang Peili (1957–), Zhang Ding (1980–), and Liu Chuang (1979–) become particularly pertinent. Their sound works, as I would like to argue, seek to detect, repurpose, exaggerate, and speculate on the nanopolitics of the state and capitalist control manifested through its increasingly distributed monumentality[1]. This nonetheless endows an anti-monumental quality to their art works. Specifically, in this last chapter, my goal is to investigate how the three artists appropriate acoustic tools into the stream of nanopolitics, how they take issue with the increasingly cloud-like, atmospheric, and ubiquitous form of control in everyday life, and how they find creative ways to negotiate with the sensology (the world market of feelings, ready-felt as Mario Perniola defines), instead of ideology, of old and new forms of governance.

Zhang Peili and Anti-Monumentality of Sound

Monumentality is normally used as an aesthetic quality of a visual object related to an authoritative power and to a collective communal sense of existence. Anti-monumentality, literally speaking, describes the aesthetic quality of arts that topples the authoritative power of official monuments, while also evoking a communal experience to some extent. An oft-cited example of anti-monumental art is the "Wrapped Reichstag" (Berlin, 1971–1995), in which the artists Christo and Jeanne Claude wrapped the German Parliament building in Berlin with more than a million square feet of fabric. That 1995 wrapping project inspired the German cultural historian Andreas Huyssen to ask, "Why is it that our prevailing notion of monumentality is so one-dimensional and itself immovably monumental that such questions usually do not even emerge?" (2003, 38) For Huyssen, the wrapping project produced a public memory of "celebrating a symbol of German democracy in all its fragility and transitoriness. The wrapping Reichstag thus became a monument to democratic culture instead of demonstration of state power" (36).

Monumentality is not just a quality limited to colossal architecture or grandiose sculptures of individual heroes, or grand symphonies by composers like Ludwig van Beethoven or Wilhelm Richard Wagner (Rheding 2017). Offering varied examples from traditional Chinese art history, the Chinese art historian Wu Hung has brought to scholarly attention cultural differences about what might be considered important and powerful. The portable but usually hidden ritual vessels known as *liqi* (ritual paraphernalia) used in ancient Chinese ritual art, the public announcement of time through bell

---

[1] Thanks to Beth M. Semel for "distributed monumentality."

and drum towers before the clock was introduced to China, the monthly ritualistic performance by the emperor to complete the cosmic meaning of the ancient Chinese architecture *Ming Tang* (Bright Hall)—all can be identified as what Wu Hung calls "monumentality without monument" (1995, 2003).

While examining contemporary art practices, the art historian Mechtild Widrich (2014) further proposes performative art as anti-monumental, and theorizes what she calls performative monuments. Performative monuments combine political needs with aesthetic solutions. Exemplars are Thomas Hirschhorn's public art project *Bataille Monument* (2002), VALIE EXPORT's performance arts *ActionPants: Genital Panic* (1969) and *Body Configuration* (1982), Marina Abramovic's performance art *Seven Easy Pieces* (2005), Richard Serra's minimalist installation *Titled Arc* (1989), Joseph Beuys' installation *Tram Stop: Monument for the Future* (1976). As Widrich argues, instead of being "authoritatively installed from above" and "being responsive to the needs of the government," such anti-monumental monuments emerge "from below" and respond to the needs of communities. Instead of being immobile, enduring, and grand, performative monuments can be temporary, precarious, small, and ephemeral (2014).

Andrea Huyssen's discussion of anti-monumentality, Wu Hung's notion of monumentality without a monument, and Mechtild Widrich's proposal of performative monuments, together offer a path toward a nuanced understanding of the anti-monumentality of Zhang Peili's sound art installation works.

Zhang Peili was born in 1957 in Hangzhou. He graduated from the Zhejiang Academy of Fine Arts (renamed China Academy of Art in 1993) in 1984 as an oil painter and was actively involved in organizing 1985's New Space Exhibition and in founding the art group together with Geng Jianyi, Wang Qiang, and Song Ling, known as the Pond Society (*Chi She*) in 1986. His first widely known work was a series of paintings of surgical gloves titled *X?* (1986–1987), which exhibited his desire to go beyond narrative painting (Krischer, 2019). Soon he turned to exploring new media of art making, producing the very first video art work in mainland China. While Zhang Peili's work has been largely explored and discussed in the realm of visual arts, in the oeuvre of his art making, sound has been used both as a medium and a strategy from the very beginning of his new media art experiments from the late 1980s. Aligned with the overall recognized aesthetics of Zhang Peili's works that are at the same time personal, political, commentary, reflective, trivial, and subversive, Zhang's sound works present a strong anti-monumental motivation, through citing and exaggerating a particular honed humming that accompanies the harmonious voice of the sovereign state, to enable the audience to become aware of the acoustic ambience haunted by the specter of total administration.

Techniques of Voice: The Monumentality of Broadcasting Tone

What does the nation-state sound like? For Chinese citizens born before the 1990s, it might be the particular tone of voice that characterized television speech, at a time when TV was still the predominant means of household media. That sound was a vocal quality—the clean, firm, and standard Chinese broadcasting tone. In China, this is known as *boyin qiang*, the broadcasting tone of voice. Zhang Peili continuously takes issue with this sound in his work. This particular politically and culturally mediated tone of voice appeared quite early in Zhang's work as a reproduced vocal quality and has also been extensively used through his more recent sound installations.

In his single channel nine-minute thirty-five-second video art piece, *Water: Standard Dictionary Version* (1991) (Figure 6.1), Zhang invited Xing Zhibing to read the word "water" in the Chinese dictionary, *Ci Hai*. Xing Zhibing's broadcasting tone of voice was considered solemn, steady, and accurate, and she has worked as the media voice/image representative of Chinese government on CCTV for over twenty-eight years (1981–2009). However, as a non-semantic part of everyday news reports, her tone of voice itself seldom drew attention. Its regularities and power only become consciously audible when news was replaced by a completely arbitrary message, in this case, her reading aloud a character in the dictionary. We

FIGURE 6.1 *Zhang Peili,* Water: Standard Dictionary Version, *video, 1991. Courtesy of the artist and SPURS Gallery.*

become aware of her voice *as a voice*, as it offers itself in citation. This strategy of dis-linkage is what Paul de Man calls "a radical estrangement between the meaning and the performance of any text" (1979, 298); it is also what Andrew Parker and Eve Sedgwick highlight from reading de Man, the "'aberrant' relation to its own reference—the torsion, the mutual perversion, as one might say, of reference and performativity" (1995, 3).

"Culture controls the voice, contours its performative capacities, and leaves deep imprints on its character—it mediates the voice, in terms of its accent, intonation, timbre, cadence, and rhythm" (Neumark, xviii). The broadcasting tone of voice delivers a *sensology* of the nation-state through normalized and standardized vocalization, which, according to *China Broadcasting* textbook, may be characterized by six qualities: normative (*gui fan xing*), solemn (*zhuang zhong xing*), agitational (*gu dong xing*), modern (*shi dai gan*), measured (*fen cun gan*), and cordial (*qin qie gan*). These six qualities define the monumentality of this broadcasting tone of voice that performs the sovereign power of the nation-state and constitutes the acoustic milieu of the collective memory of a particular Zeitgeist in Chinese history. Zhang Peili's sound art works remind us of how the performative force of the power-saturated voice shapes how we may remember an era—through its distributed, ubiquitous ambient sound, a dispersed anti-monumental monumentality.

In *Unsuitable Place to Stay* (2017), installed in an art space known as the Bunker—a 1941 building originally constructed to house the offices of the Northern China Area Army commander-in-chief, Yasuji Okamura, during the second Sino-Japanese war—this broadcasting voice is heard again. Once audience members enter the main door of the Bunker leading to an underground space, the door automatically locks itself behind them for five minutes. To lock the audience up was an unrealized idea of Zhang Peili when he created his very first video work, a three-hour long documentary, *30×30* (1988). For *30×30*, His plan was to lock viewers inside the exhibition room until they finished watching the video. It never actualized because the viewers constantly asked him to fast-forward the video. This idea was finally implemented as a crucial part of the work *Unsuitable Place to Stay*. Once locked up inside, one hears a female broadcasting voice, counting down the remaining time,

> You have five minutes . . . you have three minutes and thirty seconds . . . you have two minutes and 45 seconds . . . three . . . two . . . one. Your time is up, please leave immediately.

There are altogether six rooms in a series connection. On the ceiling of each room is installed a microwave induction-controlled vintage tungsten incandescent bulb. The movement of an audience activates the bulb; if one stays still for a few seconds, the light will turn off. Sound is programmed so that the voice appears intermittently nearby and distant. When it comes to count down to ten, all speakers play together and the voice reaches its ultimate volume. The work seems to be a fractal piece of the larger social political system in which everyone lives. Control is omnipresent and no one gets to escape. Ironically, during the time of the exhibition of this work, the city of Beijing launched its campaign to evict migrant workers referred to as "low-end population" from the city on a few days of notice.

The affective power of this piece partly derives from the space of its exhibition *The Bunker*. As Zhang Peili commented during an interview, "The space is strong enough; the sound work is just to make its strength more visible." The larger architectural context for the Bunker was the presidential palace (renovated from the prince palace in Qing Dynasty) of the Chinese warlord and politician Duan Qiriu when he became the acting chief executive (1924–1926) of the Republic of China established on January 1, 1912, after the Xinhai Revolution in 1911, overthrowing the last imperial dynasty— Qing dynasty—in China. After 1949, the place was used as the campus site for Renming University of China. Now it is officially registered as the site of Duan Qi Rui's Government, located at Zhang Zizhong road #3. The political and military history of the architecture adds a special sensation and a strong personality to the art space. In 2017, Beijing-based curator Peng Xiaoyang rented from Renming University of China the underground space and turned it to a nonprofit art space named the Bunker. The Bunker was run by an academic curatorial committee of Qin Siyuan, Dong Bingfeng, and Li Feng. The space blocks out network signal and cellphone signals and remains completely dark with no natural lights coming in. In May 2020, the Bunker Art space announced its closing because its landlord Renming University of China decided to turn the whole place to a patriotic education base. Since its opening, the Bunker has operated as an incubator for sound works. So far, it has exhibited sound works including Jiang Zhuyun's installation *Out of Void* (2017), Guo Xi's narrative-based sound installation *The Neighbors Upstairs* (2017), Zhang Ding's installation *Broad Daylight* (2018), and Yan Jun's *Time Section* (2018).

The familiar official broadcasting tone of voice is also used in Zhang's recent sound work *Sound Mattress* (2018) (Figure 6.2). This time the voice reports names of three selected groups: delegates to the National People's Congress, the wanted, and missing children. Speakers hidden inside of the mattresses get activated when one lies down on the mattress. Zhang explains in an interview:

> The three groups of people are typical. Names by themselves could not touch one's nerve, but the identities of the three groups make people sensitive. For me, they represent three social groups that most easily draw people's attention and provoke imaginations. Delegates to the National People's Congress and the wanted are two opposing power forces.

FIGURE 6.2 *Zhang Peili,* Sound Mattress, *Boers Li Gallery, Beijing, 2018. Courtesy of the artist and SPURS Gallery.*

However, they sometimes convert into each other. Missing children on the other hand are still not yet completely social individuals. They need to be protected by adults. Identities and the social structure from which identities develop have the tendency to be mutually transformative. I believe, under different circumstances and time periods, these identities can turn into its very opposite. Groups that seem to be irrelevant to each other may have very complicated relations in actual lives. Therefore, they are often paradoxical, especially when juxtaposed in a normal setting. I hope to communicate this kind of discomfort and confusion through the neutral, solemn and systematic broadcasting voice. The quilt and pillow that were hanging on the wall, attached with strong nails, also gave people this sense of uneasiness.[2]

What Zhang did not mention in the interview is the particular body posture the work demands from its audience, that is, to lie down. Lying down is hardly a comfortable gesture in an exhibition opening in public galleries in China. The mechanism of the work has effortlessly turned a potentially passive and indifferent spectator to an active participant, vulnerable at the same time, in a sound event, adding more layers to the uneasiness the work sets out to evoke.

---

[2]https://mp.weixin.qq.com/s/O6UfqXv7Hp9eQDlyOqmS1Q

From Repetition to Citation

Zhang Peili's sound works present the evolution of the state's voice, from the time of the revolution's enthusiastic voice to the sexless solemn voice of the iron curtain period, and to younger and creative voices. Before Zhang turned his attention to speech, repetition had already been a strategy he had used in earlier artworks.

For example, in his debut video work *30×30* (1988), he repeatedly smashed a mirror of dimension 30×30 cm into pieces and then repaired it by gluing fragments back together. Later, he repeatedly washed a live chicken with soap and water in *Document on "Hygiene" No.3* (1991). In 1993, Zhang Peili made a set of twenty-five silver gelatin prints titled *Continuous Reproduction*. He took a photo of a propaganda image of a peasant girl printed in *China's Newspaper* in the 1970s. He developed the photo and then took a photo of it again. The process was repeated twenty-five times until the photo became grainy enough to show an abstract effect. Using the same technical strategy, Zhang created the video installation *Focal Distance* in 1996. The original video documentation of the flow of traffic at a typical intersection of fifteen minutes was played on a video monitor, which was recorded by the artist and displayed on the second video monitor. The second monitor was then recorded showing the recorded video of the first and the result was displaced on the third monitor. There were all together eight monitors placed in a straight line showing videos with an escalating blurring effect. The video image eventually become abstract and painterly. The sound also grew abstract. In 2008, Zhang applied the same method to a piece of popular English-Chinese translation software. He used the software to translate a few Chinese sayings into English and put the English translation back into the software to get a Chinese translation. He repeated the operation until the meaning of the original Chinese saying got lost. The result of those translations was put in sequence and projected onto a screen.

From camera, to video recorder, to translation software, Zhang challenges the uses of new media tools that are made to store and deliver messages (sometimes these messages are claimed as realities or even truth).

Looping the content documented on a medium back into itself is one way to examine the medium and question the ways it can be manipulated. After 2000, Zhang began to use old films as the material for his work. He was particularly interested in feature films made between 1950 and 1970s in China. In 1942, Mao Zedong (Chairman Mao) made his speech at the Yan'an Forum on Literature and Art and called for making art for the sake of people. To answer to the call of Mao, feature films, usually in the form of celebrative comedy, were made as propaganda pieces for the Party to educate the masses. In these films, one sees all positive characters without villains. The main character was often a model of a good man or woman, presenting happiness and positivity, manifesting the socialist/communist utopian of serving the people.

In *Last Words (2003)*, Zhang selected scenes of the final moments and last words of dying heroes depicted in films made between 1950s and 1970s and edited the clips into a single flow. Climax after climax of last words of dying heroes creates a dramatic and tiring aesthetic experience. In *Happiness*(2006) (Figure 6.3), a single scene of a crowd frenetically applauding a public speaker was cut out from a didactic moral film. Through editing both the audio and video tracks, it becomes clear that the crowd, overcome with emotion, is not actually responding to the words of the speaker but rather sinks into a mindless frenzy. The collage of all-positive and happy moments exposes the absurdity of the socialist sensology during the cultural revolutionary time.

Besides repetition, the artistic strategy applied in this series of work can be understood through the notion of the performativity of citation, a notion Derrida developed out of J.L Austin's speech-act theory. For J.L Austin, voice needs to be recognized as a performative action of words. In his canonical work in performance studies, *How to Do Things With Words*, he writes,

> The term "performative" will be used in a variety of cognate ways and constructions much as the term "imperative" is. The name is derived, of course, from "perform," the usual verb with the noun "action": it indicates that the issuing of the utterance is the performing of an action— it is not normally thought of as just saying something. (1962, 6)

In developing his theory of the speech-act, however, Austin excludes the performative utterance. He considers that "a performative utterance will,

FIGURE 6.3 *Zhang Peili,* Happiness, *Single Channel video, 2006. Courtesy of the artist and SPURS Gallery.*

for example, be in a peculiar way hollow or void if said by an actor on the stage, or if introduced in a poem, or spoken in soliloquy" (1962, 22). Jacques Derrida, instead, argues that performative utterances on stage and ordinary speech-act performance share a generalized iterability (Parker and Segdwick 1995, 4; Derrida 1988). For Derrida, the iterability (duplicity or citationality) of any spoken or written mark is the very reason that a mark can function at all. Therefore, a performative utterance can be successful with or without the constraints of any context and authorial intention. Derrida developed the notion of "citational grafting" to further his point, confirming that signs or marks can be appropriated and relocated in unforeseen contexts and cited in unexpected ways, to suggest the transgressivity in performative utterances used outside of its context. As he put emphatically, "It is that (normal/abnormal) without which a mark could not even have a function called 'normal.' What would a mark be that could not be cited? Or one whose origins would not get lost along the way?" (Derrida 1988)

Citation therefore can be a subversive performative act. *last words* and *happiness* do exactly this: performing what is being said; performing the saying of it. Cultural-specific speeches (ways of speaking) are cited, grafted onto other contexts, revealing the citationality, intrinsically performative nature, and the deconstructible identity of the propaganda machine of the Party-state.

Control as an Art Regime

Another theme that threads through Zhang's works is control. In *Mute (2008)*, *The Rolling Box (2018)*, *Access Control System (2018)*, Zhang creates installation-based cybernetic art that evokes questions of social control or media control. With these works, the artist seems to be playing the role of a doctor who diagnoses the sickness or problem of the social system. This reveals Zhang's idea of the kind of relation art should establish with its audience. Instead of entertaining the public or to be consumed, art should introduce a regime to reduce the numbness and schadenfreude of the public crowd. For Zhang, this regime is control. Zhang lists four conditions for a control regime (Huang and Wang, 2008, 372),

1. To remove any ornamental, entertaining, dramatic, or journalistic characters.
2. To set a rigorous and neutral rule to guide experience.
3. To make sure all participation are voluntary.
4. To prevent any art-irrelevant power or factor from affecting the artwork.

Works created under these conditions cannot be collected.

FIGURE 6.4 *Zhang Peili*, Collision of Harmonies, *Installation, Boers Li Gallery, Beijing, 2014. Courtesy of the artist and SPURS Gallery.*

Feedback, an important concept in cybernetics, also an important sound material often used in electronic and experimental music, is also an acoustic strategy often used by Zhang. In *Collision of Harmonies* (2014) (Figure 6.4), two loudspeakers are installed on the pulley track on the high ceiling, facing each other. On top of each loudspeaker is installed a shotgun microphone. Two loudspeakers move slowly toward each other. While they are further apart, one hears women (from one side) and men (from the other side) singing in bel-canto. As the two speakers move closer, a piercing feedback noise is generated and becomes an increasingly unbearable high-frequency droning sound. Two approaching speakers stop moving when fluorescent tubes piled up underneath all lighten up. Piercing noise and blinding lights fill up the room and last for about twenty seconds. Then the two speakers slowly move apart; the high-frequency feedback noise gradually returns to singing voices. Without using any words this time, Zhang uses the mechanism of audio feedback to teach a lesson about harmony. Harmony, as one of the state ideologies and an essential moral value in Confucianism, is in fact in continuity with noise and heralds violence/noise that is inherent to the harmony machine. This work still fits into Zhang's persistent interest in putting state ideology in question, making the all-too-familiar (i.e., slogans and propaganda ideologies) unfamiliar, making the state ambience simultaneously absurd, monstrous, violent, and weak, through a series of artistic operations.

A question remains: why singing bel-canto, a seemingly foreign material, is quite different from Zhang's use of a familiar broadcasting voice? Bel-canto is not a popular form in contemporary Chinese mass culture, but it has an interesting relation with official Chinese culture before the 1980s. Bel-canto was introduced to China after the May Fourth movement in 1919, also known as the New Culture movement, or the Chinese renaissance. However, Chinese language makes it very difficult to articulate in the bass register when singing bel-canto. To accommodate Mao's call for making arts for the sake of people, Chinese singers combined techniques in ethnic singing and Chinese operas with bel-canto to develop a unique singing category, known as Chinese national vocal art, popularized as a singing art throughout China. Using bel-canto singing further contextualizes the work in a particular historical period, evoking even more complex acoustic experience for certain kinds of audiences.

The mechanism of feedback is used again in *A Standard, Uplifting, and Distinctive Circle Along with its Sound System* (2015). Zhang collected eight domestically made radio sets between 1970s and 1980s, and placed them in a circle. In the middle of the circle, he placed a motor-driven shotgun microphone, which was connected to two horn speakers installed on the wall behind. The microphone spun at a slow speed and when it was directed toward a specific radio, it played out the content of that radio through the two horn speakers. Otherwise, it is mixed radio sounds serving as the background noise.

As the primary medium for distributing the central government's messages, radio played a crucial part in the state's propaganda regime from the early 1940s to the 1990s. It also provided opportunities for rebellion through channels of enemy radio. An updated version of *A Standard, Uplifting, and Distinctive Circle Along with its Sound System* is *Sound Installation with Transistor Radio and Trumpet Speaker* (2019) (Figure 6.5), a work made for the opening exhibition of the West Bund Oil Tank Art Center in Shanghai. Forty-five recycled radio sets were set up on forty-five display stands arranged in a spiral circle, playing jingles of forty-five radio programs of different countries and regions. These jingles were programmed to play at intervals of solo and orchestra, through eight trumpet speakers hanging around the circle.

The anti-monumentality of Zhang Peili's sound installation arts gain its subversive power through citing, looping, and grafting of the official tone of voice that resonates among generations born before the new millennium. For those who do not share the same collective memory, the critical force of the work can still be vividly felt through the materiality and mechanism of the sound work itself, intriguing different interpretations drawing from one's own life experience.

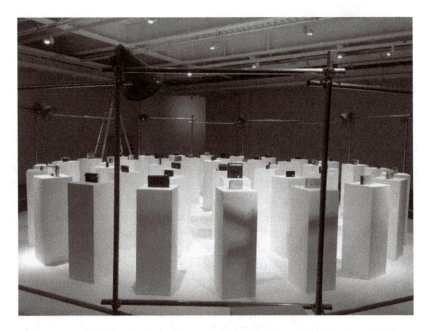

FIGURE 6.5 *Zhang Peili,* Sound Installation with Transistor Radio and Trumpet Speaker, *installation, West Bund Oil Tank Art Center, 2019. Courtesy of the artist and SPURS Gallery.*

Zhang Ding and the Military-Entertainment-Art Complex

Drawing from the German media theorist Friedrich Kittler's tracing of media's origin to military development, Steve Goodman in *Sonic Warfare: Sound, Affect, and the Ecology of Fear* (2012) presents a history of weaponized sound technology. Goodman writes, "If war saturates modern societies right down to the microphysical fabric, then it does so using an array of distributed processes of control, automation, and a both neurophysical and affective mobilization: the military-entertainment complex as a boot camp therefore, optimizing human reaction speeds, fabricating new reflexes for a postcybernetic condition. Media technologies discipline, mutate, and preempt the affective sensorium. Entertainment itself becomes part of the training" (34).

Goodman's use of the term "military-entertainment complex" unveils an unsettling vision of the military condition of modernity and the repurposing of military technology in the arts and culture. Inspired by Goodman's writing in *Sonic Warfare*, the Hong Kong artist Samson Young carried out a project titled *For Whom the Bell Tolls: A Journey into the Sonic History of*

Conflict (2015), taking a two-month field trip to gather knowledge of bells over six continents. The result is a rich archive of bell recordings, bell sound drawings, and sound composition. While Young's artistic response to the military-entertainment complex is analytical, the anti-war and anti-violence Mexican artist Pedro Reyes's method is more tactical. In *Palas Por Pistolas* (2008), Reyes collected 1,527 guns from donors and melted them down to shovels to plant 1,527 trees. In *Disarm* (2012), Reyes melted donated weapons into musical instruments and invited audience to perform music with them. Zhang Ding's sound works can also be seen as a response to the military-entertainment complex. But different from Young's analytical and archivist approach, neither working as an artist-magician, Zhang Ding adds positive feedback to the complex, resonating with what Kittler suggests: "Play to the powers that be their own melody" (1999, 110).

Zhang Ding studied oil painting at the Northwest Minority University in Lanzhou (1998–2003) before going to Hangzhou to study under Zhang Peili and Geng Jianyi in 2003, when they launched the new media art pilot program (see Chapter 2). After making his first round of sound installation works, *N Kilometers towards the West* (2006) and *Tool No.1* (2007), Zhang Ding in 2012 created another sound installation *Control Club*, the

FIGURE 6.6 *Zhang Ding,* Boxing 1&2, 2007, *Video Installation. Courtesy of Zhang Ding Studio.*

name of which was later used for his art label. The sound installation
Control Club was then used to set up the performance stage in shows
Zhang Ding and his team curated. The concept of installation-turned-
show is essentially different from oft-seen interactive sound installations
that can be turned into instruments to be played by either the artist or
audience, such as the Chinese-French artist Chen Zhen's *Jue Chang* Series,
Taiwan artist Wang Chung-kun's *Sound of Bottles* (2007/2008) (see more
in Chapter 2).

Zhang Ding's solo exhibition *Tools* at ShanghART gallery in Shanghai in
2007 was considered a turning point in his art career. In Zhang Ding's words,
he began to find his way toward apprehending and responding to the world
after *Tools. Tools* consists of three works, *Tool No.1, Tools-2,* and *Boxing
No.1&2* (Figure 6.6). *Boxing No.1&2* is a two-channel three-minute video
installation, showing Zhang Ding's bare fist punching three cacti with sharp
spiky thorns. *Tools-2* consists of two mixed-media installations (Figure 6.7).

FIGURE 6.7 *Zhang Ding,* Tools-2, 2007, *Interactive Installation. Courtesy of
Zhang Ding Studio.*

One is a half-cut crate filled with cacti, intersecting with long sharp steel knives. The other is a kinetic system with a cactus plant suspended through steel wire in the middle of a circle of twelve steel tubes. On top of each tube is a watering can, filled with water. The weight of the cactus plant pulls the watering can to water itself. The heavier the plant gets, the more it gets watered. One way of understanding these works can be: while a head-on crash with the cactus will only lead to the boxer's self-destruction, while the cutting steel knives hardly destroy the cacti, water can easily and gradually kill the cactus without sweat and blood.

On the left of *Boxing No.1&2* is *Tool No.1* (Figure 6.8). Megaphones were fixed inside of twenty-four secondhand green refrigerators with a yellow foaming agent filling spaces in between. All the loud-hailers were connected to a detonator placed in front of the refrigerators, once triggered leashing an explosive and ear deafening noise. The ruined display of the refrigerators and unexpected eruption of loud noise contrasts with the repetition of fist fighting the cactus and water splashing down on the cactus, forming an awe-ridden yet strangely empowering self-circulating system with an atmosphere of myth, crime and rebellion.

The exhibition *Tools* was a prelude of Zhang Ding's continuous creation of systems that border on control and anti-control.

FIGURE 6.8 *Zhang Ding,* Tools-1, 2007, *Interactive Sound Installation. Courtesy of Zhang Ding Studio.*

Sound Installations: *Control Club* (2012), *Om* (2014), *Safe House* (2018)

The installation *Control Club* (2012) (Figure 6.9) was commissioned by the twelfth Biennale de Lyon, displayed in a separate space from the main exhibition site, which used to be a boiler room. Measuring 490x500x500cm, *Control Club* is a tower-shaped stage, with the bottom two layers installed with subwoofers, the middle four layers with speakers, and a traditional Chinese bronze bell hanging on the top. Bell sounds, natural sounds, sounds of everyday life, military music, and classical music were played through the installation with an escalating frequency. The work's description reads, "In the compulsive frenzy brought on by this monumental stage, a world driven to chaos by excessive control is made manifest, and thus Control Club, in form and function, represents a diseased landscape of contemporary culture."

In following years, Zhang Ding made a series of speaker-installations titled *OM* (2014) (Figure 6.10), consisting of woofers, full range speakers, and a machine-controlled Chinese cymbal and drum. In the meantime, he expanded to incorporate social infrastructure in his work, including using the public lighting system and CCTV in a recent exhibition titled *Safe House* in Beijing (2018). *Safe House* consists of three separate installations, *Safe House #1* (Fig.65), *Safe House#2*, *Safe House#3* (Figure 6.11) exhibited

FIGURE 6.9 *Zhang Ding,* Control Club, *2013, Sound Installation. Courtesy of Zhang Ding Studio.*

FIGURE 6.10 *Zhang Ding, OM, 2014, Sound Installation. Courtesy of Zhang Ding Studio.*

FIGURE 6.11 *Zhang Ding,* Safe House #1, 2018, *Mechanical-kinetic Installation, lighting installation, sound installation. Courtesy of Zhang Ding Studio.*

simultaneously at three different art venues[3]. *Safe House #1* transforms a public light widely used in Chinese public squares into huge eyeball trackers. *Safe House #2* is a black mobile cube hung with two pair of sunglasses as if the character from the *Men in Black* films are guarding the door. *Safe House #3*, a sound installation with LF electrodeless lamps used in public squares in China, is exhibited in the Bunker. Zhang Ding painted the entire underground room units with white paint. Sounds were played in five separate rooms, escalating into an ambient futuristic electronic music, with a simple piano melody. Safe house is a secret location for hiding in the real world. The exhibition, with three locations, three installations, makes one wonder which one promises a sensual experience of safety: extreme darkness or extreme brightness, hypnotic symphony or electronic drone?

These large-scale speaker-installations and infrastructure-installations, like the bronze bell and drum installed in Beijing bell and drum tower, begin to accumulate a sense of monumentality. However, instead of coopting monumental voice as in Zhang Peili's sound works, Zhang Ding chooses experimental and improvisational music, which are associated with the notion of freedom and hence give expression to what the artist subtly advocates, that is, developing one's own system of anti-control.

Club Shows: *Orbit of Rock* (2014), *Enter the Dragon* (2015), *Control Club* (2016)

In March 2014, Zhang Ding's installation *Orbit* was exhibited in The Armory Show in New York. A month later in April he used *Orbit* and a two-dimensional installation titled *Sound Absorber* to stage the show *Orbit of Rock* at ShanghART Beijing. Shiny black sculptures of *Orbit* and the wall-sized golden *Sound Absorber* with a burnt texture, transformed the white space of ShangART gallery into a venue for a live rock music concert, replicating a monumental show in rock music history, the Moscow tour of the heavy-metal music show *Monsters of Rock*. *Monsters of Rock* was sponsored by Time Warner Inc., taking place at a former site of Soviet military exercises known as Tushino Airfield in September 28, 1991. An article in the *New York Times* reported that an estimated 150,000 people attended the show; helicopters circled close to the crowds and more than 1,000 militiamen guarded the stage.[4] The show was a big success and some rock music fans even claimed that it was rock music that caused the final fall of the Iron Curtain. Zhang Ding wanted to replicate the monumental

---

[3]See video documentation of exhibition *Safe House* at https://www.youtube.com/watch?time_continue=295&v=RVneejWF4u8&feature=emb_logo
[4]https://www.nytimes.com/1991/09/29/world/heavy-metal-groups-shake-moscow.html

sentiment of this legendary concert by organizing *Orbit of Rock* together with Yan Jun[5]. Local Beijing rock bands were invited to perform thirteen classical rock songs by four bands: Pantera, The Black Crows, Metallica, and AC/DC. The show attracted a large audience, mixed with art goers and metal rock fans, far exceeding the spatial capacity of the art space. The concert itself was a success, but Zhang Ding quickly realized that a monumental emotion is not to be copied or discursively communicated. It has to be acoustically enacted through performative rituals in carefully contextualized platforms.

The year after, in October 2015, Zhang Ding staged *Enter the Dragon* at ICA in London[6]. Considering the cultural differences between China and the UK, Zhang Ding decided not to replicate *Orbit of Rock* as originally suggested by ICA. "They (Londoners) do not have a socialist background. We have very different musical cultures. We (the Chinese) learned about Western rock music much later compared to the British people. The legend of the Moscow concert, a music festival believed to disintegrate a social regime, is ineffective to the British."[7] Instead, Zhang Ding decided to recreate the final scene from Bruce Lee's film *Enter the Dragon* (1973), from where the exhibition's title is adapted. He reused the installation *Sound Absorber* and created rotating mirrored sculptures particularly for the venue of ICA. The idea of using mirrors came from the last scene of the movie when Bruce Lee has entered a mirrored room looking for his enemies but only finds himself. Collaborating with NTS radio, Zhang Ding invited twenty-five artists and musicians of various music genres from Europe, the United States and Asia, to perform in his "immersive installation live house" every day for fifteen days during the duration of the project. The space was described as "a hybrid of a sci-fi discotheque and a futuristic super club." Musicians and artists were encouraged to collaborate to improvise and experiment. In May 2016, Zhang Ding was invited back to Shanghai to stage his project *Enter the Dragon II* at K11 Art Museum and later *Enter the Dragon III* at the contemporary art cluster *Gillman Barracks* in Singapore in September 2016.

The Art label *Control Club* was founded in 2014 but launched its first show in November 11, 2016.[8] The location of the show was a historical ruin, which used to be the Columbia Country Club and Old American Navy Club, as well as a mansion for Sun Ke, the son of the leader of Chinese republican revolution Sun Yat-Sen, built in the 1920 by Hungarian architect

---

[5]See video documentation of *Orbit of Rock* at https://www.youtube.com/watch?time_conti nue=957&v=520xe0Lr7lQ&feature=emb_logo
[6]See video documentation of *Enter the Dragon* at https://www.youtube.com/watch?time_conti nue=1&v=Hi4ecZvG5OA&feature=emb_logo
[7]https://news.artron.net/20160818/n858636.html
[8]see video documentation of the debut project of Control Club at https://www.youtube.com/ watch?v=vYBsaYgvPlg

Lazlo Hudec. The compound became a biological research institute after the Second World War and remained closed until 2016. One of the largest real estate companies, *Vanke,* rented this place and renovated it as office space and creative space for art and cultural events. For the majority of the audience, it was their first time to step into this mysterious architecture. Zhang Ding invited the experimental musician Wang Fan to perform live music through his speaker-installation *Control Club*, altogether sixteen channels with ten frequency ranges and fifty-nine speakers. The date of the debut show, November 11, was undoubtedly far from random. It is the annual Chinese "cyber Black Friday," with consumers spending about US$17.8 billion over one day in the "control club" of online shopping platforms of *Alibaba* empire in 2016.

The Military-Entertainment-Art Complex

Zhang Ding's installations are now widely called by art media journalists "mood sculpture" in the sense that his sculptures often create a strong mood-atmosphere for the audience. The use of light and sound in each show does make one think of the current trendy genre, ambient art, which can be related to La Monte Young and Marian Zazeela's *Dream House* in 1982, James Turrell's light installations, and more recent large-scale audiovisual installations exemplified by the Japanese artist Ryoji Ikeda. Ambient art in recent years seems to grow increasingly immersive to the extent of overwhelming and disorienting. With ecstasy very much becoming a ready-felt, these ambient artworks tend to create a pseudo-cosmic world in which one is supposed to lose oneself. However, while the term "mood sculpture" may speak to the sound and light effects of Zhang's speaker-installations, it misses the most unique aspect of these installations.

In music venues such as a livehouse or a concert hall, loudspeakers were often installed in invisible or less visible places. Zhang Ding's sound installations *Control Club*, *Om*, *Safe House*, when functioning as loudspeakers in live music shows of *Orbit of Rock*, *Enter the Dragon*, *Control Club*, are on the contrary, rather visible to the extent that they form pillars and define the force field of the entire space. During the show, people walk around them, rest against them, or even rest inside (the ground level of the installation *Control Club* are spacious enough for a person to snuggle up). These speaker-installations are reminiscent of ancient ritual artifacts (*liqi*) used in Chinese ritual art as Wu Hung describes. The sound of collective free improvising or experimental music has transformed the installation from being a symbol of power to power itself. Since its invention, the loudspeaker has been used both as a military-political weapon and a domestic-entertainment device. The dual role is magically enacted in Zhang Ding's installations-based highly ritualized "control club" shows, in which acoustic monuments of speaker-installations become channels for free expression.

In Zhang Ding's art works and projects, we see a transition from "object-oriented" to "system-oriented" way of art making. While it is difficult for a Chinese artist to get access to the state infrastructure, the artist creates an art system that simulates the infrastructure to build the military-entertainment-art complex, which is often simultaneously entertaining, aggressive and empowering. Making installations with system-thinking, to paraphrase an example from Deleuze and Guattari, is like a spider making a web with the fly code in its head (1987, 314). While remaining as an independent work, the installation can be grouped into a larger system of art. To recall what Kittler proposes, "Every culture has its zones of preparation that fuse lust and power, optically, acoustically, and so on. Our discos are preparing our youths for a retaliatory strike" (1999, 140). Is it possible to see *Control Club*, both the installation and the shows, as creating one kind of such zone? Perhaps, Zhang Ding is preparing himself and his audience, through meticulously designed art-parties, applying the same nanopolitical strategy, for a future retaliation.

Comparing with Zhang Peili's anti-monumental sound installations that often launch a direct critique of power structures, Zhang Ding's monumental speaker-installations ambiguate its critique underneath its military-entertainment-art complex. It is a game of control and anti-control. However, a further question needs to be kept in mind. That is, is it the same desire for power that gives rise to both qualities of monumentality and anti-monumentality?

Liu Chuang and the (Im)Possibility of Not Being Governed

Zhang Peili and Zhang Ding's installation-based sound works direct our attention to the particular power-saturated tone of voice and to multiple roles played by acoustics tools (i.e., radio, trumpet speakers, loudspeakers) in military and civilian cultures, in public and private life, in control and anti-control manoeuvres. Liu Chuang shares with Zhang Peili and Zhang Ding a similar antiauthoritarian and anti-totalitarian political commitment. Liu Chuang's video-based installation points us to an almost imperceptible control being deployed on the planetary level through global political, economic, and technological forces. Like the trumpet or stereo speakers, the invention of the Internet began with military purposes; it later became a space of free flows of information and communication for everyday life. However, it has not taken long for us to realize that internet technology is far from liberating. Information may suggest an ever-stronger yet invisible system of control.

Liu Chuang graduated from Hubei Institute of Fine Arts studying oil painting in 2001. After living in Shenzhen and trying out small businesses in advertising and screen-print making for six years, he moved to Beijing to become a full-time artist in 2007. In 2017, during the time of Beijing's campaign of forced eviction of migrant workers, Liu moved to Shanghai. Liu's art works often provoke institutional critiques in a reflective and poetic way through installations, videos, and performances. Both his video arts *Untilted (Dance Partner)* (2010) and *Untitled (History of Sweat)* (2007) question the nanopolitical atmosphere imposed and naturalized as part of everyone's everyday routine.

In *Untitled: History of Sweat* (2007), Liu installed an air conditioner in reverse, with the indoor unit outdoors, and outdoor unit indoors. On the floor of the gallery, there then appeared a small puddle of water: the condensed vapor processed from the sweat of audience members. The subtlety of the work nonetheless challenges one to think of the nanopolitics of perspiration, the intangible force in the atmospheric. Perspiration control is more than a biological need but a modernization of the air and the human body conditioned through a set of aesthetic, economic, and racial biases. The work can also be seen as an anti-habitual practice in which one's affective relation to the air conditioner is put into question; it diverts the audience to attend to the nanopolitical ambience of modernization that is often naturalized and desired. Another work, *Untitled (Dance Partner)* (2010) is a one-channel video of five minutes and fifteen seconds, the first artwork Liu Chuang made after moving to Beijing from Shenzhen. In the video, two cars of the same model drive at the minimum speed limit on a highway in Beijing, bordering on almost disrupting the normal order on highway driving. The slow speed does not cause a traffic jam, but is immediately judged as a wrong doing. Liu Chuang questions this judgment, showing how the traffic law gives forms to a moral law that makes everyone feel it is one's responsibility to obey the rules. But why does one have to get punished or reprimanded when not following the rule or when behaving abnormally?

Liu Chuang's investigation into how everyday life ambience—the air or the flow of traffic—is controlled and shaped by politics, technology, and the market continues in *BBRI (No.1 of Blossom Bud Restrainer)* (2015), a video work that traces how plants become a part of the process of modernization. *BBRI* is the name of a plant hormone applied to restrain trees from blossoming in China. Trees are systematically controlled to fit into urban planning and to meet spectacle needs of a city. But at the same time, the video shows how trees as a part of nature have power often beyond the control of humans. For example, increasing quantities of catkins produced by these trees as the result of the plant hormone cause breathing problems and burning them may lead to wildfire. Such "atmospheric attunement" to its endangerment, to borrow from Timothy Choy's words, is prevalent in Liu Chuang's art making (Choy and Zee 2015, 2018).

The process of questioning how institutional, technological, and capitalist power penetrates and transforms individuals' everyday life is also the process of speculating on the possibility and impossibility of not being controlled and governed. Different from a romantic desire for freedom, Liu Chuang's desire for anarchy is not overly optimistic but entangled with doubt and restraint.

Bitcoin Mining and Field Recordings of Ethnic Minorities (2018)

In 2017, the state television broadcaster China Central Television news programs released an in-depth report on Bitcoin mining in China. By then, China's Bitcoin mining accounted for 70 percent of the globally mined Bitcoins. Most Bitcoin factories were built in provinces of Sichuan and Guizhou where hydroelectricities are much cheaper than in other places. Bitcoin is a decentralizing peer-to-peer digital currency invented in 2008 by a person under the name of Satoshi Nakamoto. As a kind of cryptocurrency, Bitcoin was originally invented to oppose the central control of banks and government authorities over money flows. Bitcoin functions as a currency in the gift economy of the cyber world, first used as a token of gratitude for one's service or work. The process of creating Bitcoin is known as "mining," using computers to solve complex computational math problems in the Bitcoin network. The miner is rewarded by Bitcoin for their work. Bitcoin mining requires electricity and hardware. With cheap hydropower or

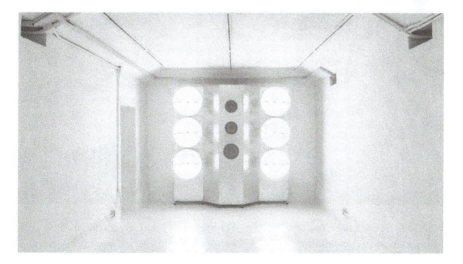

FIGURE 6.12 *Zhang Ding, Safe House #3, 2018, Audiovisual Installation. Courtesy of Zhang Ding Studio.*

wind-power generated electricity and local hardware manufacturing at a lower cost, China soon dominates the Bitcoin mining market.

This news inspired Liu Chuang to conduct a two-year research project on Bitcoin mining in China, collaborating with the contemporary art and film studies scholar Yang Beichen. The result is a three-channel forty-minute video installation titled *Bitcoin Mining and Field Recordings of Ethnic Minorities* (Figure 6.13) and an installation titled *Gluttonous Me* (Figure 6.14).

The video is a complex, speculative, and poetic narration with a dense reference to academic works. Over forty minutes, the work charts close and distant connections among Bitcoin, telegraphs in late Qing Dynasty, state power, currency, minorities, railways, dams, sci-fi films, field recordings of ethnic music, atomic bomb, and ancient Chinese bronze bell *Wushe*. As the video unfolds, images of optical power cables built in high mountains and hydropower plants in southwest China reveal the symbiotic relation between the decentralizing Bitcoin and the infrastructure of the nation-state. New technology has to rely on the seemingly outdated infrastructure after all. Every October when Sichuan province enters the drought season, Bitcoin mining factories need to migrate to Xin Jiang, which have cheaper electricity through wind powered plants. In spring, they move to Inner Mongolia to

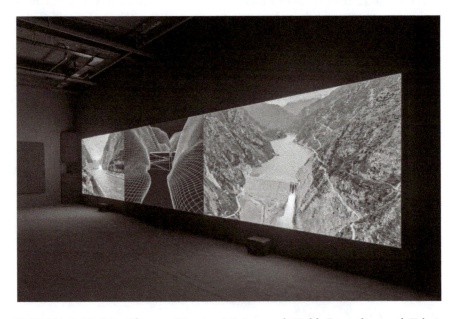

FIGURE 6.13 *Liu Chuang,* Bitcoin Mining and Field Recordings of Ethnic Minorities, *video installation 2018. 3 Channel Videos, 4k, 5.1 sound, 40 minutes. Installation view at Protocinema, Commissioned for Cosmopolis #1.5: Enlarged Intelligence with the support of the Mao Jihong Arts Foundation. Courtesy of the artist and Antenna Space.*

FIGURE 6.14 *Liu Chuang*, Gluttonous Me, *Installation, 2018. EVD, It's an all-in-one home entertainment system (walnut cabinet, Atman TV, amplifier, PC computer, 7 JBL loudspeakers, 1 JBL bass speaker, 7.1 surround sound system, plastic lampshades, LED light control system, mirror with aluminum alloy frame) Digital video, color, sound, 28'37". EVD: 2300 × 1550 × 500 mm, Mirror With Aluminum Alloy Frame: 7200 × 3000 × 500 mm × 2. Commissioned for Cosmopolis #1.5: Enlarged Intelligence with the support of the Mao Jihong Arts Foundation. Courtesy of the artist.*

take advantage of coal-fire power stations. In summer, mining machines are shipped back to Sichuan when the rain season comes.

Liu Chuang uses the Zomi language to narrate in the film, with both Chinese and English subtitles. Locations of Bitcoin mining overlaps with regions of southwest China, which is part of highland areas of southeastern part of Asia, geographically referred to as Zomia by the Dutch historian Willem Van Schenedel (2002). The American anthropologist James C. Scott in his book *The Art of Not Being Governed* (2009), as the video quotes, describes the ethnic group of Zomia as "barbaric by design"; people of Zomia have fled from the governing of Chinese empires for over two thousand years, forming their own language, cultural customs, and remaining stateless. In modern times, the government built roads, airports, train stations through mountains to reduce the cost of governing the borders. Bombs used in building the infrastructures far exceeds the amount used in wars. As noise reduction technology advances, all can be conducted more "quietly" without noticing. Noiselessness can be the result of even more extreme form of control.

Speaking through Zomi language is apparently a strategic choice, showing the artist's quasi-anthropological stance. However, Liu Chuang does not take a celebrative stance, but a critical and speculative one.

Through Zomia's relation to ancient Chinese empires, the narrative transitions from Zomian ethnic singing to a story of ancient Chinese chime bells *wushe* and Emperor Zhoujing (544–522 BC). It was a time when music was believed to be directly in connection with the cosmos and had political and moral functions. The *wushe* bell was believed to be able to make sounds of thunder and earthquake but it had never been built before because its large size makes its casting challenging. The emperor believed that the sound of the *wushe* bell would bring him an omnipotent power. In order to have enough metal for its casting, the emperor ordered the collection of currencies made of copper, reducing its weight and increasing its value and hence leading to inflation. The sound of *wushe* was overpowering; the harmony of the society was disturbed. Emperor Zhoujing died two years later. As civilian wisdom reveals, disharmonious sound from metal prophetically indicates war or disaster. The disharmony of music foretells the disharmony of the state.

Liu Chuang does not intend to conduct field recordings of ethnic minorities as indicated in the work title. The artist quotes the American folk singer Pete Seeger in the video, critiquing anthropologists who made field recordings as just "moving music from one grave to another, from the site of cultural extinction to a museum." Archives of these field recordings, as the video continues to narrate, are useful for creating fictional works, as in Spielberg's movie *Close Encounters of the Third Kind*. But in another sense, what Liu Chuang does is a field recording of the changing acoustic experience of contemporary Zomian people under the introduction of digital devices and technologies, with EVD as an example.

At the end of the video, it becomes clearer how the two seemingly irrelevant subjects, Bitcoin and ethnic minorities, connect. Both are anarchic and intentionally operate against central hegemonic control. Both adopt the style of nomad for basic survival. Both seem to lose their rebellious spirits and sync back to what they set out to escape from, at the lure of the promise of good life of global capitalism. Zomian people now send voice recordings of their ethnic singing to each other through the mobile application WeChat.

The video for the most of the time employs a birds-eye-view perspective of landscapes and an upward camera angle that meanders from the cloud floating above the dams to telegraph lines, to a mountain view of highlands and to archival video of the planet and cosmos. The sense of an anthropological field becomes difficult to pinpoint. Listened from a celestial level, what one hears, as the works may imply, is pure drone.

Gluttonous Me (2018)

The installation *Gluttonous Me* simulates a multifunctional home entertainment system made in China, one particularly targeted at minority groups at the beginning of the new millennium. Factories in Shenzhen took advantage of their electronic production line to assemble an electronic equipment called EVD, putting television, radio, tape recorder, DVD, karaoke, bluetooth, Wi-Fi, and a sound-to-light synchronization system all together. The installation consists of a TV set, amplifiers, PC computers, JBL bass speakers, 7.1 surround sound system, plastic lampshades, LED light control system, and a mirror with aluminum alloy frame, all installed in one walnut cabinet. As the voice-over in the video *Bitcoin Mining and Field Recordings of Ethnic Minorities* narrates in Zomi language, "EVD was initially conceived as a visual technology to help the deaf and the hearing-impaired learn music, but was then used to digitize the nervous system of minority ethnic groups. . . . The modernization that took the *Han* a century, we achieved in just 30 years."

The intention, or perhaps more accurately, the concern of the artist becomes clear. Just like what the Master laments in the *Analects of Confucius*, the text in *which* the Chinese expression for gluttonous (*baoshi zhongri*) (饱食终日) first appeared, "Hard is it to deal with who will stuff himself with food the whole day, without applying his mind to anything good!" First the *Han* youth, now the minority youth, are fed by digital technology, busily occupied by bits of information and eventually lose the ability to even think of rebellion and resistance.

Both *Bitcoin Mining and Field Recordings of Ethnic Minorities* and *Gluttonous Me* again showcase how nanopolitics of the nation-state and the global capitalist economy shapes the nervous system, the body gestures, the attention mode, sensual perceptions, and psychological and political desires. The artist Liu Chuang does not provide answers but raises a question that also apply to sound works by Zhang Peili and Zhang Ding: how do we negotiate with what has already been shaping, changing, and synchronizing us, the digital shimmering, the data cloud, the humming acoustic infrastructure?

Conclusion – *Qi*-Thinking, or Cybernetics: A Way of Going On

In the early fifteenth century, Emperor Yongle ordered a foundry master to cast a new bell. But the foundry master failed repeatedly to achieve the most perfect casting and this made the emperor furious. The emperor threatened to punish the master. When hearing that her father's life was endangered, the daughter jumped into the molding pot where the molten metal was poured into, making herself a permanent part of the bronze bell. The father desperately reached to catch his daughter and only grasped one of her shoes. The bell was perfect. For ordinary Beijingers, every time the bell was struck, it gave the sound of *xie* (the sound of the Chinese character for shoe) as if the daughter is looking for her missing shoe.[9]

The story reveals the quotidian wisdom of recognizing the bell as an assemblage of power-violence-communication. Folktales have been a weapon of the powerless civilians to pass their wisdom and their critique of those who abuse their power. So is art.

The challenge is that the task of detecting such power and violence is becoming increasingly difficult when they become the background, the ambient, and the peripheral, sometimes under the guise of something extremely beautiful, innocent, and ethereal. Like the cloud, as Tung-Hui Hu sharply argues, used as both an idea and a visual reference in today's networked society, in fact enables a resurgence of violence and indexes a reemergence of sovereign power (2015).

Sound, both audible and inaudible, suggests a cybernetically integrated system that comprises matter, energy, and information. Zhang Peili, Zhang Ding, and Liu Chuang, through their idiosyncratic means of art making, exercise to different extents a sensory critique of the sound of ubiquitous control. Humming is the acoustic counterpart of the cloud. If cybernetic control is imbedded in today's military and governmental regime, it can also empower the individuals in detecting such regime, to become a "weapon of the weak" (Scott 1985).

*   *   *

Control is not only about restraining; it also means steering, cultivating, and predicting. Chinese classic *Yi Ching*, which informs the philosophy of *qi*, reveals an art of being attentive to not only the nowness but also the past, the future, the peripheral, and the subliminal. Despite the historical and cultural differences, cybernetics, "the science of steermanship," shares a similar way of thinking (Pickering, 2010). Cybernetics, ever since its inception in late 1940s, has grabbed the attention of the artworld in the West. The best example might be the legendary exhibition *Cybernetic Serendipity* curated by Jasia Reichardt at ICA London in 1968 and later toured in United States, showing works by artists, musicians, engineers, and mathematicians. The term serendipity, as the press release for the London exhibition notes, was used to "describe the faculty of making happy chance discoveries." Although this explicit passion for system theory and cybernetics in the 1960s

---

[9]I read this folktale from Wu Hung's article "Monumentality of Time: Giant Clocks, the Drum Tower, the Clock Tower" (2013).

and 1970s cooled down, its influence in the arts is enduring. Conceptual art, minimal art, experimental music, and net art more or less inherit from system-thinking and cybernetics, integrating technology, art, and life.

System theory and cybernetics' application in military and industry should never become a reason for its neglect in the arts. In China, cybernetics as a system of knowledge remains largely a subject in hard science introduced and led by scientist Qian Xuesen until recently, when scholars, including the curator Zhang Ga and scholar Yuk Hui and Bernard Stiegler, popularize the vocabulary of and knowledge related to cybernetics in China's contemporary art world through exhibitions, workshops, and lecture series. Through this "new" Western discourse, the ancient and long forgotten *qi*-thinking in contemporary China can be re-visioned and reimagined. There is no time more fitting than now to develop an organic holistic worldview of *qi* (Zhang Zai), an immanent mind (Bateson), or cybernetic brain (Pickering), for us to be able to stay alert, to go on living, to care for the self and the other, when the system is failing to.

GLOSSARY OF TERMS

bigu 辟谷 grain avoidance

chang Xiao 长啸 transcendental whistling, chanting, roaring

cheng 诚 creativity

chimei wangliang 魑魅魍魉 ghost, monsters, demons

dan 淡 bland in taste

dan 澹 quiet, peaceful and slow

de 德 virtue

gan 感 resonance

guai li luan shen 怪力乱神 prodigies, force, disorder and gods

gui 鬼 ghost

gu shen 谷神 the creative indeterminacy of the valley

gui-shen 鬼神 ghost-spirits, movements of contraction and expansion

hongyun tuoyue 烘云托月 to bring moon to the fore by depicting clouds

huanghu 恍惚 elusive, evasive

huwei tuotai 互为脱胎 mutual birth

jian 间 a space to let pass and to let connect

jing 敬 reverence

jing qi 精气 the most refined form of *qi*

li 礼 ritual, rites

liang zhi 良知 intuitive knowledge

lv guan 律管 humming tubes

moqi 默契 tacit resonance

ren 仁 humanness

shanshui 山水 mountain-water

sheng 声 sound

shi 势 the advantage of position or force

shidai qu 时代曲 a unique music genre that combines Chinese folk music with American Jazz originated in Shanghai in the 1920s

tianren ganying 天人感应 resonance between the heaven and the human

wu 无 non-presence

wu 巫 shamanism

wu 舞 dance

xian wang shuo hui 弦望朔晦 crescent, full, new, and dark

xian 仙 immortals or sages

xiang 象 the intensity and propensity of the shapeless

xing 性 nature, instinct

xu 虚 emptiness

xuanxue 玄学 metaphysics

yangbanxi 样板戏, "model opera" during the Cultural Revolution

yinyun 氤氲 diffusive with thick clouds of *qi*; the state of organism mutually breathing life into one another; a wildly shimmering heat; chaos

yin 音 notes

you 幽 inward expandedness

yue 乐 music

zao 噪 noise

BIBLIOGRAPHY

Allen, Barry. 2015. *Vanishing into Things: Knowledge in Chinese Tradition.* Cambridge, MA: Harvard University Press.

Ames, Roger T., and David L. Hall, eds. 2001. *Focusing the Familiar: A Translation and Philosophical Interpretation of the Zhongyong.* Honolulu: University of Hawai'i Press.

Arquilla, John, and David F. Ronfeldt. eds. 2001. *Networks and Netwars: The Future of Terror, Crime, and Militancy.* Santa Monica, CA: Rand.

Attali, Jacques. 1985. *Noise: The Political Economy of Music.* Theory and History of Literature, vol. 16. Minneapolis: University of Minnesota Press.

Austin, John L. 1962. *How to Do Things with Words: The William James Lectures Delivered at Harvard University in 1955.* Edited by James O. Urmson. 1. ed., [repr.]. Cambridge, MA: Harvard University of Press.

Barad, Karen. 2003. "Posthumanist Performativity: Toward an Understanding of How Matter Comes to Matter." *Signs* 28 (3): 801. doi:10.1086/345321

Bateson, Gregory. 1972. *Steps to an Ecology of Mind: Collected Essays in Anthropology, Psychiatry, Evolution, and Epistemology.* Chicago: University of Chicago Press.

Battier, Marc, and Lin-Ni Liao. 2018. "Electronic Music in East Asia," in *The Routledge Research Companion to Electronic Music: Reaching Out with Technology,* edited by Simon Emmerson. Abingdon, Oxon and New York: Routledge.

Beck, Guy L. 1993. *Sonic Theology: Hinduism and Sacred Sound.* Delhi: Motilal Banarsidass Publishers.

Belgrad, Daniel. 2019. *The Culture of Feedback: Ecological Thinking in Seventies America.* Chicago: The University of Chicago Press.

Berque, Augustin. 2013. *Thinking through Landscape.* Translated by Anne-Marie Feenberg-Dibon. London and New York: Routledge.

Bishop, Claire. 2012. *Installation Art: A Critical History.* Reprinting of the ed. 2005. London: Tate Publ.

Boden, Jeanne. 2015."笑对生活—解读耿建翌回顾展" 丰静帆译。关于耿建翌，高士明编辑。杭州: 中国美术学院出版社，56–65.

Boyle, James. 1997. "Foucault in Cyberspace: Surveillance, Sovereignty, and Hardwired Censors." *University of Cincinnati Law Review.*

Braga, Adriana. 2016. "Mind as Medium: Jung, McLuhan and the Archetype." *Philosophies* 1 (3): 220–7.

Butler, Judith. 2006. *Gender Trouble: Feminism and the Subversion of Identity.* Routledge Classics. New York: Routledge.

Butler, Judith. 2011. *Bodies That Matter: On the Discursive Limits of "Sex."* Routledge Classics. Abingdon, Oxon; New York: Routledge.

Carrette, Jeremy R., and Richard King. 2005. *Selling Spirituality: The Silent Takeover of Religion.* London and New York: Routledge.

Cavarero, Adriana. 2005. *For More than One Voice: Toward a Philosophy of Vocal Expression.* Stanford, CA: Stanford University Press.

Cecchetto, David. 2013. *Humanesis: Sound and Technological Posthumanism.* Posthumanities 25. Minneapolis: University of Minnesota Press.

Chan, Wing-Tsit, ed. 1973. *A Source Book in Chinese Philosophy.* 1. Princeton paperback ed., 4. print. Princeton, NJ: Princeton University Press.

Chang, Peter M. 2006. *Chou Wen-Chung: The Life and Work of a Contemporary Chinese-Born American Composer.* Composers of North America, no. 25. Lanham, MD: Scarecrow Press.

Chao, Mei-pa. 1937. "The Trend of Modern Music." *T'ien Hsia Monthly* 4 (March): 269–86.

Chen, Cheng-Yih. 1996. *Early Chinese Work in Natural Science: A Re-Examination of the Physics of Motion, Acoustics, Astronomy and Scientific Thoughts.* Hong Kong: Hong Kong University Press.

Cheng, Chung-Ying. 1987. "Li and Chi in the I Ching: A Reconsideration of Being and Non-Being in Chinese Philosophy." *Journal of Chinese Philosophy* 14 (1): 1–38.

Cheng, Zhongying, and Nicholas Bunnin, eds. 2002. *Contemporary Chinese Philosophy.* Malden, MA: Blackwell Publishers.

Choy, Timothy. 2018. "Tending to Suspension: Abstraction and Apparatuses of Atmospheric Attunement in Matsutake Worlds." *Social Analysis* 62 (4). Berghahn Journals: 54–77.

Choy, Timothy, and Jerry Zee. 2015. "Condition—Suspension." *Cultural Anthropology* 30 (2): 210–23.

Clark, Paul, Laikwan Pang, and Tsan-Huang Tsai, eds. 2016. *Listening to China's Cultural Revolution: Music, Politics, and Cultural Continuities.* Chinese Literature and Culture in the World. Houndmills, Basingstoke, and Hampshire: Palgrave Macmillan.

Coggins, Owen. 2018. *Mysticism, Ritual, and Religion in Drone Metal.* London: Bloomsbury Academic.

Corbin, Alain. 1998. *Village Bells: Sound and Meaning in the Nineteenth-Century French Countryside.* European Perspectives. New York: Columbia University Press.

Corris, Michael, ed. 2004. *Conceptual Art: Theory, Myth, and Practice.* New York: Cambridge University Press.

Cox, Christoph. 2018. *Sonic Flux: Sound, Art, and Metaphysics.* Chicago and London: The University of Chicago Press.

Cox, Christoph, and Daniel Warner, eds. 2017. *Audio Culture: Readings in Modern Music.* Revised ed. New York: Bloomsbury Academic, an imprint of Bloomsbury Publishing Inc.

Cullen, Christopher. 1990. "The Science/Technology Interface in Seventeenth-Century China: Song Yingxing on 'Qi' and the 'Wu Xing.'" *Bulletin of the School of Oriental & African Studies* 53 (2): 295–318.

Darter, Tom. 1982. "John Cage." *Keyboard* 8 (9): 18–29.

Dayal, Geeta. 2009. *Brian Eno's Another Green World*. 33 1/3. New York, NY ; London: Continuum.

Deleuze, G., and Guattari, F. 1987. *A Thousand Plateaus: Capitalism and Schizophrenia*. Minneapolis: University of Minnesota Press.

De Man, Paul. 1979. *Allegories of Reading: Figural Language in Rousseau, Nietzsche, Rilke, and Proust*. New Haven, CT: Yale University Press.

Derrida, Jacques. 1988. *Limited Inc*. Evanston, IL: Northwestern University Press.

Dolar, Mladen. 2006. *A Voice and Nothing More*. Short Circuits. Cambridge, MA: MIT Press.

Duchamp, Marcel. 1973. *Salt Seller: The Writings of Marcel Duchamp*. New York: Oxford University Press.

Dunbar-Hester, Christina. 2010. "Listening to Cybernetics: Music, Machines, and Nervous Systems, 1950–1980." *Science, Technology, & Human Values* 35 (1): 113–39.

Duve, Thierry de. 1991. *Pictorial Nominalism on Marcel Duchamp's Passage from Painting to the Readymade*. Theory and History of Literature, vol. 51. Minneapolis: University of Minnesota Press.

Edwards, E. D. 1957. "'Principles of Whistling'– 嘯 旨 Hsiao Chih-Anonymous." *Bulletin of the School of Oriental and African Studies, University of London* 20 (1/3). Cambridge University Press: 217–29.

Erlmann, Veit. 2010. *Reason and Resonance: A History of Modern Aurality*. New York and Cambridge, MA: Zone Books and Distributed by MIT Press.

Flynt, Henry. 1961. "Essay: Concept Art," in *An Anthology of Chance Operations*, edited by La Monte Young. New York: La Monte Young & Jackson Mac Low, 1963.

Farina, Almo, and S. H. Gage, eds. 2017. *Ecoacoustics: The Ecological Role of Sounds*. First ed. Hoboken, NJ: John Wiley & Sons, Inc.

Fazenda, Bruno, Chris Scarre, Rupert Till, Raquel Jiménez Pasalodos, Manuel Rojo Guerra, Cristina Tejedor, Roberto Ontañón Peredo et al. 2017. "Cave Acoustics in Prehistory: Exploring the Association of Palaeolithic Visual Motifs and Acoustic Response." *The Journal of the Acoustical Society of America* 142 (3): 1332–49.

Feng, You-Lan. 1948. "Chinese Philosophy and a Future World Philosophy." *The Philosophical Review* 57 (6). Duke University Press: 539–49. doi:10.2307/2181795

Fink, Robert Wallace. 2005. *Repeating Ourselves: American Minimal Music as Cultural Practice*. Berkeley: University of California Press.

Foster, Hal. 1995. "The Artist as Ethnographer?" in *The Traffic in Culture: Refiguring Art and Anthropology*, edited by George E. Marcus and Fred R. Myers, 302–9. Berkeley: University of California Press.

Gladston, Paul, Robin Peckham, Robin Peckham, and Venus Lau, eds. 2012. *Zhang Peili: Certain Pleasures (Que Qie de Kuai Gan: Zhang Pei Li)*. 1st ed. Min Sheng Mei Shu Guan Shu Xi Minsheng Art Museum Series. Hong Kong: Blue Kingfisher.

Goodman, Steve. 2010. *Sonic Warfare Sound, Affect, and the Ecology of Fear*. Cambridge, MA: The MIT Press.

Gottschalk, Jennie. 2016. *Experimental Music since 1970*. New York and London: Bloomsbury Academic.

Groom, Simon, Karen Smith, and Zhen Xu, eds. 2007. *The Real Thing: Contemporary Art from China*. Liverpool and London: Tate Liverpool. In association with Tate Pub.; Distributed in the U.S. and Canada by Harry N. Abrams.

Hall, David L., and Roger T. Ames. 1995. *Anticipating China: Thinking through the Narratives of Chinese and Western Culture*. Albany: State University of New York Press.

Hallock, Jennifer. 2015. *Under the Sugar Sun*. Weare, NH: Little Brick Books.

Haraway, Donna Jeanne. 2016. *Staying with the Trouble: Making Kin in the Chthulucene*. Experimental Futures: Technological Lives, Scientific Arts, Anthropological Voices. Durham, NC: Duke University Press.

Harrison, Charles, and Charles Harrison. 2003. *Conceptual Art and Painting: Further Essays on Art & Language*. Cambridge, MA and London: MIT Press.

Hay, John. 1985. "The Rock and Chinese Art." *Orientations* 16 (12): 16–32.

Helmreich, Stefan, Sophia Roosth, and Michele Ilana Friedner. 2015. *Sounding the Limits of Life: Essays in the Anthropology of Biology and Beyond*. Princeton Studies in Culture and Technology. Princeton, NJ: Princeton University Press.

Howes, David, ed. 2005. *Empire of the Senses: The Sensual Culture Reader*. Sensory Formations Series. Oxford and New York: Berg.

Huang, Siu-Chi. 1968. "Chang Tsai's Concept of Ch'i." *Philosophy East and West* 18 (4): 247. doi:10.2307/1398403

Hui, Yuk. 2016. *The Question Concerning Technology in China: An Essay in Cosmotechnics*. Falmouth: Urbanomic Media Ltd.

Huyssen, Andreas. 2003. *Present Pasts: Urban Palimpsests and the Politics of Memory*. Cultural Memory in the Present. Stanford, CA: Stanford University Press.

Ilfeld, Etan J. 2012. "Contemporary Art and Cybernetics: Waves of Cybernetic Discourse within Conceptual, Video and New Media Art." *Leonardo* 45 (1): 57–63. doi:info:doi/10.1162/LEON_a_00326

Ingold, Tim. 2000. *The Perception of the Environment: Essays on Livelihood, Dwelling & Skill*. London and New York: Routledge.

Ingold, Tim. 2007. "Against Soundscape," in *Autumn Leaves: Sound and the Environment in Artistic Practice*, edited by Angus Carlyle, 10–13. Paris: Association Double-Entendre in association with CRISAP.

Jullien, François. 1999. *The Propensity of Things: Toward a History of Efficacy in China*. 1. paperback ed. New York: Zone Books.

Jullien, François. 2004. *In Praise of Blandness: Proceeding from Chinese Thought and Aesthetics*. New York: Zone Books.

Jullien, François. 2009. *The Great Image Has No Form, or On the Nonobject through Painting*. Translated by Jane Marie Todd. Chicago: The University of Chicago Press.

Jullien, François. 2015. *De l'être Au Vivre: Lexique Euro-Chinois de La Pensée*. Bibliothèque Des Idées. Paris: Gallimard.

Jullien, François. 2018a. *Living off Landscape: Or, the Unthought-of in Reason*. Global Aesthetic Research. Lanham, MD: Rowman & Littlefield International.

Jullien, François. 2018b. *Cong Cunyou dao Shenghuo: Ouzhou Sixiang yu Zhongguo Sixiang de Juli. (De l'être au vivre : lexique euro-chinois de la pensée)*. Translated by Zhuo Li. Shanghai: Dongfang Chuban Zhongxin.

Jung, Carl Gustav. 1980. *The Archetypes and the Collective Unconscious.* Princeton, NJ: Princeton University Press.

Jung, Carl Gustav. 1981. *The Archetypes and the Collective Unconscious (Collected Works of C.G. Jung Vol.9 Part 1).* Translated by R. F. C. Hull. Princeton, NJ: Princeton University Press.

Kasoff, Ira E. 1984. *The Thought of Chang Tsai (1020-1077).* Cambridge Studies in Chinese History, Literature, and Institutions. Cambridge and New York: Cambridge University Press.

Keane, Michael, ed. 2016. *Handbook of Cultural and Creative Industries in China.* Handbooks of Research on Contemporary China. Cheltenham: Edward Elgar.

Kelly, Caleb. 2009. *Cracked Media: The Sound of Malfunction.* Cambridge, MA: MIT Press.

Kerber, Robert C. 2006. "If It's Resonance, What Is Resonating?" *Journal of Chemical Education* 83 (2): 223. doi:10.1021/ed083p223.

Kett, Robert J. 2015. "Monumentality as Method: Archaeology and Land Art in the Cold War." *Representations* 130 (1): 119–51. doi:10.1525/rep.2015.130.1.119

Kim, Jung-Yeup. 2015. *Zhang Zai's Philosophy of Qi: A Practical Understanding.* Lanham, MD: Lexington Books.

Kittler, Friedrich A. 1999. *Gramophone, Film, Typewriter.* Writing Science. Stanford, CA: Stanford University Press.

Kosuth, Joseph. 1975 [2008]. "Artist as Anthropologist" (extracts) in *The Everyday*, edited by Stephen Johnstone. Documents of Contemporary Art. London: Cambridge, MA: Whitechapel; MIT Press.

Kouwenhoven, Frank. 1990. "Mainland China's New Music (1): Out of the Desert." *Chime: Newsletter of the European Foundation for Chinese Music Research*, no. 2 (autumn): 59–82.

Krauss, Rosalind, Denis Hollier, Annette Michelson, H. Foster, S. Kolbowski, M. Buskirk, and B. Buchloh. 1994. "The Reception of the Sixties." *OCTOBER*, no. 69 (SUM): 3–21.

Krischer, Olivier. ed. 2019. *Zhang Peili: From Painting to Video = Zhang Peili: Cong Hui Hua Dao Lu Xiang.* Acton, ACT: ANU Press.

Kuriyama, Shigehisa. 1999. *The Expressiveness of the Body and the Divergence of Greek and Chinese Medicine.* New York: Zone Books.

LaBelle, Brandon. 2015. *Background Noise: Perspectives on Sound Art.* Second ed. New York: Bloomsbury Academic.

Landy, Leigh. 2018. "The Three Paths: Cultural Retention in Contemporary Chinese Electroacoustic Music," in *The Routledge Research Companion to Electronic Music: Reaching out with Technology*, edited by Simon Emmerson. Abingdon, Oxon and New York: Routledge.

Laozi, and Victor H. Mair. 1990. *Tao Te Ching: The Classic Book of Integrity and the Way.* New York: Bantam Books.

Latour, Bruno. 2017. *Facing Gaia: Eight Lectures on the New Climatic Regime.* Translated by Catherine Porter. Cambridge and Medford, MA: Polity.

Li, Jianhong. 2010. *Liner notes to Twelve Moods.* Beijing: C.F.I. Records, CFI 001-CD.

Li, Qiuxiao. 2019. "Characteristics of Early Electronic Music Composition in China's Mainland," in *Electroacoustic Music in East Asia*, edited by Marc Battier and Kenneth Fields. London and New York: Routledge.

Li, Zehou. 2018. *The Origins of Chinese Thought: From Shamanism to Ritual Regulations and Humaneness*. Translated by Robert A. Carleo. Modern Chinese Philosophy, vol. 17. Leiden and Boston: Brill.

Licht, Alan. 2019. *Sound Art Revisited*. New York: Bloomsbury Academic, Bloomsbury Publishing Inc.

Lippard, Lucy R. 1997. *Six Years: The Dematerialization of the Art Object from 1966 to 1972*. Berkeley: University of California Press.

Lucier, Alvin, ed. 2017. *Eight Lectures on Experimental Music*. Middletown, CT: Wesleyan University Press.

Lucy, Niall. 2004. *A Derrida Dictionary*. Malden, MA: Blackwell Pub.

Mangalwadi, Vishal. 1977. *The World of Gurus*. New Delhi: Vikas Publication House.

McCullough, Malcolm. 2013. *Ambient Commons: Attention in the Age of Embodied Information*. Cambridge, MA: The MIT Press.

McLuhan, Marshall, and Wilfred Watson. 1970. *From Cliche to Archetype*. New York: Viking Press.

Morton, Timothy. 2013. *Hyperobjects: Philosophy and Ecology after the End of the World*. Posthumanities 27. Minneapolis: University of Minnesota Press.

Mowitt, John. 2015. *Sounds: The Ambient Humanities*. Oakland: University of California Press.

Murdoch, Iris, and Peter J. Conradi. 1999. *Existentialists and Mystics: Writings on Philosophy and Literature*. A Penguin Book. New York: Penguin.

Needham, Joseph. 1965. *Science and Civilisation in China Physics and Physical Technology Vol.4: Physics and Physical Technology. Part II: Mechanical Engineering*. print. Cambridge: Cambridge University Press.

Nelson, Susan E. 1998/1999. "Picturing Listening: The Sight of Sound in Chinese Painting." *Archives of Asian Art* 51: 30–55.

O'Callaghan, Casey. 2007. *Sounds: A Philosophical Theory*. Oxford and New York: Oxford University Press.

Parker, Andrew, Eve Kosofsky Sedgwick, and English Institute, eds. 1995. *Performativity and Performance*. Essays from the English Institute. New York: Routledge.

Pettman, Dominic. 2017. *Sonic Intimacy: Voice, Species, Technics (or, How to Listen to the World)*. Stanford, CA: Stanford University Press.

Pickering, Andrew. 2010. *The Cybernetic Brain: Sketches of Another Future*. Chicago and London: University of Chicago Press.

Pignarre, Philippe, Isabelle Stengers, and Andrew Goffey. 2011. *Capitalist Sorcery: Breaking the Spell*. Houndmills, Basingstoke, Hampshire and New York: Palgrave Macmillan.

Polanyi, Michael, and Amartya Sen. 2009. *The Tacit Dimension*. Chicago and London: University of Chicago Press.

Prendergast, Mark J. 2000. *The Ambient Century: From Mahler to Trance: The Evolution of Sound in the Electronic Age*. 1st US ed. New York: Bloomsbury.

Price, Peter. 2011. *Resonance: Philosophy for Sonic Art*. New York, NY: Atropos Press.

Pu, Songling, and John Minford. 2006. *Strange Tales from a Chinese Studio*. London: Penguin.

Ramey, Joshua Alan. 2012. *The Hermetic Deleuze: Philosophy and Spiritual Ordeal*. New Slant: Religion, Politics, and Ontology. Durham: Duke University Press.

Rehding, Alexander. 2017. *Music and Monumentality Commemoration and Wonderment in Nineteenth-Century Germany*. Oxford: Oxford University Press.

Reznikoff, Iégor, and Michel Dauvois. 1988. "La Dimension Sonore Des Grottes Ornées." *Bulletin de La Société Préhistorique Française*, no. 8: 238.

Roquet, Paul. 2016. *Ambient Media: Japanese Atmospheres of Self*. Minneapolis: University of Minnesota Press.

Scarre, Chris J. 1989. "Painting by Resonance." *Nature (London)* 338, 382.

Schulze, Holger. 2018. *The Sonic Persona: An Anthropology of Sound*. New York: Bloomsbury Academic, an imprint of Bloomsbury Publishing Inc.

Schwartz, Benjamin Isadore. 1985. *The World of Thought in Ancient China*. Cambridge, MA: The Belknap Press of Harvard University Press.

Scott, James C. 1985. *Weapons of the Weak: Everyday Forms of Peasant Resistance*. New Haven: Yale University Press.

Shi, Tao. 2007. *Shitao Huayu Lu* (石涛画语录) (*Comments on Painting*). Translated by Yu Jianhua. Nanjing: Jiangsu Meishu Chubanshe.

Silver, Micah. 2014. *Figures in Air: Essays toward a Philosophy of Audio*. Los Angeles: Inventory Press.

Sivin, Nathan. 1978. "On the Word 'Taoist' as a Source of Perplexity. With Special Reference to the Relations of Science and Religion in Traditional China." *History of Religions* 17 (3/4): 303–30.

Sivin, Nathan. 1987. *Traditional Medicine in Contemporary China: A Partial Translation of Revised Outline of Chinese Medicine (1972): With an Introductory Study on Change in Present Day and Early Medicine*. Science, Medicine, and Technology in East Asia, vol. 2. Ann Arbor: Center for Chinese Studies, University of Michigan.

Sloterdijk, Peter. 2017. *The Aesthetic Imperative: Writings on Art*. English ed. Malden, MA: Polity.

Steintrager, James A., and Rey Chow, eds. 2019. *Sound Objects*. Durham, NC: Duke University Press.

Sunder Rajan, Kaushik, ed. 2012. *Lively Capital: Biotechnologies, Ethics, and Governance in Global Markets*. Experimental Futures. Durham, NC: Duke University Press.

Tang, Chün-i. 1956. "Chang Tsai's Theory of Mind and Its Metaphysical Basis." *Philosophy East and West* 6 (2): 113–36.

Tanizaki, Jun'ichirō, 1977. *In Praise of Shadows*. Translated by Thomas J. Harper and Edward Seidensticker. Sedgwick: Leete's Island Books.

The Nanopolitics Group. 2012. "Nanopolitics: A First Outline of Our Experiments in Movement." *Lateral: Journal of The Cultural Studies Association*. (1) https://csalateral.org/section/mobilisations-interventions-and-cultural-policy/nanopolitics/

Tu, Weiming. 2010. "An 'Anthropocosmic' Perspective on Creativity." *Procedia—Social and Behavioral Sciences*, The Harmony of Civilization and Prosperity for All: Selected Papers of Beijing Forum (2004–2008), 2 (5): 7305–11. doi:10.1016/j.sbspro.2010.05.084

Van Gulik, Robert Hans. 1969. *The Lore of the Chinese Lute: An Essay in the Ideology of the Ch'in*. Tokyo and Rutland: Sophia University Tokyo in cooperation with the Charles E. Tuttle Company.

Viola, Bill. 2013. "The Sound of One Line Scanning," in *Sound by Artists*, edited by Dan Lander and Micah Lexier, 39–54. Toronto: Charivari Press and Blackwood Gallery.

Wang, Hefei. 2019. "Exploration and Innovation, the Chinese Model of the Musicacoustica-Beijing Festival," in *Electroacoustic Music in East Asia*, edited by Marc Battier and Kenneth Fields. London and New York: Routledge.

Wang, Jing. 2015. "Utopian Impulses in China's Sound Culture: The Raying Temple Subculture Collective." *Journal of Popular Music Studies* 27 (1): 2–24.

Wang, Jing. 2016. "Affective Listening as a Mode of Coexistence: The Case of China's Sound Practice." *Representations* 136 (1): 112–31. doi:10.1525/rep.2016.136.1.112

Wang, Jing. 2018. "On Acoustic Milieus." *Communication and the Public* 3 (4): 283–9. doi:10.1177/2057047318812570

Wang, Jing. 2019. "Throbbing Crowds: Of Dancing Grannies and Acoustic Milieus in Contemporary China." *Social Science Information* 58 (2): 377–89. doi:10.1177/0539018419843808

Ward, Frazer. 1997. "Some Relations between Conceptual and Performance Art." *Art Journal* 56 (4): 36–40. doi:10.2307/777718

Weibel, Peter, ed. 2019. *Sound Art: Sound as a Medium of Art*. Cambridge, London: The MIT Press.

Weller, Robert P. 2006. *Discovering Nature: Globalization and Environmental Culture in China and Taiwan*. Cambridge and New York: Cambridge University Press.

Widrich, Mechtild. 2014. *Performative Monuments: The Rematerialisation of Public Art*. Rethinking Art's Histories. Manchester and New York: Manchester University Press.

Wiener, Norbert. 1948. *Cybernetics: Or Control and Communication in the Animal and the Machine*. New York and Paris: John Wiley& Sons, Inc., Hermann& Cie.

Wu, Hung. 1995. *Monumentality in Early Chinese Art and Architecture*. Stanford, CA: Stanford University Press.

Wu, Hung. 2013. "Monumentality of Time: Giant Clocks, the Drum Tower, the Clock Tower," in *Monuments and Memory, Made and Unmade*, edited by Robert Nelson, Margaret Olin. University of Chicago Press, 2013.

Wu, Hung. 2014. *Contemporary Chinese Art: A History, 1970s>2000s*. London and New York: Thames & Hudson.

Yan, Jun. 2017. "RE-INVENT: Experimental Music in China," in *Audio Culture: Readings in Modern Music*. Revised ed., edited by Christoph Cox, and Daniel Warner, 1111–46. New York, NY: Bloomsbury Academic, an imprint of Bloomsbury Publishing Inc.

Yan, Jun. 2019. "An Audience of Six in Chengdu—The Wire." *The Wire Magazine—Adventures In Modern Music*. Accessed May 18. https://www.thewire.co.uk/in-writing/columns/audience-in-chengdu-yan-jun

Yao, Dajuin. 2019. "Sound Art in China: Revolutions Per Minute," in *Sound Art: Sound as a Medium of Art*, edited by Peter Weibel, 644–53. MIT Press.

Yin, Yi. 2017. "Urban Space as Resource and Practice Field for Sound Art." *Communication and the Public* 2 (4): 365–70.

Young, Samson. 2007. "Reconsidering Cultural Politics in the Analysis of Contemporary Chinese Music: The Case of Ghost Opera." *Contemporary Music Review* 26 (5–6): 605–18.

Young, Samson. 2009. "The Voicing of the Voiceless in Tan Dun's 'The Map': Horizon of Expectation and the Rhetoric of National Style." *Asian Music* 40 (1). University of Texas Press: 83–99.

Yu, Ying-Shih. 1987. "'O Soul, Come Back!' A Study in The Changing Conceptions of The Soul and Afterlife in Pre-Buddhist China." *Harvard Journal of Asiatic Studies* 47 (2): 363. doi:10.2307/2719187

Zhang, Xiaofu. 2019. "The Power of Arterial Language in Constructing a Musical Vocabulary of One's Own: Inheriting the Inspiration and Gene of Innovation in Electroacoustic Music from Chinese Culture," in *Electroacoustic Music in East Asia*, edited by Marc Battier and Kenneth Fields. London and New York: Routledge.

Zhuangzi, Burton Watson. 2013. *The Complete Works of Zhuangzi*. New York: Columbia University Press.

奥·菲奥凡诺夫. 1955. 原子狂人音乐。禾金译。人民音乐，第6期。 (奥·菲奥凡诺夫 (Soviet Union). 1955. "Yuanzi Kuangren Yinyue" Translated by He, Jin in *People's Music*, No. 6).

蔡仲德. 2003. 中国美学音乐史. 北京: 人民音乐出版社。 (Cai, Zhongde. 2003. *Zhongguo Meixue Yinyueshi*. Beijing: People's Music Publishing House).

杜而未. 1977. 中国古代宗教系统: 帝道后土研究。台湾学生书局。 (Du, Erwei. 1977. *Zhongguo Gudai Zongjiao Xitong: Di Dao Hou Tu Yanjiu*. Taiwan Xuesheng Shuju).

冯时. 2007. 中国天文考古学. 北京: 中国社会科学出版社。 (Feng, Shi. 2007. *Zhongguo Tianwen Kaogu Xue*. Beijing: China Social Sciences Press).

傅汗. 1956. "无调性," 人民音乐, 第2期。 (Fu, Han. 1956. "Wu Diaoxing" in *People's Music*. No. 2).

高士明.主编. 2015. 关于: 耿建翌. 杭州: 中国美术学院出版社. (Gao, Shiming. ed. 2015. *Guanyu: Geng Jianyi*. Hangzhou: China Academy of Art Press).

韩冬. 1979. 国内电子琴试制简况。乐器科技，第3期。 (Han, Dong. 1979. "Guonei Dianziqin Shizhi Jiankuang" in *Yueqi Keji*, No. 3).

李豐楙. 1997. 六朝隋唐仙道類小說研究. 台北市: 台灣學生. (Li, Fengmao. 1997. *Liuchao Suitang Xiandaolei Xiaoshuo Yanjiu*. Taipei: Taiwan Xuesheng).

李豐楙. 2010. 神话与变异: 一个"常与非常"的文化思维. 北京: 中华书局. (Li, Fengmao. 2010. *Shenhua yu Bianyi: Yige "Chuang yu Feichang" de Wenhua Siwwei*. Beijing: Zhonghua Book Company).

李欧梵. 2017. 中国文化传统的六个面向. 中华书局. (Lee, Leo Ou-fan. 2017. *Zhongguo Wenhua Chuantongde Liuge Mianxiang*. Beijing: Zhonghua Book Company).

羅悦全 主编. 2015. 造音翻土: 戰後臺灣聲響文化的探索. 远足文化. (Luo, Yuequan, ed. 2015. *ALTERing NATIVism : Sound Cultures in Post-war Taiwan*. Yuanzu Wenhua.

李泽厚. 1999. 历史本体论·己卯五说. 生活·读书·新知三联书店. (Li, Zehou. 1999. *Lishi Bentilun Ji Mao Wu Shuo*. Beijing: SDX Joint Publishing Company).

李泽厚. 2015. 由巫到礼, 释礼归仁. 生活·读书·新知三联书店. (Li, Zehou. 2015. *You Wu Dao Li, Shi Li Gui Ren*. Beijing: SDX Joint Publishing Company).

牟宗三. 2007. 中国哲学的特质. 罗义俊 编 上海: 上海古籍出版社. (Mou, Zongsan. 2007. *Zhongguo Zhexue de Tezhi*. edited by Yijun Luo. Shanghai: Shanghai Classics Publishing House.)

石涛. 2007 石涛画语录. 俞剑华注释. 南京: 江苏美术出版社. (Shi, Tao. 2007. *Shitao Huayulu. Yu Jianhua Zhushi*. Nanjing: Jiangsu Meishu Chubanshe),

王博. 1993. 老子思想的史官特色. 大陆地区博士论文丛刊 55. 北京: 文津出版社. (Wang, Bo. 1993. *Laozi Sixiangde Shiguan Tese*. Dalu Diqu Boshi Lunwen Congkan 55. Beijing: Wenjin Publishing House).

Kurokawa, Masayuki. 2014. *Eight Aesthetic Consciousness of Japan* (Chinese edn), trans. Wang Chaoying and Zhang Yingxing. Shi Jia Zhuang: Hebei Fine Arts Publishing House.

吴南星. 1961. "电子音乐剧原来如此," 前线。第24期。Wu, Nanxing. 1961. "Dianzi Yinyue Yuanlai Ruci" in *Qianxian*. No. 24).

廖明君, 萧梅。2008. "巫乐'研究的新探索" 民族艺术, 第3期。

小野沢 精一，福永光司，山井涌，编辑. 2007.
气的思想：中国自然观与人的观念的发展. 翻译，李庆. 上海人民出版社. (Onozawa, Seiichi, Fukunaga, Koji, and Yamanoi, Yū, eds. 2007. *Qi de Sixiang: Zhongguo Ziranguan yu rende Guanniande Fazhan*. Translated by Li qing. Shanghai: Shanghai People's Publishing House).

意佳, 严伟. 1979. 我国电子乐器在发展. 人民音乐, Z1期。Yi, Jia, and Yan, Wei. 1979. "Woguo Dianzi Yueqi Zaifazhan" in *People's Music*. No. Z1).

余英时. 2014. 论天人之际: 中国古代思想起源试探. 北京: 中华书局. (Yu, Ying-shih. 2014. *Lun Tianren Zhiji: Zhongguo Gudai Sixiang Qiyuan Shitan*. Beijing: Zhonghua Book Company).

颜峻, 路易斯·格蕾 (Louise Gray). 2007. 都市发声: 城市·声音环境. 上海: 上海人民出版社. (Yan, Jun, and Gray, Louise, eds. 2007. *Sound and the City*. Shanghai: Shanghai People's Publishing House).

周建萍. 2015. 中日古典审美范畴比较研究. 北京: 中国社会科学出版社. (Zhou, Jianping. 2015. *Zhongri Gudian Shenmei Fanchou Bijiao Yanjiu*. Beijing: China Social Sciences Press).

黄专, 王景编. 2008. 张培力艺术工作手册. 广州: 岭南美术出版社. (Huang, Zhuan, and Wang, Jing, eds. 2008. *Artisic Working Manual of Zhang Peili*. Guangzhou: Lingnan Fine Arts Publishing House).

张小夫. 2012. "对中国电子音乐发展脉络的梳理与评估." 艺术评论, no. 04: 27–40. (Zhang, Xiaofu. 2012. "Dui Zhongguo Dianzi Yinyue Fazhan Mailuode Shuliyu Pinggu." *Yishu Pinglun*, no. 04: 27–40).

赵汀阳. 2019. 历史·山水·渔樵. 生活·读书·新知三联书店. (Zhao, Tingyang. 2019. *Lishi Shanshui Yuqiao*. Beijing: SDX Joint Publishing Company).

周贇. 2014.《正蒙》诠译. 北京: 知识产权出版社 (Zhou, Yun. 2014. *Zheng Meng Quan Yi*. Beijing: Intellectual Property Publishing House.).

INDEX